The Wisdom of
JOHN ADAMS

The Wisdom of

JOHN ADAMS

EDITED BY
KEES DE MOOY

PHILOSOPHICAL LIBRARY

 CITADEL PRESS
Kensington Publishing Corp.
www.kensingtonbooks.com

CITADEL PRESS books are published by

Kensington Publishing Corp.
850 Third Avenue
New York, NY 10022

Titles included in the Wisdom Library are published by arrangement with Philosophical Library.

All Kensington titles, imprints, and distributed lines are available at special quantity discounts for bulk purchases for sales promotions, premiums, fund-raising, educational, or institutional use. Special book excerpts or customized printings can also be created to fit specific needs. For details, write or phone the office of the Kensington special sales manager: Kensington Publishing Corp., 850 Third Avenue, New York, NY 10022, attn: Special Sales Department, phone 1-800-221-2647.

CITADEL PRESS is a Reg. U.S. Pat. & TM Off.
The Citadel Logo is a trademark of Kensington Publishing Corp.

First Wisdom Library printing: February 2003

10 9 8 7 6 5 4 3 2 1

Printed in the United States of America

Library of Congress Control Number: 2002110878

ISBN 0-8065-2465-0

(4 September 1820)

My plain writings have been misunderstood by many, misrepresented by more, and vilified and anathematized by multitudes who never read them. They have, indeed, nothing to recommend them but stubborn facts, simple principles, and irresistible inferences from both, without any recommendation from ambitious ornaments of style, or studied artifices of arrangement; notwithstanding all which, amidst all the calumnies they have occasioned, I have the consolation to know, and the injustice I have suffered ought to excuse me in saying, that they have been translated into the French, German, and Spanish languages; that they are now contributing to introduce representative governments into various nations of Europe, as they have before contributed to the introduction and establishment of our American constitutions, both of the individual states and the nation at large; and that they are now employed, and have been, in assisting the South Americans in establishing their liberties, from the days of Miranda to this hour. I may say, with Lord Bacon, that I bequeath my writings to foreign nations, and to my own country, after a few generations shall be past.

(WJA X 392)

CONTENTS

INTRODUCTION

The *Wisdom of John Adams* consists of fifteen chapters of quotations grouped thematically into four sections. The quotations within each chapter are arranged chronologically, allowing the reader to follow the progress of historical events and monitor the evolution of Adams's thinking over time. The selections are presented as they were written, with minor adjustments where eighteenth-century spelling, punctuation, or grammar conventions have obscured the meaning of a passage. The capitalization of words within sentences has likewise been eliminated to reflect modern usage. Editorial insertions are separated from the text with square brackets. Brief introductions to selected passages have been provided where necessary to place quotes in context. As a further aid to the reader, a Timeline with important biographical and historical events has been inserted after the Introduction.

John Adams was born on October 30, 1753, in Braintree (now Quincy), Massachusetts. He was educated at Harvard and began a lifelong study of history, government, and political philosophy. At the start of his career as a young lawyer in Boston, Adams found himself at the center of trade and legal controversies that eventually drove the American colonies into open revolt. He quickly rose to prominence in Massachusetts politics and became associated with many of the central figures of the American Revolution, including John Dickinson, James Otis, and Samuel Adams, his second cousin. Throughout this turbulent period, John Adams envisioned glorious prospects for a United States, but debates over independence moved far too slowly for his liking. "There is always more smoke than fire," he impatiently confided to his wife, Abigail, "more noise than music." As a delegate to the First and Second Congresses, Adams was a tireless worker, serving on so many committees that he claimed he did "more business than any other member of that house." His steadfast efforts and prodigious talents were recognized and respected by the other members of Congress, so much so that they sent him abroad to negotiate treaties with France and Holland, and, as the war was drawing to a close, the Treaty of Paris that formally ended the conflict with Great Britain. After the war, whether in his capacity as the first ambassador to Great Britain, a two-term vice president under Washington, the second president of the United States, or as an aging statesman at home in Quincy, Adams continued to revisit the Revolution to clarify its significance and reinforce its lessons.

Adams's personality was shaped by his New England heritage and upbringing, his religious and philosophical education, and his experiences in what he referred to as the "flowery meadows" and "dismal swamps" of life. His background made him look skeptically and critically at himself and the world around him. He constantly analyzed his own and others' shortcomings in the belief that "he is not a wise man, and is unfit to fill any important station in society, that has left one passion in his soul unsubdued." Vanity, avarice, luxury, ambition, and envy were to be weeded out, while virtue, honor, justice, and temperance gained his approbation.

The Unitarian religion, with its focus on personal responsibility and respect for other faiths, helped to shape Adams's temperament. He derived solace from his belief in God, and was convinced that "all good men are Christians." He believed in the separation of church and state, but did not hesitate during his presidency to declare a day of "solemn humiliation, fasting and prayer; that the citizens of these States, abstaining on that day from their customary worldly occupations, offer their devout addresses to the Father of mercies." He also professed that, despite its many shortcomings, religion was essential to a well-ordered society. Matters beyond man's comprehension were best left to God's Providence, and as he approached his own demise, he often meditated on the promise of life after death.

John Adams married Abigail Smith in 1764. Though not formally schooled, she was a highly intelligent woman who shared his love of reading and writing. She was his closest friend and confidante, and with her he shared his greatest joys and sorrows. Their marriage lasted fifty-four years, until Abigail's death of typhoid fever. During his political career, Adams was separated from his wife for long periods, sometimes years, and in his letters to her, he would unburden himself of his cares and yearn for her comforting presence. He wrote to her about everything that crossed his mind, from affairs of state to the moral education of their children. The resulting correspondence is unparalleled in American letters. Every letter shows his deep and abiding respect and love for her. In a sentiment that he often repeated, he wrote that "all the friendship I have for others is far unequal to that which warms my heart for you. The most agreeable time that I spend here is in writing to you, and conversing with you, when I am alone."

Adams developed his considerable political talent and reputation by reading every book on history, government, and political theory that he could find, debating in the circuit courts throughout New England, publishing anonymous works on the rights of American colonists, and working his way into a leading role in Congress during the American Revolution. Adams was chosen to be part of the committee to draft the Declaration of Independence, but he deferred the task to his young friend, Thomas Jefferson. By the time he became the first ambassador to Great Britain, his vast experience in domestic and international politics set him apart from almost every other man in America. Only George Washington, the military hero of the Revolution, received more votes in the first presidential election of the new nation. As the second-place finisher, Adams became vice president and served his superior faithfully for two terms. In his position as president of the Senate, he exercised a level of control that has remained unmatched to this day. He often lectured the assembled senators, and during the thirty-one times that competing factions were locked in a tie, he cast the deciding ballot.

During his vice presidency, Adams watched the development of political parties with contempt, stating that he had no desire to "wound my own mind by engaging in any party, and spreading prejudices, vices, or follies." When it became likely that he would become the next chief executive, Adams feared becoming "the butt of party malevolence," and having witnessed firsthand the animosity among Washington's administration, he found the prospect of becoming president "bitter, nauseous, and unwhole-some." In the contentious election of 1796, John Adams defeated his popular rival Thomas Jefferson by only three votes. In a bipartisan gesture that was intended to provide continuity in government, he made a fateful decision to retain all of Washington's cabinet. It was as if he had forgotten his own dictum, that "gratitude, friendship, unsuspecting confidence, and all the most amiable passions in human nature, are the most dangerous guides in politics." Alexander Hamilton, a former secretary of the treasury and popular leader of the Federalist Party, despised Adams and undermined his power at every opportunity by having disloyal cabinet members report government affairs directly to him.

Without a war to galvanize the nation and lacking the even disposition that made George Washington so successful in office, Adams struggled against divisive elements within his own government. His popularity surged briefly during the XYZ Affair and the resulting undeclared naval war with France, but he made policy decisions that were roundly criticized. Adams used the opportunity of what became known as the Quasi-War to rebuild the American navy, which had been scrapped after the Revolution, and he signed the Alien and Sedition Acts to protect the nation from the perceived threat of large numbers of French immigrants living in the United States. Vice President Jefferson, who resisted the naval buildup and saw France as an American ally, attacked Adams's policies anonymously in the press and secretly advised French negotiators to stall the peace talks. Meanwhile, Alexander Hamilton skillfully maneuvered himself into the leadership of the new American Army and simultaneously encouraged Adams's cabinet to derail the peace negotiations. His plans for glory were dashed by the Treaty of Mortefontaine, which ended the Quasi-War before it had escalated into an all-out conflict.

Adams was defeated for a second term by a very narrow margin. Attacks in the press by Jefferson and Hamilton, the political backlash against the Alien and Sedition Acts, and uncertainty over peace with France all contributed to his defeat. Adams seemed only too glad to get out of Washington, leaving the capital hours ahead of Jefferson's inauguration. In his retirement, Adams struggled to rebuild his reputation with an unfinished autobiography and in hundreds of letters to the *Boston Patriot*. Despite his efforts to vindicate himself, the negative writing campaigns by Jefferson, Hamilton, and other authors succeeded in keeping Adams low on the list of successful American presidents, behind the likes of Washington, Jefferson, and others who followed. It was only in the late part of the twentieth century that there was a resurgence of interest and attempted rehabilitation of the reputation of a man who, after all, was one of the Founding Fathers.

Adams's writings reveal a man who was profoundly dedicated to his country. Despite his personal fears and limitations, he was able to attain the highest political office in the United States. He labored to provide an enduring legacy for future generations, convinced that America "appears to me to exhibit a uniform, general tenor of character for intelligence, integrity, patience, fortitude, and public spirit." Although he was generally optimistic about the prospects for the nation, he warned that the fifty-year period since the signing of the Declaration of Independence was "destined in future history to form the brightest or the blackest page, according to the use or the abuse of those political institutions by which they shall in time to come be shaped by the *human mind.*" In a supremely ironic twist of fate, Adams died on July 4th, 1826, the anniversary of the event that he had sacrificed so much to achieve, and a lifetime to preserve.

TIMELINE OF JOHN ADAMS'S LIFE, WITH SIGNIFICANT HISTORICAL EVENTS

1735   **John Adams born October 30 in Braintree (now Quincy), Massachusetts.**

1751   **Attends Harvard University, graduates in 1755.**

1754   French and Indian War (1754–63).
Benjamin Franklin proposes Plan of Union at the Albany Congress.

1755   **Briefly teaches grammar school in Worcester, Massachusetts.**

1756   **Begins law studies.**

1758   **Admitted to the Suffolk County bar.**

1763   France cedes Canada to Great Britain at the end of the French and Indian War.

1764   **Marries Abigail Smith, couple move next to Adams's parents in Braintree.**
Practices law in Boston and travels the New England court circuit.
Sugar Act passed by British Parliament.
James Otis publishes "The Rights of the British Colonies Asserted and Proved."
Boston merchants institute a boycott of British luxury goods.

1765   **Chosen surveyor of highways in Braintree.**
Daughter Abigail (Abby) Adams born.
Publishes "A Dissertation on the Canon and the Feudal Law."
Drafts the "Braintree Instructions."
Stamp Act and Quartering Act imposed on the American colonies.
Stamp Act Congress convenes in New York City.

1766   **Elected a selectman in Braintree.**
        British Parliament repeals the Stamp Act, but signs Declaratory
        Act on same day.

1767   **Son John Quincy Adams born.**
        Townsend Revenue Acts signed by British Parliament.

1768   John Hancock's sloop *Liberty* seized by Boston customs officials.
        Writes "Instructions of the Town of Boston."
        British warships arrive in Boston Harbor to suppress rioting.
        Four regiments of British troops occupy Boston.
        Cousin Samuel Adams writes Circular Letter denouncing "taxa-
        tion without representation."
        Daughter Susanna Adams born.

1769   Virginia Resolves presented in Virginia House of Burgesses.

1770   **Baby Susanna Adams dies.**
        Boston Massacre occurs on March 5, British soldiers kill five
        civilians.
        Charles Adams born.
        **Successfully defends British troops implicated in the Boston
        Massacre.**
        Elected to the Massachusetts legislature.
        Townsend Acts repealed.

1771   **Temporarily retires from politics.**

1772   **Son Thomas Boylston Adams born September 15.**
        British customs schooner *Gaspee* burned by Rhode Island
        colonists in June.
        Committee of Correspondence established by Samuel Adams.

1773   **Elected to the Massachusetts Governor's Council.**
        Tea Act takes effect May 10.
        **Governor Hutchinson removes Adams from Council for sym-
        pathizing with patriots.**
        Boston Tea Party occurs December 16.

1774   Coercive ("Intolerable") Acts and Boston Port Bill signed by
        Parliament.
        British General Thomas Gage places Massachusetts under mili-
        tary rule.

New Quartering Act imposed.

General Gage seizes Massachusetts arsenal of weapons at Charlestown.

Appointed a delegate to the First Continental Congress held at Philadelphia.

Attends session of Congress from September through October.

1775 **Publishes "Novanglus" essays in the *Boston Gazette* from January to April.**

Battles of Lexington and Concord fought on April 19, start of American Revolution.

Massachusetts Congress mobilizes an army of 13,600 soldiers.

Serves in the Second Continental Congress.

Adams proposes George Washington to lead the Continental Army on June 15.

Battle of Bunker (actually Breed's) Hill, Boston, fought on June 17.

Olive Branch Petition sent by Congress, refused by King George III.

Elected to the Massachusetts Council.

Appointed Chief Justice of Massachusetts, but does not serve.

1776 Thomas Paine's "Common Sense" published in Philadelphia.

Delegate to the Second Continental Congress in Philadelphia February to October.

American troops bombard British positions in Boston March 2–3.

Writes "Thoughts on Government."

Appointed President of the Board of War.

Assists in writing the Resolves of Congress of May 10.

Part of the committee that results in the creation of the American Navy.

Appointed to the committee to draft the Declaration of Independence.

Jefferson prepares draft of Declaration, Adams and Franklin make minor changes.

Declaration of Independence adopted by Congress on July 2, signed on July 4.

Serves on peace delegation, British Admiral Howe's terms rejected.

Franklin, Jefferson, and Silas Deane sent as commissioners to France.

Fearing a British attack, Congress abandons Philadelphia for Baltimore.

1777   Attends second Continental Congress from January to November.
Congress returns to Philadelphia after victories by General Washington.
Abigail gives birth to stillborn daughter Elizabeth Adams.
Elected commissioner to France with Benjamin Franklin and Arthur Lee.
Congress relocates to York, Pennsylvania, when British troops threaten Philadelphia.
Major American victory at Saratoga by generals Horatio Gates and Benedict Arnold.
Congress adopts the Articles of Confederation on November 15.

1778   Treaties between America and France signed in Paris on February 6.
John and his son John Quincy Adams sail to France.
Lives at Passy with Benjamin Franklin.
Gains an audience with Louis XVI.
British troops abandon Philadelphia, Congress returns.
France declares war against Great Britain on July 10.
Congress appoints Benjamin Franklin the sole diplomatic representative in France.

1779   Learns that his joint commission is superseded by the appointment of Franklin.
Sails back to Boston from France with John Quincy Adams.
Recommends the founding of the American Academy of Arts and Sciences.
Spain forms alliance with the United States and declares war on England.
Chosen as a representative to the Massachusetts Constitutional Convention.
Drafts the Massachusetts Constitution, which is adopted in 1780.
Appointed a minister plenipotentiary to negotiate peace with Great Britain.
Sails for France with John Quincy and Charles Adams.
Forced to land on the coast of Spain due to a leaking ship.

1780   Arrives with his two sons in Paris after a two-month journey.
        Directed by Congress to raise money in the Netherlands for
        the war effort.
        Writes "Letters from a Distinguished American," published in
        1782.
        Arrives in the Netherlands with John Quincy and Charles
        Adams.
        Appointed by Congress to sign a treaty of commerce with the
        Netherlands.

1781   Congress adds Franklin, Jefferson, John Jay, and Henry
        Laurens to peace commission.
        Publishes a memorial encouraging the Netherlands to recog-
        nize the United States.
        Articles of Confederation ratified on March 1.
        French fleet defeats British fleet off Yorktown, Virginia, in
        September.
        British General Cornwallis surrenders to George Washington at
        Yorktown on October 19.

1782   British House of Commons votes to cease war in America.
        Lord Rockingham initiates negotiations with American peace
        commission in Paris.
        The Netherlands formally recognizes the United States on
        April 19.
        Negotiates a loan of five million guilders from Dutch bankers.
        Signs treaty of amity and commerce with the Netherlands.
        Preliminary peace treaty signed with British representative in
        Paris on November 30.

1783   Treaty of Paris signed by the United States and Great Britain
        on September 3.
        Travels to London with John Quincy Adams.
        American Continental Army disbanded.

1784   Congress ratifies the Treaty of Paris on January 14.
        Adams, Franklin, and Jefferson negotiate treaties with
        European and African nations.
        Abigail Adams and daughter Abby sail to London to join John
        and John Quincy.
        John, Abigail, Abby, and John Quincy travel to France, live
        near Paris.

1785   Named the first United States ambassador to Great Britain.
        Family travels to London, England, while John Quincy returns
        to Boston.
        Gains audience with King George III (see Appendix).
        Signs a treaty of amity and commerce with Prussia.
        Charles Adams enters Harvard University.
        Last ship in the United States Navy sold.

1786   John Quincy Adams enters Harvard University.
        With Thomas Jefferson, negotiates treaties with Tripoli,
        Portugal, and England.
        Travels with Thomas Jefferson through the English country-
        side.
        Thomas Boylston Adams enters Harvard University.
        Travels to the Netherlands with wife, Abigail, to ratify treaty
        with Prussia.

1787   Constitutional Convention begins deliberations in Philadelphia
        in May.
        Northwest Ordinance signed.
        Final draft of the Constitution approved and signed by Congress
        on September 17.
        Federalist Papers begin to be published in favor of the new
        Constitution.
        Anti-Federalists call for modifications to the Constitution, in-
        cluding a Bill of Rights.
        **Congress recalls Adams to the United States at his request in
        October.**
        **Publishes "A Defense of the Constitutions of the United
        States."**

1788   **John and Abigail Adams return to Braintree, Massachusetts.**
        Massachusetts legislature declares slavery illegal.
        Constitution ratified in June.
        U.S. government temporarily moved to New York City.

1789   Congress convenes in New York City.
        George Washington elected the first president of the United
        States.
        **Elected vice president, sworn into office on April 21 in New
        York.**
        Serves as president of the United States Senate.
        Outbreak of the French Revolution.

Twelve amendments to the Constitution submitted to Congress
on September 25.

1790   **Begins publishing "Discourses on Davila" in the *Gazette of
        the United States*.
        Moves with Abigail to Philadelphia.**
        Benjamin Franklin dies.
        President George Washington selects a parcel on the Potomac
        River for the new capital city.

1791   **Elected President of the American Academy of Arts and
        Sciences.**
        Bill of Rights adopted by Congress on December 15.

1792   France declared a republic.

1793   George Washington elected to a second four-year term.
        Elected to second term as vice president.
        Louis XVI and Marie Antoinette guillotined.

1794   Whisky Rebellion put down by federal troops.

1795   **Debates over Jay's Treaty results in the emergence of two dis-
        tinct national parties:
        Federalists (Washington, Adams, Hamilton) and Democrat-
        Republicans (Jefferson, Madison).**

1796   **Elected president of the United States, defeats Thomas
        Jefferson by three votes.
        Thomas Jefferson becomes vice president.
        Retains all four cabinet secretaries from George Washington's
        administration:
        Secretary of State Timothy Pickering (MA)
        Secretary of the Treasury Oliver Wolcott, Jr. (CT)
        Secretary of War James McHenry (MD)
        Attorney General Charles Lee (VA)**

1797   **Inaugurated president on March 4 (see Appendix for First
        Inaugural Speech).
        Sends peace mission to France to reinforce the neutral status
        of the United States.**

1798   **French minister attempts to secure bribes from Americans in
        the XYZ Affair.**

Quasi-War begins between the United States and France.
Proposes creation of a Department of the Navy, Congress approves.
Navy expands to over fifty ships by 1800.
Yellow fever epidemic hits Philadelphia.
Conducts presidential duties from home in Quincy.
Alien and Sedition Acts signed in July.
Nominates George Washington to command army of 10,000 men.
Alexander Hamilton attempts to become second-in-command of army.
Minister Elbridge Gerry returns from France, claims the French want to negotiate.
Hamilton plots to use army to conquer French possessions in Florida and Louisiana.

1799   Sends second peace mission to France.
American frigate *Constellation* captures French ship *L'Insurgent*.
George Washington dies December 14, 1799.

1800   American frigate *Constellation* defeats French man-of-war *La Vengeance*.
News arrives that Napoleon Bonaparte is the new leader of the French Republic.
James Callender, supported by Jefferson, assaults Adams in the *Richmond Examiner*.
Callender charged, tried, and jailed under provisions of the Sedition Act.
Secretary of War James McHenry forced to resign for opposing his policies.
Secretary of State Timothy Pickering dismissed for the same reason.
Pardons John Fries, Pennsylvanian leader of a small riot against federal taxation.
U.S. government moves from Philadelphia to Washington in June.
Quasi-War ends with the Treaty of Mortefontaine.
Adams attacked in "A Letter from Alexander Hamilton."
Moves into the new President's House on November 1.
Charles Adams dies in New York City on November 30.
Narrowly defeated in the presidential election.

1801 Thomas Jefferson and Aaron Burr tied in electoral votes.
      Appoints John Marshall Chief Justice of the Supreme Court.
      Congress votes for Thomas Jefferson on the thirty-sixth ballot.
      Jefferson inaugurated March 4, Adams leaves for Braintree
      before the inauguration.
      Returns to his family, farming, reading, and writing.
      Jefferson releases everyone jailed under the Alien and Sedition
      Acts and cuts the Navy.
      James Callender reveals that he was paid by Jefferson to de-
      fame Adams.
      Callender also claims that Jefferson had children by his slave
      Sally Hemings.

1802 **Begins writing his autobiography.**
      John Quincy Adams elected to the U.S. Senate.

1803 Louisiana Purchase.

1804 Aaron Burr kills Alexander Hamilton in a duel.
      Jefferson elected to a second term.
      Napoleon made Emperor of France.

1807 **Stops writing his autobiography.**
      Embargo Act.

1809 President James Madison inaugurated.
      For three years, recounts his presidency in over 300 letters to
      the Boston *Patriot*.

1811 **Daughter Abigail diagnosed with breast cancer.**
      Battle of Tippecanoe.

1812 **Resumes a correspondence with Thomas Jefferson after an**
      eleven-year hiatus.
      War declared against Great Britain (War of 1812).

1813 James Madison elected to second term as president.
      Daughter Abigail Adams Smith dies of cancer.

1814 British forces burn the Capitol and President's House.
      War of 1812 ends with the Treaty of Ghent.

1815 Napoleon defeated at Waterloo.

1817   President James Monroe inaugurated.
        John Quincy Adams appointed secretary of state.

1818   **Abigail Adams dies of typhoid fever on October 28.**

1820   Missouri Compromise.

1821   James Monroe reelected.

1823   Monroe Doctrine.

1824   **Sits for portrait by Gilbert Stuart.**
        John Quincy Adams elected president by the House of
        Representatives.

1825   **John Quincy Adams inaugurated.**

1826   **Dies in Quincy on July 4, the fiftieth anniversary of the**
        Declaration of Independence.
        Thomas Jefferson had died at Monticello approximately two
        hours earlier.

Sources: **Massachusetts Historical Society,** *Encyclopedia Americana.*

Part I

THE ROAD TO FREEDOM

1

Prelude to Lexington and Concord

(August 1765)
Beginning in 1765, British Parliament circumvented colonial legislatures by passing a series of direct taxes.

The prospect now before us in America, ought in the same manner to engage the attention of every man of learning, to matters of power and of right, that we may be neither led nor driven blindfolded to irretrievable destruction. Nothing less than this seems to have been meditated for us, by somebody or other in Great Britain. There seems to be a direct and formal design on foot, to enslave all America. . . . It seems very manifest from the Stamp Act itself, that a design is formed to strip us in a great measure of the means of knowledge, by loading the press, the colleges, and even an almanac and a newspaper, with restraints and duties; and to introduce the inequalities and dependencies of the feudal system, by taking from the poorer sort of people all their little subsistence, and conferring it on a set of stamp officers, distributors, and their deputies.

(WJA III 463-64)

(18 December 1765)
In October, nine of the thirteen colonies convened the Stamp Act Congress.

That enormous engine, fabricated by the British Parliament, for battering down all the rights and liberties of America, I mean the Stamp Act, has raised and spread through the whole continent a spirit that will be recorded to our honor with all future generations.

(WJA II 154)

(18 December 1765)

The people, even of the lowest ranks, have become more attentive
to their liberties, more inquisitive about them, than they were
ever before known or had occasion to be; innumerable have been
the monuments of wit, humor, sense, learning, spirit, patriotism,
and heroism, erected in the several colonies and provinces in the
course of this year. Our presses have groaned, our pulpits have
thundered, our legislatures have resolved, our towns have voted;
the crown officers have everywhere trembled, and all their little
tools and creatures been afraid to speak and ashamed to be seen.

(WJA II 154)

(27 December 1765)

If there is anyone who cannot see the tendency of [the Stamp] Act
to reduce the body of the people to ignorance, poverty, dependence, his want of eyesight is a disqualification for public employment. Let the towns and the representatives, therefore,
renounce every stamp man and every trimmer next May.

(WJA II 167)

(31 December 1765)

The national attention is fixed upon the colonies; the religion, administration of justice, geography, numbers, etc., of the colonies,
as a fashionable study. But what wretched blunders do they make
in attempting to regulate them. They know not the character of
Americans.

(WJA II 170)

(1 January 1766)

This year brings ruin or salvation to the British Colonies. The eyes
of all Americans are fixed on the British Parliament. In short,
Britain and America are staring at each other; and they will probably stare more and more for some time.

(WJA II 170)

(17 June 1768)

Introductory paragraph of "Instructions of the Town of Boston to their Representatives," addressed to Governor Hutchinson of Massachusetts. On the same day in 1766 that the British Parliament repealed the Stamp Act, they passed the Declaratory Act, which effectively swept away the authority of colonial legislatures. The following year, Parliament passed the Townsend Revenue Acts, which established taxes on glass, lead, paints, paper, and tea.

After the repeal of the late Stamp Act, we were happy in the pleasing prospect of a restoration of that tranquility and unanimity among ourselves, and that harmony and affection between our parent country and us, which had generally subsisted before that detestable act. But with the utmost grief and concern, we find that we flattered ourselves too soon, and that the root of bitterness is yet alive. The principle on which that act was founded continues in full force, and a revenue is still demanded from America.

(WJA III 501)

(17 June 1768)

In May, Boston customs officials seized John Hancock's ship Liberty, *causing extensive rioting. British warships were stationed in Boston Harbor, and troops were sent to occupy the town.*

Under all these misfortunes and afflictions . . . it is our fixed resolution to maintain our loyalty and duty to our most gracious Sovereign, a reverence and due subordination to the British Parliament, as the supreme legislative in all cases of necessity, for the preservation of the whole empire, and our cordial and sincere affection for our parent country; and to use our utmost endeavors for the preservation of peace and order among ourselves; waiting with anxious expectations, for a favorable answer to the petitions and solicitations of this continent for relief. At the same time, it is our unalterable resolution, at all times, to assert and vindicate our dear and invaluable rights and liberties, at the utmost hazard of our lives and fortunes; and we have a full and rational confidence that no designs formed against them will ever prosper.

(WJA III 502)

(31 December 1772)
In June, the British revenue schooner Gaspee *ran aground in Narragansett Bay, Rhode Island, and was burned to the waterline by colonists. A lengthy trial ensued, during which no witnesses would came forward.*

This evening at Mr. Cranch's . . . Mr. Collins, an English gentleman, was there, and in conversation about the high commission court for inquiring after the burners of the *Gaspee* in Providence, I found the old warmth, heat, violence, acrimony, bitterness, sharpness of my temper and expression, was not departed. I said there was no more justice left in Britain than there was in hell; that I wished for war, and that the whole Bourbon family was upon the back of Great Britain; avowed a thorough disaffection to that country; wished that any thing might happen to them, and, as the clergy prayed of our enemies in time of war, that they might be brought to reason or to ruin.

(WJA II 308)

(17 December 1773)
Angry over the Tea Act, a group of Bostonians disguised themselves as Indians and dumped cargos of tea from three ships.

Last night, three cargoes of Bohea tea were emptied into the sea. . . . This destruction of the tea is so bold, so daring, so firm, intrepid and inflexible, and it must have so important consequences, and so lasting, that I cannot but consider it as an epoch in history.

(WJA II 323)

(14 May 1774)
Parliament responded to the Boston Tea Party by closing the port, dissolving the Massachusetts legislature, and placing the province under military rule.

We begin almost to wish that Europe could forget that America was ever discovered, and America could forget that Europe ever existed.

(WJA IX 338)

(1774)

License of the press is no proof of liberty. When a people are corrupted, the press may be made an engine to complete their ruin; and it is now notorious, that the ministry are daily employing it, to increase and establish corruption, and to pluck up virtue by the roots. Liberty can no more exist without virtue and independence, than the body can live and move without a soul.

(WJA IV 31)

(25 June 1774)

We have not men fit for the times. We are deficient in genius, in education, in travel, in fortune, in every thing. I feel unutterable anxiety. God grant us wisdom and fortitude! Should the opposition be suppressed, should this country submit, what infamy and ruin! God forbid. Death in any form is less terrible!

(WJA II 338)

(20 June 1774)

There is a new and a grand scene open before me; a congress. This will be an assembly of the wisest men upon the continent, who are Americans in principle, that is, against the taxations of Americans by authority of Parliament. I feel myself unequal to the business.

(WJA II 338)

(July 1774)

I confess myself to be full of fears that the ministry and their friends and instruments will prevail, and crush the cause and friends of liberty. The minds of that party are so filled with prejudices against me that they will take all advantages, and do me all the damage they can. These thoughts have their turns in my mind, but in general my hopes are predominant.

(FL 7)

(6 July 1774)

How much profaneness, lewdness, intemperance, etc., have been
introduced by the [British] army and navy and revenue; how
much servility, venality, artifice, and hypocrisy have been introduced among the ambitious and avaricious by the British politics
of the last ten years. In short, the original faulty causes of all the
vices which have been introduced are the political innovations of
the last ten years.

(FL 13)

(6 July 1774)

We very seldom hear any solid reasoning. I wish always to dis-
cuss the question without all painting, pathos, rhetoric, or flourish of every kind. And the question seems to me to be, whether
the American colonies are to be considered as a distinct community so far as to have a right to judge for themselves when the fundamentals of their government are destroyed or invaded, or
whether they are to be considered as a part of the whole British
empire, the whole English nation, so far as to be bound in honor,
conscience, or interest by the general sense of the whole nation.

(FL 16)

(6 July 1774)

It is a fundamental, inherent, and unalienable right of the people,
that they have some check, influence, or control in their supreme
legislature. If the right of taxation is conceded to Parliament, the
Americans have no check or influence left.

(FL 16)

(26 September 1774)
*Adams was one of fifty-six delegates from twelve colonies to the First
Continental Congress.*

The commencement of hostilities is exceedingly dreaded here [in
Philadelphia]. It is thought that an attack upon the troops, even
though it should prove successful and triumphant, would cer-

tainly involve the whole continent in a war. . . . If Boston and Massachusetts can possibly steer a middle course between obedience to the acts and open hostilities with the troops, the exertions of the colonies will procure a total change of measures and full redress for us.

(WJA I 155)

(7 October 1774)
Militias were formed throughout the colonies in response to the policies of the British Parliament.

There is a great spirit in the Congress. But our people must be peaceable. Let them exercise every day in the week if they will, the more the better. Let them furnish themselves with artillery, arms, and ammunition. Let them follow the maxim which you say they have adopted, "In times of peace prepare for war." But let them avoid war *if possible—if possible*, I say.

(FL 44)

(January–April 1775)
Adams published a series of articles in the Boston Gazette *under the pseudonym "Novanglus," in response to articles by a Loyalist writer who argued for staying united with Britain.*

The most sensible and jealous instances of resistance have placed it beyond a doubt, that their rulers had formed settled plans to deprive them of their liberties; not to oppress an individual or a few, but to break down the fences of a free constitution, and deprive the people at large of all share in the government, and all the checks by which it is limited.

(WJA IV 17)

(January 1775)

A union of the colonies might be projected, and an American legislature; for, if America has three millions of people, and the whole dominions, twelve millions, she ought to send a quarter part of all the members to the house of commons; and, instead of holding parliaments always at Westminster, the haughty members of Great Britain must humble themselves, one session in four, to cross the Atlantic, and hold the parliament in America.

(WJA IV 116)

(January–April 1775)

Now, let me ask you, if the Parliament of Great Britain had all the natural foundations of authority, wisdom, goodness, justice, power, in as great perfection as they ever existed in any body of men since Adam's fall; and if the English nation was the most virtuous, pure, and free that ever was; would not such an unlimited subjection of three millions of people to that parliament, at three thousand miles distance, be real slavery?

(WJA IV 28)

(January–April 1775)

Are there not fifty bays, harbors, creeks, and inlets upon the whole coast of North America, where there is one round the island of Great Britain? Is it to be supposed, then, that the whole British navy could prevent the importation of arms and ammunition into America, if she should have occasion for them to defend herself against the hellish warfare that is here supposed?

(WJA IV 40)

(January–April 1775)

Opposition, nay, open, avowed resistance by arms, against usurpation and lawless violence, is not rebellion by the law of God or the land.

(WJA IV 57)

(January–April 1775)

A settled plan to deprive the people of all the benefits, blessings, and ends of the contract, to subvert the fundamentals of the constitution, to deprive them of all share in making and executing laws, will justify a revolution.

(WJA IV 16)

2

The American Revolution

(2 May 1775)
Adams stopped writing his "Novanglus" letters when, on April 19, the Battles of Lexington and Concord were fought.

It is arrogance and presumption, in human sagacity, to pretend to penetrate far into the designs of Heaven. The most perfect reverence and resignation becomes us, but I cannot help depending upon this, that the present dreadful calamity of that beloved town [Boston] is intended to bind the colonies together in more indissoluble bonds, and to animate their exertions at this great crisis in the affairs of mankind. It has this effect in a most remarkable degree, as far as I have yet seen or heard. It will plead with all America with more irresistible persuasion than angels trumpet-tongued.

(FL 51–2)

(8 May 1775)
The Second Continental Congress began meeting in Philadelphia on May 10, 1775.

Our prospect of a union of the colonies is promising indeed. Never was there such a spirit. Yet I feel anxious, because there is always more smoke than fire—more noise than music.

(FL 55)

11

(29 May 1775)

Colonel [George] Washington appears at Congress in his uniform, and, by his great experience and abilities in military matters, is of much service to us. O that I were a soldier! I will be. I am reading military books. Everybody must, and I will, and shall, be a soldier.

(FL 59)

(17 June 1775)
On June 15, John Adams nominated George Washington to lead the Continental Army.

I can now inform you that the Congress have made choice of the modest and virtuous, the amiable, generous, and brave George Washington, Esquire, to be General of the American army, and that he is to repair, as soon as possible, to the camp before Boston. This appointment will have a great effect in cementing and securing the union of these colonies. . . . I hope the people of our province will treat the General with all that confidence and affection, that politeness and respect, which is due to one of the most important characters in the world. The liberties of America depend upon him, in a great degree.

(FL 65–6)

(18 June 1775)

We shall have a redress of grievances or an assumption of all the powers of government, Legislative, executive, and judicial, throughout the whole continent, very soon.

(FL 67)

(24 July 1775)
Two days after Washington was chosen to lead the army, Royal Navy ships bombarded Charlestown, Massachusetts, and British troops led a charge that became immortalized as the Battle of Bunker Hill. Abigail and John Quincy Adams watched the smoke of the Charlestown fires from the hill beside their home in Braintree. The letter containing this passage, addressed to Abigail Adams, was intercepted by the British and published in England.

The business I have had upon my mind has been as great and important as can be entrusted to man, and the difficulty and intricacy of it prodigious. When fifty or sixty men have a constitution to form for a great empire, at the same time that they have a country of fifteen hundred miles in extent to fortify, millions to arm and train, a naval power to begin, an extensive commerce to regulate, numerous tribes of Indians to negotiate with, a standing army of twenty-seven thousand men to raise, pay, victual, and officer, I really shall pity those fifty or sixty men.

(FL 85)

(24 July 1775)
On July 8, Congress formulated a last-ditch appeal to King George III for a peaceful way out of the crisis. The Olive Branch Petition was sent to England, but George III refused to read it, commenting that the insurgency of the American colonies had to be suppressed by "the most decisive exertions."

We ought to have had in our hands, a month ago, the whole legislative, executive, and judicial of the whole continent, and have completely modeled a constitution; to have raised a naval power, and opened all our ports wide; to have arrested every friend of government on the continent, and held them as hostages for the poor victims in Boston; and then opened the door as wide as possible for peace and reconciliation.

(WJA I 179)

(7 October 1775)

From my earliest entrance into life, I have been engaged in the public cause of America; and from first to last I have had upon my mind a strong impression that things would be wrought up to their present crisis. I saw from the beginning that the controversy was of such a nature that it never would be settled, and every day convinces me more and more. This has been the source of all the disquietude of my life. It has lain down and risen up with me these twelve years. The thought that we might be driven to the sad necessity of breaking our connection with Great Britain, exclusive of the carnage and destruction, which it was easy to see must attend the separation, always gave me a great deal of grief. And even now I would cheerfully retire from public life forever, renounce all chance for profits or honors from the public, nay, I would cheerfully contribute my little property, to obtain peace and liberty. But all these must go, and my life too, before I can surrender the right of my country to a free constitution.

(FL 104–5)

(13 October 1775)

We have few hopes, excepting that of preserving our honor and our consciences untainted, and a free constitution for our country. Let me be sure of these, and amidst all my weaknesses, I cannot be overcome. With these, I can be happy in extreme poverty, in humble insignificance, may I hope and believe, in death. Without them, I should be miserable with a crown upon my head, millions in my coffers, and a gaping, idolizing multitude at my feet.

(FL 109)

(23 October 1775)

The tremendous calamities already felt, of fire, sword, and pestilence, may be only harbingers of greater still. We have no security against calamity here. This planet is its region. The only principle is to be prepared for the worst events.

(FL 117)

(11 February 1776)
In February, the Second Continental Congress reconvened and began taking up the issue of independence.

In such great changes and commotions, individuals are but atoms. It is scarcely worthwhile to consider what the consequences will be to us. What will be the effect upon present and future millions, and millions of millions, is a question very interesting to benevolence, natural and Christian. God grant that they may, and I firmly believe they will, be happy.

(FL 133)

(18 February 1776)

Reconciliation if practicable, and peace if attainable, you very
well know, would be as agreeable to my inclinations and as advantageous to my interest, as to any man's. But I see no prospect,
no probability, no possibility. And I cannot but despise the understanding which sincerely expects an honorable peace, for its
credulity, and detest the hypocritical heart which pretends to expect it, when in truth it does not.

(FL 135)

(18 February 1776)

The events of war are uncertain. We cannot insure success, but we
can deserve it.

(FL 135)

(12 April 1776)
*On this day, the North Carolina assembly empowered their delegates to vote
for independence.*

This is not independency, you know. What is? Why, government
in every colony, a confederation among them all, and treaties with
foreign nations to acknowledge us a sovereign state, and all that.
When these things will be done, or any of them, time must discover. Perhaps the time is near, perhaps a great way off.

(FL 153)

(17 May 1776)
*On May 10, Congress passed a resolution that paved the way to a declara-
tion of independence, and an amendment was passed five days later.*

Great Britain has at last driven America to the last step, a complete separation from her; a total, absolute independence, not
only of her Parliament, but of her crown, for such is the amount of
the resolve of the 15th.

(FL 173)

(May 1776)

We are in the very midst of a revolution the most complete, unexpected, and remarkable of any in the history of nations.

(WJA I 223)

(12 June 1776)
To John Lowell.

I am weary, and must ask leave to return to my family, after a little time, and one of my colleagues at least must do the same, or I greatly fear do worse. You and I know very well the fatigues of practice at the bar, but I assure you this incessant round of thinking and speaking upon the greatest subjects that ever employed the mind of man, and the most perplexing difficulties that ever puzzled it, is beyond all comparison more exhausting and consuming.

(WJA IX 393)

(22 June 1776)

The only question is concerning the proper time for making an explicit declaration in words. Some people must have time to look around them; before, behind, on the right hand, and on the left; then to think, and, after all this, to resolve. Others see at one intuitive glance into the past and the future, and judge with precision at once. But remember, you cannot make thirteen clocks strike precisely alike at the same second.

(WJA IX 401-2)

(23 June 1776)

It is now universally acknowledged that we are and must be independent. But still, objections are made to a declaration of it. It is said that such a declaration will arouse and unite Great Britain. But are they not already aroused and united, as much as they will be?

(WJA IX 409)

(23 June 1776)

A committee is appointed to prepare a confederation of the colonies, ascertaining the terms and ends of the compact, and the limits of the Continental Constitution; and another committee is appointed to draw up a declaration that these colonies are free and independent States. And other committees are appointed for other purposes, as important. These committees will report in a week or two, and then the last finishing strokes will be given to the politics of this revolution. Nothing will remain after that but war. I think I may then petition my constituents for leave to return to my family, and leave the war to be conducted by some others who understand it better. I am weary, thoroughly weary, and ought to have a little rest.

(WJA IX 410)

(26 June 1776)
On June 3, John Adams was made president of the Board of War.

The Congress have been pleased to give me more business than I am qualified for, and more than, I fear, I can go through, with safety to my health. They have established a board of war and ordnance and made me President of it, an honor to which I never aspired, a trust to which I feel myself vastly unequal.

(FL 189)

(3 July 1776)
On July 2, the Declaration of Independence was adopted by Congress.

Yesterday, the greatest question was decided which ever was debated in America, and a greater, perhaps, never was nor will be decided among men. A Resolution was passed without one dissenting colony "that these United Colonies are, and of right ought to be, free and independent States, and as such they have, and of right ought to have, full power to make war, conclude peace, establish commerce, and to do all other acts and things which other States may rightfully do." You will see, in a few days, a Declaration setting forth the causes which have impelled us to this mighty revolution, and the reasons which will justify it in the sight of God and man.

(FL 191–92)

(3 July 1776)

Britain has been filled with folly, and America with wisdom; at least, this is my judgment. Time must determine. It is the will of Heaven that the two countries should be sundered forever. It may be the will of Heaven that America shall suffer calamities still more wasting, and distresses yet more dreadful. If this is to be the case, it will have this good effect at least. It will inspire us with many virtues which we have not, and correct many errors, follies, and vices which threaten to disturb, dishonor, and destroy us.

(FL 191–92)

(3 July 1776)
Though adopted on July 2, the Declaration of Independence was not signed until July 4.

The second day of July, 1776, will be the most memorable epoch in the history of America. I am apt to believe that it will be celebrated by succeeding generations as the great anniversary festival. It ought to be commemorated as the day of deliverance, by solemn acts of devotion to God Almighty. It ought to be solemnized with pomp and parade, with shows, games, sports, guns, bells, bonfires, and illuminations, from one end of this continent to the other, from this time forward forevermore.

You will think me transported with enthusiasm, but I am not. I am well aware of the toil and blood and treasure that it will cost us to maintain this Declaration and support and defend these States. Yet, through all the gloom, I can see the rays of ravishing light and glory. I can see that the end is more than worth all the means. And that posterity will triumph in that day's transaction, even although we should rue it, which I trust in God we shall not.

(FL 193–94)

(15 July 1776)

Independence is, at last, unanimously agreed to in the New York Convention. You will see, by the newspapers enclosed, what is going forward in Virginia and Maryland and New Jersey. Farewell! farewell! farewell! infatuated, besotted step-dame.

(FL 202)

(29 July 1776)

If a confederation should take place, one great question is, how we shall vote. Whether each colony shall count one; or whether each shall have a weight in proportion to its number, or wealth, or exports and imports, or a compound ratio of all. Another is, whether Congress shall have authority to limit the dimensions of each colony, to prevent those, which claim by charter, or proclamation, or commission to the south sea, from growing too great and powerful, so as to be dangerous to the rest?·

(FL 205)

(19 August 1776)

I wish every man upon the continent was a soldier, and obliged, upon occasion, to fight, and determined to conquer or die. Flight was unknown to the Romans. I wish it was to Americans. There was a flight in Quebec, and worse than a flight at the Cedars. If we do not atone for these disgraces, we are undone.

(WJA IX 432)

(February 1777)

We must no longer reason nor deliberate. We only want concord and steadiness. The lot is cast. If we prove victorious, we shall be a just, free, and sovereign people. If we are conquered, we shall be traitors, perjured persons, and rebels.

(WJA I 262)

(13 April 1777)

Disease has destroyed ten men for us where the sword of the enemy has killed one.

(FL 260)

(27 April 1777)

I am more concerned about our revenue than the aid of France. Pray let the loan offices do their part, that we may not be compelled to make paper money as plenty, and, of course, as cheap as oak leaves. There is so much injustice in carrying on a war with a depreciating currency that we can hardly pray with confidence for success.

(WJA IX 463)

(27 May 1777)

Retaliation we must practice in some instances, in order to make our barbarous foes respect, in some degree, the rights of humanity. But this will never be done without the most palpable necessity.

(FL 279)

(27 July 1777)
To his ten year old son, John Quincy.

If it should be the design of Providence that you should live to grow up, you will naturally feel a curiosity to learn the history of the causes which have produced the late revolution of our government. No study in which you can engage will be more worthy of you.

(FL 284)

(24 August 1777)

Discipline in an army is like the laws in civil society. There can be no liberty in a commonwealth where the laws are not revered and most sacredly observed, nor can there be happiness or safety in an army for a single hour where the discipline is not observed.

(FL 299)

(2 September 1777)

My toast is, a short and violent war. They would call me mad and rash, etc., but I know better. I am as cool as any of them, and cooler too, for my mind is not inflamed with fear nor anger, whereas I believe theirs are with both.

(FL 305)

(21 September 1777)
General Washington suffered a defeat at the Battle of Brandywine, and was forced to retreat toward Philadelphia. Congress fled, and on September 26, British troops entered the city.

O Heaven! Grant us one great soul! One leading mind would extricate the best cause from that ruin which seems to await it for the want of it. We have as good a cause as ever was fought for; we have great resources; the people are well tempered; one active, masterly capacity, would bring order out of this confusion, and save this country.

(WJA II 439)

(21 April 1778)
Adams was elected by Congress to serve on the joint commission to the French Court. In February, he and John Quincy sailed to France, where they resided in Passy with Benjamin Franklin.

It is with much grief and concern that I have learned, from my first landing in France, the disputes between the Americans in this kingdom; the animosities between Mr. Deane and Mr. Lee; between Dr. Franklin and Mr. Lee; between Mr. Izard and Dr. Franklin, between Dr. Bancroft and Mr. Lee; between Mr. Carmichael and all. It is a rope of sand. I am at present wholly untainted with these prejudices, and will endeavor to keep myself so. Parties and divisions among the Americans here must have disagreeable, if not pernicious, effects.

(WJA III 138)

(3 December 1778)

We may call it obstinacy or blindness, if we will, but such is the state of parties in England, so deep would be the disgrace, and

perhaps so great the personal danger to those who have commenced and prosecuted this war, that they cannot but persevere
in it at every hazard; and nothing is clearer in my mind, than that
they never will quit the United States until they are either driven
or starved out of them.

(WJA VII 70–71)

(15 December 1778)
To Mercy Otis Warren, while Adams was a minister in France.

As to portraits, Madam, I dare not try my hand as yet. But my design is to retire, like my friend, and spend all my leisure hours in
writing a history of this revolution, and, with a hand as severe as
Tacitus, I wish to God it was as eloquent, draw the portrait of
every character that has figured in the business. But, when it is
done, I will dig a vault, and bury the manuscript, with a positive
injunction that it shall not be opened till a hundred years after my
death.

(WJA IX 475-6)

(2 April 1779)

America . . . can sustain the war, although it will be irksome and
grievous, infinitely better than England. America grows more
powerful, more numerous, more brave, and better disciplined
every year of the war, and more independent too, both in spirit
and circumstances. Their trade, it is true, does not flourish as it
did, but their agriculture, arts, and manufactures increase in proportion to the decline of their trade.

(WJA VII 143)

(22 April 1779)
*Franklin was appointed by Congress to be the sole minister to the French
court, so John and John Quincy Adams sailed back to Boston in June.*

The pleasure of returning home is very great. But I confess it is a
mortification to leave France. I have just acquired enough of the
language to understand a conversation, as it runs at a table, at
dinner or at supper, and to conduct all my affairs myself, in mak-

ing journeys through the country, with the postmasters, postilions, tavern keepers, etc., etc.

(WJA III 195–96)

(4 November 1779)
After a short time at home, Congress decided to send Adams back to France to conduct peace negotiations with the British ambassador in Paris.

I had yesterday the honor of receiving . . . two commissions, appointing me Minister Plenipotentiary from the United States, to negotiate peace and commerce with Great Britain. . . . Peace is an object of such vast importance, the interests to be adjusted in the negotiations to obtain it are so complicated and so delicate, and the difficulty of giving even general satisfaction is so great, that I feel myself more distressed at the prospect of executing the trust, than at the thought of leaving my country, and again encountering the dangers of the seas and of enemies. Yet, when I reflect on the general voice in my favor, and the high honor that is done me by this appointment, I feel the warmest sentiments of gratitude to Congress, and shall make no hesitation to accept it, and devote myself without reserve or loss of time to the discharge of it.

(DC IV 337-38)

(12 May 1780)

Our alliance with France is an honor and a security which have ever been near to my heart.

(WJA VII 165)

(13 May 1780)

All schemes of reconciliation with America, short of independence, and all plans for peace with America, allowing her independence separate from her allies, are visionary and delusive, disingenuous, corrupt, and wicked. America has taken her equal station, and she will behave with as much honor as any of the nations of the earth.

(WJA VII 168)

(13 May 1780)

The Americans at this day have higher notions of themselves than ever. They think they have gone through the greatest revolution that ever took place among men; that this revolution is as much for the benefit of the generality of mankind in Europe as for their own.

(WJA VII 168)

(17 August 1780)

No facts are believed, but decisive military conquests; no arguments are seriously attended to in Europe, but force. It is to be hoped, our countrymen, instead of amusing themselves any longer with delusive dreams of peace, will bend the whole force of their minds to augment their navy, to find out their own strength and resources, and to depend on themselves.

(WJA VII 248)

(14 October 1780)

Fighting is the thing. Fighting will do the business. Defeats will prove the way to victories. Patience! Patience!

(WJA VII 315)

(6 February 1781)

Combinations, political arrangements, and magnificent parade will not do with the English in their present state of intoxication. Nothing but hard blows, taking their fleets of merchant ships, and burning, taking, sinking, or destroying their men-of-war, will bring them to reason.

(WJA VII 367)

(19 July 1781)

There are no "American Colonies" at war with Great Britain. The power at war is the United States of America. . . . The word *colony*, in its usual acceptation, implies a metropolis, a mother country, a

superior political governor, ideas which the United States have
long since renounced forever.

(WJA VII 447)

(25 August 1781)

Our dear country will go fast asleep in full assurance of having
news of peace by winter, if not by the first vessel. Alas! What a
disappointment they will meet. I believe I had better go home and
wake up our countrymen out of their reveries about peace.

(WJA VII 460)

(15 October 1781)
*In September, the French navy defeated the British fleet off Yorktown,
Virginia, and one month later, General Cornwallis surrendered to General
Washington, thus ending the war. News of the defeat did not reach England
for several weeks.*

The present ministers must die off, and the King too, before there
will be any treaty between Britain and America. The nation will
stand by the King and ministry through every loss, while they
persevere; whereas both would sink into total contempt and
ridicule, if they were to make peace.

(WJA VII 471)

(5 February 1782)

Be it remembered, the present revolution, neither in America nor
Europe, has been accomplished by elegant bows, nor by fluency
in French, nor will any great thing ever be affected by such accomplishments alone.

(WJA VIII 39)

(12 February 1782)
To Count de Vergennes, the French minister of foreign affairs.

I have now the honor to acquaint you, that on the 29th day of
September last, the Congress of the United States of America did
me the honor to elect me their plenipotentiary to negotiate a

peace with Great Britain, and also negotiate a treaty of commerce with that kingdom; and Mr. Francis Dana, member of Congress, and of the Council of Massachusetts Bay, secretary to both commissions.

(WJA III 259)

(6 April 1782)
In February, the British Parliament voted for an end to war with the United States.

Never was an empire ruined in so short a time, and in so masterly a manner. Their affairs are in such a state, that even victories would only make their final ruin more complete.

(WJA VII 565)

(13 May 1782)
Peace negotiations between the American delegation and Richard Oswald, the British minister in Paris, dragged on for many months.

There are at this moment so many politicians piddling about peace, general and separate, that I am sick to death of it. Why is there not one soul in Europe capable of seeing the plainest thing in the world? Any one of the neutral powers saying to the rest, "America is one of us, and we will share in her commerce. Let us all as one declare it." These words once pronounced, peace is made, or, at least, soon and easily made. Without it, all may nibble and piddle and dribble and fribble, waste a long time, immense treasures, and much human blood, and they must come to it at last.

(WJA VII 584)

(13 August 1782)

There is but one way to negotiate with Englishmen, that is, clearly and decidedly; their fears only govern them. If we entertain an idea of their generosity or benevolence towards us, we are undone. They hate us, universally, from the throne to the footstool, and would annihilate us, if in their power, before they would treat with us in any way.

(WJA VII 610)

(6 September 1782)
Though Adams wrote regular letters to Congress, he rarely received replies or encouragements.

My correspondence with Congress and their ministers in Europe is a great deal of work; in short, I am weary, and nobody pities me. Nobody seems to know anything about me. Nobody knows that I do anything or have anything to do.

(WJA IX 513)

(2 November 1782)

Almost every moment of this week has been employed in negotiation with the English gentlemen concerning peace. We have made two propositions; one the line of forty-five degrees; the other, a line through the middle of the lakes. And for the bound between Massachusetts and Nova Scotia, a line from the mouth of Saint Croix to its source, and from its source to the highlands.

(WJA III 300)

(3 November 1782)

The present conduct of England and America resembles that of the eagle and the cat. An eagle scaling over a farmer's yard, espied a creature that he thought a hare; he pounced upon him and took him up in the air; the cat seized him by the neck with her teeth, and round the body with her fore and hind claws. The eagle finding himself scratched and pressed, bids the cat let go and fall down. No, says the cat, I won't let go and fall; you shall stoop and set me down.

(WJA III 302)

(9 December 1782)
In conversation with British diplomat Richard Oswald after a preliminary peace treaty had been signed between the United States and Great Britain on November 30.

We slid from one thing to another into a very lively conversation upon politics. He asked me what the conduct of his Court and nation ought to be in relation to America. I answered, "The alpha and the omega of British policy towards America was summed up in this one maxim: See that American independence is independent; independent of all the world; independent of yourselves, as well as of France; and independent of both, as well as of the rest of Europe. Depend upon it, you have no chance for salvation but by setting up America very high. Take care to remove from the American mind all cause of fear of you. No other motive but fear of you will ever produce in the Americans any unreasonable attachment to the House of Bourbon."

(WJA III 344)

(18 February 1783)
Adams was angry over the degree of negotiating authority granted by Congress to the French minister Vergennes.

I have omitted my Journal and several things of some consequence; but I am weary, disgusted, affronted, and disappointed. This state of mind I must alter, and work while the day lasts. I have been injured, and my country has joined in the injury; it has basely prostituted its own honor by sacrificing mine. But the sacrifice of me was not so servile and intolerable as putting us all under guardianship. Congress surrendered their own sovereignty into the hands of a French minister. Blush! Blush! Ye guilty records! Blush and perish! It is glory to have broken such infamous orders. Infamous, I say, for so they will be to all posterity. How can such a stain be washed out? Can we cast a veil over it and forget it?

(WJA III 359)

(16 June 1783)
Adams suffered from two major illnesses while conducting diplomatic affairs in Holland.

The connections I have formed in Holland may be of use to the public wherever I may be, in America or elsewhere, as well as even in that country itself. Those connections will readily become those of any minister Congress may send there. It cost me all my happiness, and had very nearly cost me my life to form them; it cost me more; it has left me in an ill state of health which I never shall fully repair. I shall carry Holland in my veins to my grave.

(WJA VIII 72)

(16 June 1783)

When the existence of our country and her essential interests were at stake, it was a duty to run all risks, to stifle every feeling, to sacrifice every interest; and this duty I have discharged with patience and perseverance, and with a success that can be attributed only to Providence. But, in time of peace, the public in less danger abroad than at home, knowing I can do more good at home, I should do a very wrong thing to remove my family to stay in Holland, merely for the sake of holding an honorable commission, making and receiving bows and compliments, and eating splendid suppers at Court.

(WJA VIII 73)

(2 August 1783)
Adams returned to Paris to help negotiate a preliminary peace treaty with Great Britain the previous November. Negotiations over the Canadian-American border, fishing rights, navigation of the Mississippi, and Loyalist debts dragged on for months, until the final treaty was signed.

The prospect of returning to Paris, and living there without my family, in absolute idleness, at a time when so many and so great things want to be done for our country elsewhere, is very disagreeable. If we must live there, waiting for the moving of many waters, and treaties are to be there negotiated with the powers of Europe. . . . I pray that we may all be joined in the business, as we are in the commission for peace, that, at least, we may have the satisfaction of knowing what is done, and of giving a hint for the public good, if any one occurs to us, and that we may not be made the sport and ridicule of all Europe, as well as those who contrive such humiliations. I declare, I had rather be door-keeper to Congress, than live at Paris as I have done for the last six months.

(WJA VIII 130)

(5 September 1783)
The Treaty of Paris marked the formal end of hostilities between the United States and Great Britain.

On Wednesday, the third day of this month, the American ministers met the British minister at his lodgings at the *Hôtel de York,*

and signed, sealed, and delivered the definitive treaty of peace
between the United States of America and the King of Great
Britain. Although it is but a confirmation or repetition of the pro-
visional articles, I have the honor to congratulate Congress upon
it, as it is a completion of the work of peace, and the best that we
could obtain. Nothing remains now to be done, but a treaty of
commerce; but this, in my opinion, cannot be negotiated without
a new commission from Congress to some one or more persons.
Time, it is easy to foresee, will not be likely to render the British
nation more disposed to a regulation of commerce favorable to
us, and, therefore, my advice is, to issue a commission as soon as
may be.

(WJA VIII 143)

3

REFLECTIONS ON THE REVOLUTION

(16 July 1786)

It is an observation of one of the profoundest inquirers into human affairs, that a revolution of government successfully conducted and completed is the strongest proof that can be given by a people of their virtue and good sense. An enterprise of so much difficulty can never be planned and carried on without abilities; and a people without principle cannot have confidence enough in each other.

(WJA III 399–400)

(4 March 1797)

When it was first perceived, in early times, that no middle course for America remained between unlimited submission to a foreign legislature and a total independence of its claims, men of reflection were less apprehensive of danger from the formidable power of fleets and armies they must determine to resist, than from those contests and dissensions, which would certainly arise, concerning the forms of government to be instituted, over the whole, and over the parts of this extensive country. Relying, however, on the purity of their intentions, the justice of their cause, and the integrity and intelligence of the people, under an overruling Providence, which had so signally protected this country from the first, the representatives of this nation, then consisting of little more than half its present numbers, not only broke to pieces the chains which were forging, and the rod of iron that was lifted up, but frankly cut asunder the ties which had bound them, and launched into an ocean of uncertainty.

(WJA IX 105)

(1802–7 Autobiography)
At the urging of John Quincy, who had just been elected to the U.S. Senate, Adams began writing his autobiography.

I was incessantly employed through the whole fall, winter, and spring of 1775 and 1776, in Congress during their sittings, and on committees on mornings and evenings, and unquestionably did more business than any other member of that house.

(WJA II 510)

(1802–7 Autobiography)
John Adams wrote the "Braintree Instructions," which were published throughout the province of Massachusetts.

This year, 1765, was the epoch of the Stamp Act. I drew up a petition to the selectmen of Braintree, and procured it to be signed by a number of the respectable inhabitants, to call a meeting of the town to instruct their representative in relation to the stamps. The public attention of the whole continent was alarmed, and my principles and political connections were well known.

(WJA II 153)

(1805)

The English were strangely infatuated with an idea that [Samuel] Adams and Hancock, Washington and Franklin, with a few others in the several States, as they had influence enough to throw off the authority of Great Britain, would have influence enough to put it on again, as a man who has strength enough to throw off his cloak, may be supposed able to throw it again over his shoulder. Nothing could be more erroneous; for none of these leaders had any influence but that which was given them by the folly and temerity of Great Britain; and if any of them had adopted and advocated any such projects as these, he would not only have lost all influence in America, but been obliged to fly to England for protection among the royalists and refugees. These speculations were, however, all rendered unnecessary. Independence had been declared two years; and all America in a manner had renounced every modification of government under Great Britain forever, fully convinced that no cordial confidence or affection could ever be restored on either side. Besides, a treaty with France had been solemnly made. America was then a virgin, and her faith sacred; and it would have been ridiculous to suppose that France would now consent that we should make a separate treaty, and become subject again to England, that the reunited kingdoms might immediately fall upon France in a new war.

(WJA III 180-81)

(8 March 1805)

All the powers of government, legislative, executive, and judiciary were at that time [late 1776] collected in one centre, and that centre was the Congress. As a member of that body, I had contributed my share towards the creation of the army, and the appointment of all the officers, and, as president of the Board of War, it was my peculiar province to superintend everything relating to the army. I will add without vanity, I had read as much on the military art, and much more of the history of war, than any American officer of that army, General Lee excepted.

(WJA III 87)

(December 1806)

When I asked leave of Congress to make a visit to my constituents and my family in November, 1777, it was my intention to decline the next election, and return to my practice at the bar. I had been four years in Congress, had left my accounts in a very loose condition, my debtors were failing, the paper money was depreciating; I was daily losing the fruits of seventeen years' industry; my family was living on my past acquisitions, which were very moderate, for no man ever did so much business for so little profit; my children were growing up without my care in their education, and all my emoluments as a member of Congress, for four years, had not been sufficient to pay a laboring man upon my farm.

Some of my friends, who had more compassion for me and my family than others, suggested to me what I knew very well before, that I was losing a fortune every year by my absence. Young gentlemen who had been clerks in my offices, were growing rich; for the prize causes, and other controversies had made the profession of a barrister more lucrative than it ever had been before. I thought, therefore, that four years' drudgery, and sacrifice of everything, were sufficient for my share of absence from home, and that another might take my place.

(WJA III 89)

(1 May 1807)

Jefferson has acquired such glory by his declaration of independence in 1776, that I think I may boast of my declaration of independence in 1755, twenty-one years older than his.

(WJA IX 592)

(9 February 1811)
To Josiah Quincy.

I ought not to object to your reverence for your fathers, as you call them, meaning, I presume, the government, and those concerned in the direction of public affairs; much less can I be displeased at your numbering me among them. But, to tell you a very great secret, as far as I am capable of comparing the merit of different periods, I have no reason to believe that we were better than you are. We had as many poor creatures and selfish beings, in proportion, among us as you have among you; nor were there then more enlightened men, or in greater number, in proportion, than there are now.

(WJA IX 630)

(24 January 1813)
On his role in the founding of the Continental Navy in 1775.

The committee appointed were John Langdon, Silas Deane, and John Adams. We met, and at once agreed to report a resolution, authorizing General Washington to fit and arm one or more vessels for the purpose.

(WJA X 27)

(28 March 1813)
Although the Declaration of Independence was unanimously signed by the members of the Second Continental Congress, there were those who did so with reservations.

They who were then members, all signed it, and, as I could not see their hearts, it would be hard for me to say that they did not approve it; but, as far as I could penetrate the intricate, internal foldings of their soul, I then believed, and have not since altered my opinion, that there were several who signed with regret, and several others, with many doubts and much lukewarmness. The measure had been on the carpet for months, and obstinately opposed from day to day. Majorities were constantly against it.

(WJA X 35)

(28 June 1813)

The *general principles* on which the fathers achieved independence, were the only principles in which that beautiful assembly of young men could unite, and these principles only could be intended by them in their address, or by me in my answer. And what were these *general principles*? I answer, the general principles of Christianity, in which all those sects were united, and the *general principles* of English and American liberty, in which all those young men united, and which had united all parties in America, in majorities sufficient to assert and maintain her independence. Now I will avow, that I then believed and now believe that those general principles of Christianity are as eternal and immutable as the existence and attributes of God; and that those principles of liberty are as unalterable as human nature and our terrestrial, mundane system. I could, therefore, safely say, consistently with all my then and present information, that I believed they would never make discoveries in contradiction to these *general principles*. In favor of these *general principles*, in philosophy, religion, and government, I could fill sheets of quotations from Frederic of Prussia, from Hume, Gibbon, Bolingbroke, Rousseau, and Voltaire, as well as Newton and Locke; not to mention thousands of divines and philosophers of inferior fame.

(WJA X 45-46)

(1813)
This handwritten footnote was added by Adams to his personal copy of Discourses on Davila.

The Declaration of Independence of 4 July, 1776, contained nothing but the Boston Declaration of 1772 and the Congress Declaration of 1774. Such are the caprices of fortune. This Declaration of Rights was drawn by the little John Adams. The mighty Jefferson, by the Declaration of Independence of 4 July, 1776, carried away the glory of the great and the little.

(WJA VI 278)

(31 August 1813)

Upon the whole, if we allow two-thirds of the people to have been with us in the revolution, is not the allowance ample? Are not two-thirds of the nation now with the administration? Divided we ever have been, and ever must be. Two-thirds always had and will have more difficulty to struggle with the one-third than with all our foreign enemies.

(WJA X 63)

(5 January 1815)
On the importance of the Boston Massacre.

If Parliament was omnipotent, could enact what statutes it pleased, and employ armies and navies, governors, counselors, and judges to interpret them, and carry them into execution, of what use could our Houses of Representatives be? And what were our religion, liberties, properties, or existence worth? . . . However slightly historians may have passed over this event, the blood of the martyrs, right or wrong, proved to be the seeds of the congregation. Not the battle of Lexington or Bunker's Hill, not the surrender of Burgoyne or Cornwallis were more important events in American history than the battle of King Street, on the 5th of March, 1770.

(WJA X 202-3)

(January 1815)

If I were to calculate the divisions among the people of America ... I should say that full one-third were averse to the revolution. These, retaining that overweening fondness, in which they had been educated, for the English, could not cordially like the French; indeed, they most heartily detested them. An opposite third conceived a hatred for the English, and gave themselves up to an enthusiastic gratitude to France. The middle third, composed principally of the yeomanry, the soundest part of the nation, and always averse to war, were rather lukewarm both to England and France; and sometimes stragglers from them, and sometimes the whole body, united with the first or the last third, according to circumstances.

(WJA X 110-11)

(29 March 1815)

The last twenty-five years of the last century, and the first fifteen years of this, may be called the age of revolutions and constitutions. We began the dance, and have produced eighteen or twenty models of constitutions, the excellences and defects of which you probably know better than I do. They are, no doubt, the best for us that we could contrive and agree to adopt.

(WJA X 149)

(5 April 1815)

The war from 4th July, 1776, to 30th November, 1782, six years and some months, was only an appeal to Heaven in defense of our sovereignty. Heaven decided in our favor; and Britain was forced not to give, grant, concede, or release our independence, but to acknowledge it, in terms as clear as our language afforded, and under seal and under oath.

(WJA X 159)

(24 April 1815)

After the battles or skirmishes of Concord and Lexington on the
19th of April, 1775, the militia of Massachusetts, Connecticut,
New Hampshire, and Rhode Island, marched to Cambridge,
Roxbury, Medford, Charlestown, etc., to drive the British army
into the sea; and if their first ardor had not been restrained by
considerations *of the Union of the Colonies,* they would have done
it.

(WJA X 162)

(30 July 1815)
To Thomas McKean, a fellow signer of the Declaration of Independence.

Who shall write the history of the American Revolution? Who can
write it? Who will ever be able to write it? The most essential doc-
uments, the debates and deliberations in Congress, from 1774 to
1783, were all in secret, and are now lost forever. Mr. Dickinson
printed a speech, which he said he made in Congress against the
Declaration of Independence; but it appeared to me very different
from that which you and I heard. Dr. Witherspoon has published
speeches, which he wrote beforehand, and delivered memoriter
as he did his sermons. But these, I believe, are the only speeches
ever committed to writing.

(WJA X 171)

(24 August 1815)
To Thomas Jefferson on the meaning of the American Revolution.

As to the history of the revolution, my ideas may be peculiar, perhaps singular. What do we mean by the revolution? The war?
That was no part of the revolution; it was only an effect and consequence of it. The revolution was in the minds of the people, and
this was effected from 1760 to 1775, in the course of fifteen years,
before a drop of blood was shed at Lexington. The records of thirteen legislatures, the pamphlets, newspapers in all the colonies,
ought to be consulted during that period, to ascertain the steps by
which the public opinion was enlightened and informed concerning the authority of parliament over the colonies.

(WJA X 173)

(5 December 1815)
On the passage of the Stamp Act in 1765.

Here, then, was a declaration of war on both sides. Here were already two nations directly and explicitly at issue concerning their fundamental laws; for if the sovereignty of the empire was vested in Parliament, a denial of its right to tax the colonies was a declaration of total independence on Parliament; and the Stamp Act was a declaration of war against the colonies, by King, Lords, and Commons. As the King had conspired with his Lords and Commons in the treasonable invasion of the legal sovereignties of the colonies, his Majesty was, upon their principles, a rebel, a traitor, and a declared enemy, and they had a right, if they pleased, "to cashier him. . . ." Nay, they had as clear a right to hang, draw, and quarter him, upon their principles, as he had upon his, notwithstanding his anointment with holy oil, to practice a similar inhumanity upon Samuel Adams and John Hancock, for which he has recorded to endless ages so ardent a desire.

(WJA X 189-90)

(1 January 1816)

From 1760 to 1766, was the purest period of patriotism; from 1766 to 1776 was the period of corruption; from 1775 to 1783 was the period of war. Not a revolutionary war, for the revolution was complete, in the minds of the people, and the union of colonies, before the war commenced in the skirmishes of Concord and Lexington on the 19th of April, 1775.

(WJA X 197)

(1 June 1817)

If statues, obelisks, pyramids, or divine honors were ever merited by men, of cities or nations, James Otis, Samuel Adams, and John Hancock, deserved these from the town of Boston and the United States. Such adulations, however, are monopolized by profligate libelers, by cringing flatterers, by unprincipled ambition, by sordid avarice, by griping usurers, by scheming speculators, by plundering bankers, by blind enthusiasts, by superstitious bigots, by puppies and butterflies, and by everything but honor and virtue.

(WJA X 261)

(5 June 1817)

James Otis, Samuel Adams, and John Hancock were the three most essential characters; and Great Britain knew it, though America does not. Great and important and excellent characters, aroused and excited by these, arose in Pennsylvania, Virginia, New York, South Carolina, and in all the other States; but these three were the first movers, the most constant, steady, persevering springs, agents, and most disinterested sufferers and firmest pillars of the whole Revolution.

(WJA X 263)

(18 September 1818)

Who, then, was the author, inventor, discoverer of independence? The only true answer must be the first emigrants, and the proof of it is in the charter of James I. When we say that Otis, Adams, Mayhew, Henry, Lee, Jefferson, etc., were authors of independence, we ought to say they were only awakeners and revivers of the original fundamental principle of colonization.

(WJA X 359)

(9 February 1821)

It is true there always existed in the colonies a desire of independence of Parliament in the articles of internal taxation and internal policy, and a very general, if not a universal opinion, that they were constitutionally entitled to it, and as general a determination, if possible, to maintain and defend it. But there never existed a desire of independence of the crown, or of general regulations of commerce for the equal and impartial benefit of all parts of the empire. . . . That the encroaching disposition of Great Britain would one day attempt to enslave them by an unlimited submission to Parliament and rule them with a rod of iron, was early foreseen by many wise men in all the States; that this attempt would produce resistance on the part of America, and an awful struggle, was also foreseen, but dreaded and deprecated as the greatest calamity that could befall them. For my own part, there was not a moment during the Revolution, when I would not have given everything I ever possessed for a restoration to the state of things before the contest began, provided we could have had any sufficient security for its continuance. I always dreaded the Revolution, as fraught with ruin to me and my family; and, indeed, it has been but little better.

(WJA X 394–95)

(24 February 1821)

The principles and sentiments and expressions of the Declaration of Independence had been so often pronounced and echoed and reechoed in that Congress for two years before, and especially for the last six months, that it will forever be impossible to ascertain who uttered them, and upon what occasion.

(WJA X 396)

(31 March 1821)

Silence, then, ye revolutionary heroes, patriots, and sages! Never boast of your superiority for services or sufferings or sacrifices! Our Hancocks and Washingtons never exceeded in disinterestedness dozens of emigrants to America two hundred years ago. In short, the whole history of America for two hundred years appears to me to exhibit a uniform, general tenor of character for intelligence, integrity, patience, fortitude, and public spirit. One generation has little pretension for boasting over another.

(WJA X 402–30)

Part II

THE PRIVATE ADAMS

4

Personal Philosophy

(12 October 1755)

Friendship, I take it, is one of the distinguishing glories of man; and the creature that is insensible of its charms, though he may wear the shape of man, is unworthy of the character.

(WJA I 24)

(19 February 1756)

No man is entirely free from weakness and imperfection in this life. Men of the most exalted genius and active minds are generally most perfect slaves to the love of fame. They sometimes descend to as mean tricks and artifices in pursuit of honor or reputation as the miser descends to in pursuit of gold. The greatest men have been the most envious, malicious, and revengeful.

(WJA II 6)

(21 February 1756)

We must be cautious and sparing of our praise, lest it become too familiar and cheap, and so, contemptible; corporal as well as disgraceful punishments depress the spirits, but commendation enlivens and stimulates them to a noble ardor and emulation.

(WJA II 6)

(27 March 1756)

The stream of life sometimes glides smoothly on through the flowery meadows and enameled plains; at other times it drags a winding, reluctant course, through offensive bogs and dismal, gloomy swamps.

(WJA II 12)

(29 April 1756)

Our proper business in this life is not to accumulate large fortunes, not to gain high honors and important offices in the state, not to waste our health and spirits in pursuit of the sciences, but constantly to improve ourselves in habits of piety and virtue.

(WJA II 14)

(15 May 1756)

Exercise invigorates and enlivens all the faculties of body and of mind; it arouses our animal spirits, it disperses melancholy; it spreads a gladness and satisfaction over our minds, and qualifies us for every sort of business, and every sort of pleasure.

(WJA II 17)

(1 April 1756)

The man who lives wholly to himself is of less worth than the cattle in his barn.

(WJA I 30)

(10 April 1756)

The man to whom nature has given a great and surprising genius, will perform great and surprising achievements. But a soul originally narrow and confined will never be enlarged to a distinguishing capacity. Such a one must be content to grovel amidst pebbles and butterflies through the whole of his life. By diligence and attention indeed, he may possibly get the character of a man of sense; but never that of a great man.

(WJA II 13)

(14 June 1756)

He is not a wise man, and is unfit to fill any important station in society, that has left one passion in his soul unsubdued. The love of glory will make a General sacrifice the interest of his nation to his own fame. Avarice exposes some to corruption, and all to a thousand meannesses and villainies destructive to society. Love has deposed lawful kings, and aggrandized the unlawful, ill deserving courtiers. Envy is more studious of eclipsing the luster of other men by indirect stratagems, than of brightening its own luster by great and meritorious actions. These passions should be bound fast, and brought under the yoke. Untamed, they are lawless bulls; they roar and bluster, defy all control, and sometimes murder their proper owner. But, properly inured to obedience, they take their places under the yoke without noise, and labor vigorously in their master's service.

(WJA II 22–23)

(1759)

Disappointments are misery. If a man takes pride and pleasure in a house, or in rich furniture, or clothing, or in any thing, how is it possible for him to be satisfied when they are lost, destroyed, consumed?

(WJA II 76)

(30 May 1760)

Several country towns, within my observation, have at least a dozen taverns and retailers. Here the time, the money, the health, and the modesty, of most that are young and of many old, are wasted; here diseases, vicious habits, bastards, and legislators, are frequently begotten.

(WJA II 85)

(29 November 1760)

Order, method, regularity in business or study, have excellent effects, both in saving of time and in bettering and improving performance. Business done in order, is done sooner and better.

(WJA II 105)

(16 December 1760)

Virtues, ambition, generosity, indulged to excess, degenerate into
extravagance, which plunges headlong into villainy and folly.

(WJA II 106)

(29 August 1763)

The greatest and best of all mankind deserve less admiration, and
even the worst and vilest deserve more candor, than the world in
general is willing to allow them.

(WJA III 432)

(29 August 1763)

There is nothing in the science of human nature more curious, or
that deserves a critical attention from every order of men so
much, as that principle which moral writers have distinguished
by the name of self-deceit. This principle is the spurious offspring
of self-love; and is, perhaps, the source of far the greatest and
worst part of the vices and calamities among mankind.

(WJA III 433)

(29 August 1763)

Indeed, it must be confessed, and it ought to be with much contrition lamented, that those eyes, which have been given us to see,
are willingly suffered by us to be obscured, and those consciences,
which by the commission of God Almighty have a rightful authority over us, to be deposed by prejudices, appetites, and passions,
which ought to hold a much inferior rank in the intellectual and
moral system. Such swarms of passions, avarice and ambition, servility and adulation, hopes, fears, jealousies, envy, revenge, malice, and cruelty, are continually buzzing in the world, and we are
so extremely prone to mistake the impulses of these for the dictates of our consciences,—that the greatest genius, united to the
best disposition, will find it hard to hearken to the voice of reason,
or even to be certain of the purity of his own intentions.

(WJA III 434-35)

(29 August 1763)

Sedition, rebellion, pedantry, desire of fame, turbulence, and malice, were always reproached to the great reformers, who delivered us from the worst chains that were ever forged by monks or devils for the human mind.

(WJA III 435)

(August 1765)

Man has certainly an exalted soul; and the same principle in human nature,—that aspiring, noble principle founded in benevolence, and cherished by knowledge; I mean the love of power, which has been so often the cause of slavery,—has, whenever freedom has existed, been the cause of freedom. If it is this principle that has always prompted princes and nobles of the earth, by every species of fraud and violence to shake off all the limitations of their power, it is the same that has always stimulated the common people to aspire at independency, and to endeavor at confining the power of the great within the limits of equity and reason.

(WJA III 448)

(29 December 1765)

A religious bigot is the worst of men.

(WJA II 169)

(7 January 1766)

To pry into a man's private life, and expose to the world all the vices and follies of youth, to paint before the public eye all the blots and stains in a man's private character, must excite the commiseration of every reader to the object, and his indignation against the author of such abuse.

(WJA II 175)

(26 April 1766)

Foresight, judgment, sagacity, penetration, etc., are but very feeble, infirm things, in these great affairs of state and war.

(WJA II 192)

(27 June 1770)

Pen, ink and paper, and a sitting posture, are great helps to attention and thinking.

(WJA II 238)

(22 June 1771)

The more I consider mankind, the more I see that every man seriously and in his own conscience believes himself the wisest, brightest, best, happiest, etc. of all mankind.

(WJA II 282)

(30 June 1772)

The rich are seldom remarkable for modesty, ingenuity, or humanity.

(WJA II 297)

(28 November 1772)

A sensible soldier is as entertaining a companion as any man whatever. They acquire an urbanity, by travel and promiscuous conversation, that is charming.

(WJA II 303)

(31 December 1772)

A character can never be supported, if it can be raised, without a good, a great share of self-government.

(WJA II 309)

(1 January 1773)

A head full of schemes, and a heart full of anxiety, are incompatible with any degree of happiness.

(WJA II 314)

(6 July 1774)

There is not a sin which prevails more universally and has prevailed longer than prodigality in furniture, equipage, apparel, and diet. And I believe that this vice, this sin, has as large a share in drawing down the judgments of Heaven as any. And perhaps the punishment that is inflicted may work medicinally and cure the disease.

(FL 14)

(7 July 1774)

So difficult is it for the frail, feeble mind of man to shake itself loose from all the prejudice and habits . . . and as long as a man adheres immovably to his own interest and has understanding or luck enough to secure and promote it, he will have the character of a man of sense, and will be respected by a selfish world. I know of no better reason for it than this, that most men are conscious that they aim at their own interest only, and that if they fail it is owing to short sight or ill luck, and therefore they can't blame, but secretly applaud, admire, and sometimes envy those whose capacities have proved greater and fortunes more prosperous.

(FL 19)

(1774)

Human nature itself is evermore an advocate for liberty.

(WJA IV 14)

(1774)

There is not in human nature a more wonderful phenomenon, nor in the whole theory of it a more intricate speculation, than in the shiftings, turnings, windings, and evasions of a guilty conscience. Such is our unalterable moral constitution, that an internal inclination to do wrong is criminal; and a wicked thought stains the mind with guilt, and makes it tingle with pain. Hence it comes to pass, that the guilty mind can never bear to think that its guilt is known to God or man, no, nor to itself.

(WJA IV 44)

(4 March 1776)

A man may have the faculty of concealing his resentment, or suppressing it, but he must and ought to feel it; nay, he ought to indulge it, to cultivate it; it is a duty. His person, his property, his liberty, his reputation, are not safe without it.

(WJA II 488)

(22 June 1776)

There are as many evils, and more, which arise in human life from an excess of diffidence, as from an excess of confidence.

(WJA IX 404)

(3 July 1776)

The furnace of affliction produces refinement in states as well as individuals. And the new government we are assuming in every part will require a purification from our vices, and an augmentation of our virtues, or they will be no blessings. The people will have unbounded power, and the people are extremely addicted to corruption and venality, as well as the great.

(FL 191–92)

(7 July 1776)

Affectation is as disagreeable in a letter as in conversation, and therefore studied language, premeditated method, and sublime sentiments are not expected in a letter. Notwithstanding which, the sublime, as well as the beautiful and the novel, may naturally enough appear in familiar letters among friends.

(FL 196)

(September 1776)

A panic in the army, when pushed to desperation, becomes heroism.

(WJA I 256)

(22 September 1776)

Unfaithfulness in public stations is deeply criminal. But there is no encouragement to be faithful. Neither profit, nor honor, nor applause is acquired by faithfulness. But I know by what. There is too much corruption even in this infant age of our republic. Virtue is not in fashion. Vice is not infamous.

(FL 228)

(21 February 1777)

Military abilities and experience are a great advantage to any character.

(FL 248)

(22 May 1777)

I am wearied to death with the wrangles between military officers, high and low. They quarrel like cats and dogs. They worry one another like mastiffs, scrambling for rank and pay like apes for nuts. I believe there is no one principle which predominates in human nature so much, in every stage of life from the cradle to the grave, in males and females, old and young, black and white, rich and poor, high and low, as this passion for superiority.

(FL 276)

(12 April 1778)

I cannot help suspecting that the more elegance, the less virtue, in all times and countries. Yet I fear that even my own dear country wants the power and opportunity more than the inclination to be elegant, soft, and luxurious.

(FL 329)

(2 June 1778)

From all that I had read of history and government, of human life and manners, I had drawn this conclusion, that the manners of women were the most infallible barometer to ascertain the degree of morality and virtue in a nation. All that I have since read, and all the observations I have made in different nations, have confirmed me in this opinion. The manners of women are the surest criterion by which to determine a republican government is practicable in a nation or not. The Jews, the Greeks, the Romans, the Dutch, all lost their public spirit, their republican principles and habits, and their republican forms of government, when they lost the modesty and domestic virtues of their women.

(WJA III 171)

(3 June 1778)

My dear countrymen! How shall I persuade you to avoid the plague of Europe? Luxury has as many and as bewitching charms on your side of the ocean as [here in France]; and luxury, wherever she goes, effaces from human nature the image of the Divinity. If I had the power I would forever banish and exclude from America all gold, silver, precious stones, alabaster, marble, silk, velvet, and lace.

(FL 334)

(2 April 1779)

When a society gets disturbed, men of great talents and good qualities are always found or made.

(WJA VII 144)

(22 May 1779)
In conversation with a French officer on board a ship bound for America.

We fell upon the subject of swearing. I asked him if the French sailors swore. He said, *chaque instant*, every moment; that Henry IV swore a great deal,—*ventre Saint-Gris*; literally, holy grey belly. . . . I told him that most of the oaths had originally relation to religion, and explained to him, zounds, G—d's wounds; s'blood and wounds, his blood and wounds, relating to Christ. He said this made him shudder. *Ma foi,*—faith,—*par dieu,* etc. It is amazing how men get the habit of using these words without thinking. I see no difference between French and English on this account.

(WJA III 208)

(18 April 1781)

An excess of modesty and reserve is an excess still.

(WJA VII 394)

(19 February 1782)

Vanity . . . is a passion capable of inspiring illusions which astonish all other men; and the Britons are, without exception, the vainest people upon earth.

(WJA VII 513)

(5 February 1782)

A man must have something in his head to say, before he can speak to effect, however ready he may be at utterance.

(WJA VIII 39)

(24 December 1782)

There are men who carry the countenance and air of boys through life.

(WJA III 351)

(21 January 1785)

I have half a mind to devote the next ten years to the making of a book upon the subject of nobility. I wish to inquire into the practice of all nations, ancient and modern, civilized and savage, under all religions,—Mohammedan, Christian, and Pagan,—to see how far the division of mankind into patricians and plebeians, nobles and simples, is necessary and inevitable, and how far it is not. Nature has not made this discrimination. Art has done it. Art may prevent it. Would it do good or evil to prevent it? I believe good, think what you will of it. . . . I believe this many-headed beast, the people, will, some time or other, have wit enough to throw their riders; and, if they should, they will put an end to an abundance of tricks, with which they are now curbed and bitted, whipped and spurred.

(WJA VIII 370)

(10 September 1785)

There are in history examples of characters wholly disinterested, who have displayed the sublimest talents, the greatest virtues, at the same time that they have made long and severe sacrifices to their country, of their time, their estates, their labor, healths, and even their lives, and they are deservedly admired and revered by all virtuous men. But how few have they been!

(WJA IX 539)

(2 June 1786)
On the discoveries of British astronomer Sir William Herschel (1738–1822).

Herschel . . . with his new glass, has discovered the most magnif-icent spectacle that ever was seen or imagined, and I suppose it is chiefly as a spectacle that his discovery is admired. If all those sin-gle, double, triple, quadruple worlds are peopled as fully as every leaf and drop is in this, what a merry company there is of us in the universe, all fellow-creatures, insects, animalcules, and all! Why are we kept so unacquainted with each other? I fancy we shall know each other better, and shall see that even cards and routs, dancing dogs, learned pigs, scientific birds, etc., are not so despi-cable things as we in our wonderful wisdom sometimes think them.

(WJA IX 550)

(1787)

Happiness, whether in despotism or democracy, whether in slav-ery or liberty, can never be found without virtue.

(WJA VI 219)

(1790–91)

A desire to be observed, considered, esteemed, praised, beloved, and admired by his fellows, is one of the earliest, as well as keenest dispositions discovered in the heart of man.

(WJA VI 232)

(11 June 1790)

Mankind have, I agree, behaved too much like horses; been rude, wild, and mad, until they were mastered, and then been too tame, gentle, and dull. . . . The great and perpetual distinction in civilized societies, has been between the rich, who are few, and the poor, who are many. When the many are masters, they are too unruly, and then the few are too tame, and afraid to speak the truth. When the few are masters, they are too severe, and then the many are too servile. This is the strict truth.

(WJA IX 570)

(1790–91)

Every man not only desires the consideration of others, but he frequently compares himself with others, his friends or his enemies; and in proportion as he exults when he perceives that he has more of it than they, he feels a keener affliction when he sees that one or more of them, are more respected than himself.

(WJA VI 233)

(1790–91)

Every personal quality, and every blessing of fortune, is cherished in proportion to its capacity of gratifying this universal affection for the esteem, the sympathy, admiration and congratulations of the public. Beauty in the face, elegance of figure, grace of attitude and motion, riches, honors, everything is weighed in the scale, and desired, not so much for the pleasure they afford, as the attention they command.

(WJA VI 235)

(1790–91)

To feel ourselves unheeded, chills the most pleasing hope, damps the most fond desire, checks the most agreeable wish, disappoints the most ardent expectations of human nature.

(WJA VI 239)

(1790–91)

A sense of duty; a love of truth; a desire to alleviate the anxieties of ignorance, may, no doubt, have an influence on some minds. But the universal object and idol of men of letters is *reputation*. It is the *notoriety*, the *celebration*, which constitutes the charm that is to compensate the loss of appetite and sleep, and sometimes of riches and honors.

(WJA VI 240)

(1790–91)

Reason holds the helm, but passions are the gales.

(WJA VI 243)

(1790–91)

Nature has ordained it, as a constant incentive to activity and industry, that, to acquire the attention and complacency, the approbation and admiration of their fellows, men might be urged to constant exertions of beneficence. By this destination of their natures, men of all sorts, even those who have the least of reason, virtue or benevolence, are chained down to an incessant servitude to their fellow creatures; laboring without intermission to produce something which shall contribute to the comfort, convenience, pleasure, profit, or utility of some or other of the species, they are really thus constituted by their own vanity, slaves to mankind. Slaves, I say again. For what a folly is it!

(WJA VI 245)

(1790–91)

As no appetite in human nature is more universal than that for honor, and real merit is confined to a very few, the numbers who thirst for respect are out of all proportion to those who seek it only by merit. The great majority trouble themselves little about merit, but apply themselves to seek for honor, by means which they see will more easily and certainly obtain it, by displaying their taste and address, their wealth and magnificence, their ancient parchments, pictures and statues, and the virtues of their ancestors; and if these fail, as they seldom have done, they have recourse to artifice, dissimulation, hypocrisy, flattery, imposture, empiricism, quackery, and bribery.

(WJA VI 250)

(1790–91)

There is a remarkable disposition in mankind to congratulate with others in their joys and prosperity, more than to sympathize with them in their sorrows and adversity.

(WJA VI 253)

(1790–91)

As rest is rapture to the weary man, those who labor little will always be envied by those who labor much, though the latter in reality be probably the most enviable.

(WJA VI 280)

(1790–91)

The controversy between the rich and the poor, the laborious and the idle, the learned and the ignorant, distinctions as old as the creation, and as extensive as the globe, distinctions which no art or policy, no degree of virtue or philosophy can ever wholly destroy, will continue, and rivalries will spring out of them.

(WJA VI 280)

(1790–91)

Narrow and illiberal sentiments are not peculiar to the rich or the poor.

(WJA VI 396)

(4 February 1794)

By the law of nature, all men are men, and not angels—men, and
not lions—men, and not whales—men, and not eagles—that is,
they are all of the same species; and this is the most that the equality of nature amounts to. But man differs by nature from man, almost as much as man from beast. The equality of nature is moral
and political only, and means that all men are independent. But a
physical inequality, an intellectual inequality, of the most serious
kind, is established unchangeably by the Author of nature; and
society has a right to establish any other inequalities it may judge
necessary for its good.

(WJA I 462)

(1798)

Reputation is of as much importance to nations, in proportion, as
to individuals. Honor is a higher interest than reputation. The
man or the nation without attachment to reputation or honor, is
undone. What is animal life, or national existence, without either?

(WJA IX 205–6)

(12 May 1798)

Among all the appearances portentous of evil, there is none more
incomprehensible than the professions of republicanism among
those who place not a sense of justice, morality, or piety, among
the ornaments of their nature and the blessings of society.

(WJA IX 193)

(23 July 1799)

There are two principles which produce a tenaciousness of rank.
One is a sense of honor and consciousness of dignity, which cannot bear disgrace or degradation; the other is a selfish vanity and
aspiring ambition, which is desirous of rising at any rate, and
leaping over the heads of all others who are higher.

(WJA VIII 671)

(24 January 1801)

A general relaxation of education and government, a general de-
bauchery as well as dissipation, produced by pestilential philosophical principles of Epicurus, infinitely more than by shows
and theatrical entertainments; these are, in my opinion, more serious and threatening evils than even the slavery of the blacks,
hateful as that is.

(WJA IX 93)

(8 March 1805)

I had met with an observation among regular officers, that
mankind were naturally divided into three sorts; one third of
them are animated at the first appearance of danger, and will
press forward to meet and examine it; another third are alarmed
of it, but will neither advance nor retreat, till they know the nature of it, but stand to meet it. The remaining third will run or fly
upon the first thought of it. If this remark is just, as I believed it
was, it appeared to me that the only way to form an army to be
confided in, was a systematic discipline, by which means all men
may be made heroes. In this manner, in time, our American army
was made equal to the veterans of France and England, and in
this way the armies of France have been made invincible hitherto,
and in the same way they will be ultimately conquered, or at
least, successfully resisted by their enemies.

(WJA III 87)

(21 May 1807)

Vanity is really what the French call it, *amour propre,* self-love, and
it is a universal passion. All men have it in an equal degree.
Honest men do not always disguise it. Knaves often do, if not always. When you see or hear a man pique himself upon his modesty, you may depend upon it, he is as vain a fellow as lives, and
very probably a great villain.

(WJA IX 598)

(27 September 1808)

We mortals cannot work miracles; we struggle in vain against the constitution and course of nature.

(WJA IX 604)

(18 February 1811)

There are no people on earth so ambitious as the people of America. The reason is, because the lowest can aspire as freely as the highest.

(WJA IX 633)

(28 August 1811)

Fifty-three years ago I was fired with a zeal, amounting to enthusiasm, against ardent spirits, the multiplication of taverns, retailers, and dram-shops, and tippling houses. Grieved to the heart to see the number of idlers, thieves, sots, and consumptive patients made for the physicians, in those infamous seminaries, I applied to the Court of Sessions, procured a committee of inspection and inquiry, reduced the number of licensed houses, etc. But I only acquired the reputation of a hypocrite and an ambitious demagogue by it. The number of licensed houses was soon reinstated; drams, grog, and sotting were not diminished, and remain to this day as deplorable as ever.

(WJA IX 637)

(22 March 1813)

Mankind, in general, and our beloved country, in particular, bear adversity much better than prosperity.

(WJA X 34)

(13 July 1813)

Inequalities of mind and body are so established by God Almighty in his constitution of human nature, that no art or policy can ever plane them down to a level. I have never read reasoning more absurd, sophistry more gross, in proof of the Athanasian creed, or transubstantiation, than the subtle labors of Helvetius and Rousseau to demonstrate the natural equality of mankind. *Jus cuique*, the golden rule, do as you would be done by, is all the equality that can be supported or defended by reason or common sense.

(WJA X 53)

(2 September 1813)

Beauty, grace, figure, attitude, movement, have, in innumerable instances, prevailed over wealth, birth, talents, virtues, and everything else, in men of the highest rank, greatest power, and, sometimes, the most exalted genius, greatest fame, and highest merit.

(WJA X 65–66)

(1814)

Inequalities are a part of the natural history of man.

(WJA VI 452)

(1814)

That all men are born to equal rights is true. Every being has a right to his own, as clear, as moral, as sacred, as any other being has. This is as indubitable as a moral government in the universe. But to teach that all men are born with equal powers and faculties, to equal influence in society, to equal property and advantages through life, is as gross a fraud, as glaring an imposition on the credulity of the people, as ever was practiced by the monks, by Druids, by Brahmins, by priests of the immortal Lama, or by the self-styled philosophers of the French revolution.

(WJA VI 453–54)

(1814)

All that men can do, is to modify, organize, and arrange the powers of human society, that is to say, the physical strength and force of men, in the best manner to protect, secure, and cherish the moral, which are all the natural rights of mankind.

(WJA VI 458)

(1814)

Individuals have conquered themselves. Nations and large bodies of men, never.

(WJA VI 485)

(1814)

The moral equality, that is, the innocence, is only at birth; as soon as they can walk or speak, you may discern a moral inequality. These inequalities, physical, intellectual, and moral, I have called sources of a natural aristocracy; and such they are, have been, and will be; and it would not be dangerous to say, they are sources of all the artificial aristocracies that have been, are, or will be.

(WJA VI 491)

(26 November 1815)
To Thomas McKean, fellow signer of the Declaration of Independence.

I must acknowledge I contemplate with pleasure the rising generation. As much secluded as I am from the world, I see a succession of able and honorable characters, from members of Congress down to bachelors and students in our universities, who will take care of the liberties which you have cherished and done so much to support.

(WJA X 182)

(26 May 1816)

I have so much sympathy and compassion for human nature, that a man or a woman may grunt and groan, screech and scream, weep, cry, or roar, as much as nature dictates under extreme distress, provided there be no affectation; for there may be hypocrisy even in these expressions of torture.

(WJA X 221)

(19 April 1817)

So far from believing in the total and universal depravity of
human nature, I believe there is no individual totally depraved.
The most abandoned scoundrel that ever existed, never yet
wholly extinguished his conscience, and, while conscience remains, there is some religion.

(WJA X 254)

(19 April 1817)

I must hate myself before I can hate my fellow men, and that I
cannot and will not do. No, I will not hate any of them, base, brutal, and devilish as some of them have been to me. From the bottom of my soul I pity my fellow men.

(WJA X 255)

(5 June 1817)

The variety of human characters is infinite. Nature seems to delight in showing the inexhaustibility of her resources. There never
were two men alike, from the first man to the last, any more than
two pebbles or two peas.

(WJA X 263)

(1 June 1818)

The greatest men have the greatest faults.

(WJA X 317)

(21 February 1819)

A drunkard is the most selfish being in the universe; he has no
sense of modesty, shame, or disgrace; he has no sense of duty, or
sympathy of affection with his father or mother, his brother or sister, his friend or neighbor, his wife or children, no reverence for
his God, no sense of futurity in this world or the other. All is swal-
lowed up in the mad, selfish joy of the moment. . . . Is it not mortifying beyond all expression that we, Americans, should exceed

all other and millions of people in the world in this degrading, beastly vice of intemperance?

(WJA X 365)

(August 1821)
Speech to cadets at West Point on the subject of glory.

There is no real glory in this world or any other but such as arises from wisdom and benevolence. There can be no solid glory among men but that which springs from equity and humanity; from the constant observance of prudence, temperance, justice, and fortitude. Battles, victories, and conquests, abstracted from their only justifiable object and end, which is justice and peace, are the glory of fraud, violence, and usurpation.

(WJA X 419)

5

INTROSPECTIONS

(1 February 1756)

I am constantly forming, but never executing, good resolutions.

(WJA II 4)

(16 February 1756)

Oh! that I could wear out of my mind every mean and base affection; conquer my natural pride and self-conceit; expect no more deference from my fellows than I deserve; acquire that meekness and humility which are the sure mark and characters of a great and generous soul; subdue every unworthy passion, and treat all men as I wish to be treated by all. How happy should I then be in the favor and goodwill of all honest men and the sure prospect of a happy immortality!

(WJA II 5)

(23 April 1756)

I have never any bright, refulgent ideas. Everything appears in my mind dim and obscure, like objects seen through a dirty glass or roiled water.

(WJA II 13)

(1 April 1756)

I am as yet very contented in the place of a schoolmaster. I shall not, therefore, very suddenly become a preacher.

(WJA I 30)

(3 May 1756)

Vanity, I am sensible, is my cardinal vice and cardinal folly.

(WJA II 16)

(21 June 1756)

I am now entering another year, and I am resolved not to neglect my time as I did last year. I am resolved to rise with the sun, and to study the Scriptures on Thursday, Friday, Saturday, and Sunday mornings, and to study some Latin author the other three mornings. Noons and nights I intend to read English authors. This is my fixed determination; and I will set down every neglect and every compliance with this resolution. May I blush whenever I suffer one hour to pass unimproved. I will rouse up my mind and fix my attention; I will stand collected within myself, and think upon what I read and what I see; I will strive, with all my soul, to be something more than persons who have had less advantages than myself.

(WJA II 23)

(25 June 1756)

Good sense is generally attended with a very lively sense and delight in applause; the love of fame in such men is generally much stronger than in other people, and this passion, it must be confessed, is apt to betray men into impertinent exertions of their talents, sometimes into censorious remarks upon others, often into little meannesses to sound the opinions of others, and, oftenest of all into a childish affectation of wit and gayety. I must own myself to have been, to a very heinous degree, guilty in this respect; when in company with persons much superior to myself in years and place, I have talked to show my learning; I have been too bold with great men, which boldness will, no doubt, be called self-conceit; I have made ill-natured remarks upon the intellectuals, manners, practice, etc., of other people; I have foolishly aimed at wit and spirit, at making a shining figure in gay company; but, instead of shining brighter, I only clouded the few rays that before rendered me visible.

(WJA II 25)

(14 August 1756)

I seem to have lost sight of the object that I resolved to pursue. Dreams and slumbers, sloth and negligence, will be the ruin of my schemes. However, I seem to be awake now; why can't I keep awake?

(WJA II 29)

(3 January 1759)

By the way, laziness, languor, inattention, are my bane.

(WJA II 59)

(3 January 1759)

What am I doing? Shall I sleep away my whole seventy years? No, by everything I swear I will renounce this contemplative, and betake myself to an active, roving life by sea or land, or else I will attempt some uncommon, unexpected enterprise in law; let me lay the plan, and arouse spirit enough to push boldly. I swear I will push myself into business; I'll watch my opportunity to speak in court, and will strike with surprise—surprise bench, bar, jury, auditors and all.

(WJA II 59–60)

(3 January 1759)

I don't see clearly the objects that I am after; they are often out of sight; motes, atoms, feathers, are blown into my eyes and blind me.

(WJA II 60)

(14 March 1759)

In such a slow, gradual ascent to fame and fortune and business, the pleasure that they give will be imperceptible; but by a bold, sudden rise, I shall feel all the joys of each at once. Have I genius enough and resolution and health enough for such an achievement?

(WJA II 64)

(8 April 1759)

Let love and vanity be extinguished, and great passions of ambition, patriotism, break out and burn. Let little objects be neglected and forgot, and great ones engross, arouse, and exalt my soul. The mind must be aroused, or it will slumber.

(WJA II 70)

(1760)

Pretensions to wisdom and virtue, superior to all the world, will not be supported by words only. If I tell a man I am wiser and better than he or any other man, he will either despise, or hate, or pity me, perhaps all three.

(WJA I 47)

(14 November 1760)

A pen is certainly an excellent instrument to fix a man's attention and to inflame his ambition. I am, therefore, beginning a new literary year in the twenty-sixth of my life.

(WJA II 100)

(18 December 1765)

I find that idleness lies between business and study; that is, the transition from the hurry of a multiplicity of business to the tranquility of what is necessary for intense study, is not easy. There must be a vacation, an interval between them, for the mind to recollect itself.

(WJA II 155)

(18 December 1765)

Thirty years of my life are passed in preparation for business; I have had poverty to struggle with, envy and jealousy and malice of enemies to encounter, no friends, or but a few, to assist me; so that I have groped in dark obscurity, till of late, and had but just become known and gained a small degree of reputation, when this execrable project [the Stamp Act] was set on foot for my ruin as well as that of America in general, and of Great Britain.

(WJA II 156)

(30 January 1768)

Am I grasping at money or scheming for power? Am I planning the illustration of my family or the welfare of my country? These are great questions. In truth, I am tossed about so much from post to pillar, that I have not leisure and tranquility enough to consider distinctly my own views, objects, and feelings. I am mostly intent, at present, upon collecting a library; and I find that a great deal of thought and care, as well as money, are necessary to assemble an ample and well-chosen assortment of books.

(WJA II 208)

(20 July 1770)

I am under no moral or other obligation to publish to the world, how much my expenses or my incomes amount to yearly. There are times when, and persons to whom, I am not obliged to tell what are my principles and opinions in politics or religion. There are persons whom in my heart I despise; others I abhor. Yet I am not obliged to inform the one of my contempt, nor the other of my detestation. This kind of dissimulation, which is no more than concealment, secrecy, and reserve, or in other words, prudence and discretion, is a necessary branch of wisdom, and so far from being immoral and unlawful, that it is a duty and a virtue.

(WJA II 249)

(5 July 1771)

I have often been surprised with claps and plaudits and hosannas, when I have spoken but indifferently, and as often met with inattention and neglect when I have thought I spoke very well; how vain and empty is breath!

(WJA II 287)

(22 September 1772)

I am determined my own life and the welfare of my whole family, which is much dearer to me, are too great sacrifices for me to make. . . . I will devote myself wholly to my private business, my office and my farm, and I hope to lay a foundation for better fortune to my children, and a happier life than has fallen to my share.

(WJA II 298)

(19 October 1772)

Thirty-seven years, more than half the life of man, are run out. What an atom, an animalcule I am! The remainder of my days I shall decline in sense, spirit, and activity. My season for acquiring knowledge is past, and yet I have my own and my children's fortune to make. My boyish habits and airs are not yet worn off.

(WJA II 299)

(24 May 1773)

I was not sent into this world to spend my days in sports, diversions, and pleasures; I was born for business, for both activity and study. I have little appetite or relish for anything else. I must double and redouble my diligence. I must be more constant to my office and my pen; constancy accomplishes more than rapidity; continual attention will do great things; frugality of time is the greatest art, as well as virtue. This economy will produce knowledge as well as wealth.

(WJA II 320)

(24 May 1773)

If I should be called in the course of Providence to take a part in public life, I shall act a fearless, intrepid, undaunted part at all hazards, though it shall be my endeavor likewise, to act a prudent, cautious, and considerate part.

(WJA II 320)

(1 July 1774)

I shall arouse myself erelong, I believe, and exert an industry, a frugality, a hard labor, that I will serve my family, if I can't serve my country. I will not lie down in despair. If I cannot serve my children by the law, I will serve them by agriculture, by trade, by some way or other. I thank God I have a head, and heart, and hands, which, once fully exerted altogether, will succeed in the world as well as those of the mean-spirited, low-minded, fawning, obsequious scoundrels who have long hoped that my integrity would be an obstacle in my way, and enable them to outstrip me in the race.

But what I want in comparison of them of villainy and servility, I will make up in industry and capacity. If I don't, they shall laugh and triumph. I will not willingly see blockheads, whom I have a right to despise, elevated above me and insolently triumphing over me. Nor shall knavery, through any negligence of mine, get the better of honesty, nor ignorance of knowledge, nor folly of wisdom, nor vice of virtue.

(FL 7)

(1 July 1774)

I am determined to be cool, if I can. I have suffered such torments in my mind heretofore as have almost overpowered my constitution, without any advantage. And now I will laugh and be easy if I can, let the contest of parties terminate as it will, let my own estate and interest suffer what it will, nay, whether I stand high or low in the estimation of the world, so long as I keep a conscience void of offense towards God and man. And this I am determined by the will of God to do, let what will become of me or mine, my country or the world.

(FL 7)

(4 July 1774)

For my own part, it has long been my resolution to avoid being concerned in counseling, or aiding, or abetting tumult or disorder; to avoid all exceptionable scribbling in the newspaper of

every kind; to avoid all passion and personal altercation or reflections. I have found it difficult to keep these resolutions exactly; all
but the last, however, I have religiously and punctiliously observed these six years.

(FL 11)

(6 July 1774)

If I have the approbation of my own mind, whether applauded or
censured, blessed or cursed, by the world, I will not be unhappy.

(FL 18)

(7 July 1774)

I shall bring home as much as I brought from home, I hope, and
not much more, I fear. I go mourning in my heart all day long,
though I say nothing. I am melancholy for the public and anxious
for my family. As for myself, a frock and trousers, a hoe and a
spade would do for my remaining days.

(FL 21)

(15 March 1775)

Being a man of desperate fortune, and a bankrupt in business, I
cannot help putting my hand to the pump, now the ship is in a
storm, and the hold half full of water; but as soon as she gets into
a calm, and a place of safety, I must leave her.

(WJA IX 355)

(23 June 1775)

I, poor creature, worn out with scribbling for my bread and my
liberty, low in spirits and weak in health, must leave others to
wear the laurels which I have sown; others to eat the bread which
I have earned; a common case.

(FL 70)

(23 October 1775)

The man who violates private faith, cancels solemn obligations,
whom neither honor nor conscience holds, shall ever be know-

ingly trusted by me. . . . Though I think a fatality attends us in some instances, yet a divine protection and favor is visible in others; and let us be cheerful, whatever happens. Cheerfulness is not a sin in any times.

(FL 117)

(4 November 1775)

I really fear I shall ruin myself for want of exercise.

(FL 122)

(25 November 1775)

Balls, assemblies, concerts, cards, horses, dogs, never engaged any part of my attention or concern. Nor am I ever happy in large and promiscuous companies. Business alone, with the intimate, unreserved conversation of a very few friends, books, and familiar correspondence, have ever engaged all my time; and I have no pleasure, no ease, in any other way.

(WJA IX 368)

(February, 1776)

I feel, upon some of these occasions, a flow of spirits and an effort of imagination, very like an ambition to be engaged in the more active, gay, and dangerous scenes; (dangerous, I say, but recall that word, for there is no course more dangerous than that which I am in). I have felt such passions all my lifetime, particularly in the year 1757, when I longed to be a lawyer. But I am too old, and too much worn with the fatigues of study in my youth, and there is too little need, in my province, of such assistance to assume a uniform.

(FL 134)

(15 April 1776)

I believe my children will think I might as well have thought and labored a little, night and day, for their benefit. But I will not bear the reproaches of my children. I will tell them that I studied and labored to procure a free constitution of government for them to solace themselves under, and if they do not prefer this to ample fortune, to ease and elegance, they are not my children, and I care not what becomes of them. They shall live upon thin diet, wear mean clothes, and work hard with cheerful hearts and free spirits, or they may be the children of the earth, or of no one, for me.

(FL 159)

(28 April 1776)

There is such a mixture of folly, littleness, and knavery in the world, that I am weary of it, and although I behold it with unutterable contempt and indignation, yet the public good requires that I should take no notice of it by word or by letter. And to this public good I will conform.

(FL 166)

(22 May 1776)

I have some thoughts of petitioning the General Court for leave to bring my family here [to France]. I am a lonely, forlorn creature here. It used to be some comfort to me that I had a servant and some horses. They composed a sort of family for me. But now, there is not one creature here that I seem to have any kind of relation to.

(FL 175)

(3 July 1776)

In private life, no one has a right to censure me for following my own inclinations in retirement, simplicity, and frugality.

(WJA IX 417)

(3 July 1776)

I have not fortune enough to support my family and, what is of more importance, to support the dignity of that exalted station. It is too high and lifted up for me who delight in nothing so much as retreat, solitude, silence, and obscurity. In private life, no one has a right to censure me for following my own inclinations in retirement, simplicity, and frugality.

(FL 190–1)

(7 July 1776)

For myself, as I never had a regular tutor, I never studied anything methodically, and consequently never was completely accomplished in anything.

(FL 197)

(18 August 1776)

I have a very tender, feeling heart. This country knows not, and
never can know, the torments I have endured for its sake. I am
glad it never can know, for it would give more pain to the benevolent and humane than I could wish even the wicked and malicious to feel.

(FL 214)

(18 August 1776)

There are very few people in this world with whom I can bear to
converse. I can treat all with decency and civility, and converse
with them, when it is necessary, on points of business. But I am
never happy in their company. This has made me a recluse and
will one day make me a hermit.

(FL 215)

(17 February 1777)

I know of no policy, God is my witness, but this: piety, humanity,
and honesty are the best policy.

(FL 247)

(16 March 1777)

As much as I converse with sages and heroes, they have very little of my love or admiration. I should prefer the delights of a garden to the dominion of a world. I have nothing of Caesar's
greatness in my soul. Power has not my wishes in her train.

(FL 250)

(26 April 1777)

Posterity! You will never know how much it cost the present generation to preserve your freedom! I hope you will make a good use of it. If you do not, I shall repent it in heaven that I ever took half the pains to preserve it.

(FL 265)

(24 December 1777)

I should have wanted no motives nor arguments to induce me to accept of this momentous trust, if I could be sure that the public would be benefited by it. But when I see my brothers at the bar here so easily making fortunes for themselves and their families, and when I recollect that for four years I have abandoned myself and mine, and when I see my own children growing up in something very like real want, because I have taken no care of them, it requires as much philosophy as I am master of to determine to persevere in public life, and to engage in a new scene, for which, I fear, I am very ill qualified.

(WJA IX 471)

(8 February 1778)

In spite of all the reflections that are cast upon human nature, and of all the satires on mankind, and especially on courts, I have ever found, or thought that I found, honesty to be the best policy. And it is as great a truth now as it was three thousand years ago, that the honest man is seldom forsaken.

(WJA IX 472)

(5 August 1778)

I will have nothing to do with designs and endeavors to run down characters, to paint in odious colors indifferent actions, excite or propagate suspicions without evidence, or to foment or entertain prejudices of any kind, if I can possibly avoid it.

(DC IV 264)

(28 February 1779)

Lessons of moderation are so much wanted, that I, even I, am obliged to become a preacher of that great virtue; but with as little success as most other preachers.

(WJA IX 479)

(26 April 1779)

There is a feebleness and a languor in my nature. My mind and body both partake of this weakness. By my physical constitution I am but an ordinary man. The times alone have destined me to fame; and even these have not been able to give me much. When I look in the glass, my eye, my forehead, my brow, my cheeks, my lips, all betray this relaxation. Yet some great events, some cutting expressions, some mean hypocrisies, have, at times, thrown this assemblage of sloth, sleep, and littleness into rage a little like a lion. Yet it is not like the lion; there is extravagance and distraction in it that still betray the same weakness.

(WJA III 197)

(9 June 1779)

Upon the whole, truth must be my shield; and if the shafts of interested malice can pierce through this, they shall pierce me.

(WJA VII 97)

(9 May 1780)

I may be thought again too sanguine. I have been too sanguine these twenty years; constantly sanguine, yet eternally right.

(WJA VII 161)

(2 December 1781)

My children shall never have the smallest soil of dishonor or disgrace brought upon them by their father, no, not to please ministers, kings, or nations. At the expense of a little of this, my children might perhaps ride at their ease through life, but dearly as I love them, they shall live in the service of their country, in her navy, her army, or even out of either in the extremest degree of poverty, before I will depart in the smallest iota from my sentiments of honor and delicacy; for I, even I, have sentiments of delicacy as exquisite as the proudest minister that ever served a monarch.

(FL 397)

(17 June 1782)

What is it to me, after having done all I can to set them right, whether other people go to Heaven or to the devil? I may howl and weep, but this will have no effect. I may then just as well sing and laugh.

(WJA IX 512)

(26 July 1782)
On his way to negotiate the Treaty of Paris, Adams toured an estate in Chantilly.

While we were viewing the statue of Montmorency, Mademoiselle de Bourbon came out into the round house at the corner of the castle, dressed in beautiful white, her hair uncombed, hanging and flowing about her shoulders, with a book in her hand, and leaned over the bar of iron; but soon perceiving that she had caught my eye, and that I viewed her more attentively than she fancied, she rose up with that majesty and grace which persons of her birth affect, if they are not taught, turned her hair off both shoulders with her hands, in a manner that I could not comprehend, and decently stepped back into the chamber, and was seen no more. The book in her hand is consistent with what I heard four years ago at the *Palais de Bourbon*, in Paris, that she was fond of reading.

(WJA III 298)

(23 January 1783)

I do not affect singularity, nor love to be in a minority, though truth and justice have sometimes obliged me to be so.

(WJA VIII 27)

(1 July 1786)

The pleasure which arises from imitation we have in looking at a picture of a landscape, a port, a street, a temple, or a portrait. But there must be action, passion, sentiment, and moral, to engage my attention very much.

(WJA III 398)

(15 January 1787)

I am no enemy to elegance, but I say no man has a right to think of elegance till he has secured substance; nor then, to seek no more of it than he can afford. That taste which, for its gratification, will commit knavery and run in debt beyond the ability to pay, merits execration. That elegance which devours honor, truth, and independency, which scorns reputations and can reconcile itself to ignominy, public or private, is a monster that Hercules ought to destroy.

(WJA I 433)

(1 March 1787)

If it lay within my power, I would take a vow to retire to my little turnip-yard, and never again quit it.

(WJA VIII 434)

(19 April 1790)

For "eminence" I care nothing; for though I pretend not to be exempt from ambition, or any other human passion, I have not been convinced from my infancy and have been confirmed every year and day of my life, that the mechanic and peasant are happier than any nobleman, or magistrate, or king, and that the higher a man rises, if he has any sense of duty, the more anxious he must be.

(WJA IX 564)

(10 March 1791)
On his ancestors.

If I could ever suppose that family pride were any way excusable, I should think a descent from a line of virtuous, independent

New England farmers for a hundred and sixty years, was a better foundation for it than a descent through royal or noble scoundrels ever since the Flood.

(WJA IX 574)

(19 May 1794)

The world is a riddle, which death, I hope, will unravel. Amidst all the trials I have gone through, I have much to be grateful for: good parents, and excellent wife, and promising children; tolerable health, upon the whole, and competent fortune; success almost without example in a dangerous, dreadful revolution, and still hopes of better times.

(WJA I 474)

(31 January 1796)

If I had got my living by my brains for seven years past, I should have had more mental power. But brains have not only been useless, but even hurtful and pernicious in my course. Mine have been idle a long time till they are rusty.

(WJA I 486)

(12 July 1796)

This Journal is commenced to allure me into the habit of writing again, long lost. This habit is easily lost, but not easily regained. I have in the course of my life, lost it several times, and regained it as often; so I will now.

(WJA III 416)

(28 July 1796)

I continue my practice of drinking a gill of cider in the morning, and find no ill, but some good effects.

(WJA III 421)

(4 August 1796)

Of all the summers of my life, this has been the freest from care, anxiety, and vexation to me, the sickness of Mrs. Adams excepted.

My health has been better, the season fruitful, my farm was well conducted. Alas! What may happen to reverse all this? But it is folly to anticipate evils, and madness to create imaginary ones.

(WJA III 422)

(4 August 1796)

Virtue is the mistress of all things. Virtue is the master of all things. Therefore a nation that should never do wrong must necessarily govern the world. The might of virtue, the power of virtue, is not a very common topic, not so common as it should be.

(WJA III 423)

(2 June 1798)

Difficulties were the inheritance to which I was born, and a double portion has been allotted to me. I have hitherto found in my integrity an impenetrable shield, and I trust it will continue to preserve me.

(WJA IX 200)

(13 September 1798)
Letter to Secretary of the Treasury Oliver Wolcott during an epidemic.

The distress of the poor at Philadelphia is so great, that I pray you to subscribe and pay for me, under the title of a friend, and to let nobody know but yourself from whom it comes, five hundred dollars.

(WJA VIII 595)

(11 April 1800)

Repose is desirable enough to me, but I have been so long a stranger to it, that I know not whether I should not find it a mortal enemy.

(WJA IX 49)

(28 December 1800)
Writing on the death of his son Charles Adams.

The affliction in my family from the melancholy death of a once beloved son, has been very great, and has required the consolation of religion, as well as philosophy, to enable us to support it. The prospects of that unfortunate youth were very pleasing and promising, but have been cut off, and a wife and two very young children are left with their grandparents to bewail a fate, which neither could avert, and to which all ought in patience to submit. I have two sons left, whose conduct is worthy of their education and connections. I pray that their lives may be spared and their characters respected.

(WJA IX 577)

(3 March 1804)

A little law, a little ethics, and a little history constitute all the circle of my knowledge, and I am too old to acquire anything new.

(WJA IX 588)

(21 February 1805)

The danger I was in [in 1768] appeared in full view before me; and I very deliberately, and, indeed, very solemnly, determined at all events to adhere to my principles in favor of my native country, which, indeed, was all the country I knew, or which had been known by my father, grandfather, or great grandfather; but, on the other hand, I never would deceive the people, nor conceal from them any essential truth, nor, especially, make myself subservient to any of their crimes, follies, or eccentricities. These rules, to the utmost of my capacity and power, I have invariably and religiously observed to this day.

(WJA II 214)

(1805)

I shall draw no characters, nor give any enumeration of my youthful flames. It would be considered as no compliment to the dead or the living. This, I will say; they were all modest and virtuous girls, and always maintained their character through life. No virgin or matron ever had cause of grief or resentment for any intercourse between me and any daughter, sister, mother, or any other relation of the female sex.

(WJA II 145)

(1 May 1807)

I never engaged in public affairs for my own interest, pleasure, envy, jealousy, avarice, or ambition, or even the desire of fame. If any of these had been my motive, my conduct would have been very different. In every considerable transaction of my public life, I have invariably acted according to my best judgment, and I can look up to God for the sincerity of my intentions. How, then, is it possible I can repent? Notwithstanding this, I have an immense load of errors, weaknesses, follies, and sins to mourn over and repent of, and these are the only afflictions of my present life.

(WJA IX 593)

(11 March 1809)

For the faculty of medicine I never had any inclination, having an aversion to sick rooms and no fondness for rising at all hours of the night to visit patients.

(WJA IX 611)

(11 March 1809)

My temper in general has been tranquil, except when any instance of extraordinary madness, deceit, hypocrisy, ingratitude, treachery or perfidy, has suddenly struck me. Then I have always been irascible enough, and in three or four instances, very extraordinary ones, too much so. The storm, however, never lasted for half an hour, and anger never rested in the bosom.

(WJA IX 613)

(13 March 1809)

I always consider the whole nation as my children; but they have almost all been unfaithful to me.

(WJA IX 615)

(12 April 1809)
To Benjamin Rush.

You advise me to write my own life. I have made several attempts, but it is so dull an employment that I cannot endure it. I
look so much like a small boy in my own eyes, that, with all my
vanity, I cannot endure the sight of the picture.

(WJA IX 616)

(28 August 1811)

It is most certain that the end of my life cannot be remote. My
eyes are constantly fixed upon it, according to the precept or advice of the ancient philosopher; and, if I am not in a total delusion,
I daily behold and contemplate it without dismay.

(WJA IX 635)

(15 October 1811)

I am as happy as ever I was in my life, as happy as I can ever expect to be in this world, and I believe as happy as any man can be,
who sees all the friends of his youth dropping off about him, and
so much sickness among his nearest relations, and who expects
himself to drop in a very short time. Public affairs move me no
more than private. I love my country and my friends, but can do
very little for either. Reconciled and resigned to my lot in public
and private, I wait with patience for a transfer to another scene.

(WJA X 3)

(21 June 1812)

I am as cheerful as ever I was; and my health is as good, excepting
a quiveration of the hands, which disables me from writing in the
bold and steady character of your letter, which I rejoice to see.
Excuse the word quiveration, which, though I borrowed it from
an Irish boy, I think an improvement in our language worthy a
place in Webster's dictionary. Though my sight is good, my eyes
are too weak for all the labor I require of them; but as this is a de-
fect of more than fifty years standing, there are no hopes of relief.

The trepidation of the hands arising from a delicacy, or, if you will, a morbid irritability of nerves, has shown itself at times for more than half a century, but has increased for four or five years past, so as to extinguish all hopes that it will ever be less.

(WJA X 16)

(31 August 1813)

In times like those in which you and I have lived, we are not masters, we can scarcely be said to be fathers, of our own families. I have three children born in Quincy, one in Boston. I have one grandson born in London, another on Long Island, another in Berlin, several in Quincy, several in New York, several in Boston, one born and died in St. Petersburg. Is this a desirable history of a family? I trow not.

(WJA X 63)

(16 July 1814)
To Thomas Jefferson.

I am bold to say, that neither you nor I will live to see the course which the "wonders of time" will take. Many years, and perhaps centuries must pass before the current will acquire a settled direction.

(WJA X 100)

(December 1814)

It seems to be generally agreed and settled among men, that John Adams is a weak and vain man. I fall down under the public opinion, the general sense, and frankly and penitently acknowledge, that I have been all my lifetime, and still am, a weak and vain man.

(WJA VI 501)

(6 March 1815)

Private letters I have preserved in considerable numbers, but they ought not to be opened these hundred years, and then, perhaps, will not be found of much consequence, except as memorials of private friendship.

(WJA X 134)

(30 March 1815)

Meantime, what shall I do with these letters and the subject of them? I have no inclination to publish them. They will remain in my letter-book, to enable my children to apologize for my memory.

(WJA X 151)

(31 March 1815)

I cannot repent of my "strong character." Whether I have one or not, I know not. I am not conscious of any character stronger than common. If I have such a nature, it was given me. I shall neither be rewarded nor punished for it. For all my foibles, strong or weak, I hold myself responsible to God and man.

(WJA X 152)

(13 July 1815)
To F. A. Vanderkemp.

You ask, "What! Have you more grandchildren about you?" Yes, I have four pretty little creatures, who, though they disarrange my writing-table, give me much of my enjoyment. Why, you seem to know nothing about me. I have grandchildren and great-grand-children, multiplying like the seed of Abraham. You have no idea of the prolific quality of the New England Adamses. Why, we have contributed more to the population of North America, and cut down more trees, than any other race; and I hope will furnish hereafter, if they should be wanted, more soldiers and sailors for the defense of their country.

(WJA X 169)

(13 July 1815)
To F. A. Vanderkemp.

My friend, what opportunities have I had to do good things, and how few have I done! I am ashamed, I grieve, I am mortified and humiliated, at the recollection of what I have been and where I have been. Yet, I have done all in my power to do, and have been overwhelmed by a dispensation, uncontrollable by any talents or virtues I possessed.

(WJA X 169)

(2 March 1816)
Reply to Thomas Jefferson's question, whether he would want to live his life again.

If I am prepared to give you an explicit answer, the question involves so many considerations of metaphysics and physics, of theology and ethics, of philosophy and history, of experience and romance, of tragedy, comedy, and farce, that I would not give my opinion without writing a volume to justify it.

(WJA X 210–11)

(3 May 1816)

I have had more comfort than distress, more pleasure than pain, ten to one; nay, if you please, a hundred to one. A pretty large dose, however, of distress and pain. But, after all, what is human life? A vapor, a fog, a dew, a cloud, a blossom, a flower, a rose, a blade of grass, a glass bubble, a tale told by an idiot, a *boule de savon*, vanity of vanities, and eternal succession of which would terrify me almost as much as annihilation.

(WJA X 214)

(12 December 1816)
On the lessons contained in his latest readings in philosophy, religion, and history

I have learned nothing of importance to me, for they have made no change in my moral or religious creed, which has, for fifty or sixty years, been contained in four short words, "Be just and good."

(WJA X 232)

(30 December 1817)

If I regret the infirmities of age, it is not because they announce the rapid approach of the end of my life, but because they disable me to associate and correspond with my friends according to their wishes and my own.

(WJA X 270)

(29 May 1818)

Mr. Binon, a French artist, from Lyon, who has studied eight years in Italy, has lately taken my bust. He appears to be an artist, and a man of letters. I let them do what they like with my old head. When we come to be cool in the future world, I think we cannot choose but smile at the gambols of ambition, avarice, pleasure, sport, and caprices here below.

(WJA X 313)

(28 November 1821)

In August, a corps of West Point cadets marched from Boston to the Adams home in Quincy. Never before, but once, in the whole course of my life, was my soul so melted into the milk of human kindness; and that one was when four or five hundred fine young fellows appeared before me in [Quincy], presenting an address and receiving my answer. On both occasions I felt as if I could lay down a hundred lives to preserve the liberties and promote the prosperity of so noble a rising generation.

(WJA X 401)

(17 September 1823)
To Thomas Jefferson, on the return of John Quincy Adams, his wife, and three sons from abroad.

As you write so easily and so well, I pray you to write me as often as possible, for nothing revives my spirits so much as your letters, except the society of my son and his family, who are now happily with me after an absence of two years.

(WJA X 411)

(7 June 1826)
To John Whitney, on his inability to attend a July 4th celebration, one month before his death

The present feeble state of my health will not permit me to indulge in the joys and festivities and solemn services of that day, on which will be completed the fiftieth year from the birth of the independence of the United States.

(WJA X 417)

6

FAITH AND RELIGION

(7 March 1756)

Honesty, sincerity, and openness I esteem essential marks of a good mind. I am, therefore, of opinion that men ought, after they have examined with unbiased judgments every system of religion, and chosen one system, on their own authority, for themselves, to avow their opinions and defend them with boldness.

(WJA II 8)

(23 May 1756)

When we consider the vast and incomprehensible extent of the material universe, those myriads of fixed stars that emerge out of the remote regions of space to our view by glasses, and the finer our glasses the more of these systems we discover; when we consider that space is absolutely infinite and boundless, that the power of the Deity is strictly omnipotent, and his goodness without limitation, who can come to a stop in his thoughts and say, hither does the universe extend and no further?

(WJA II 18)

(29 May 1756)

Habits of contemplating the Deity and his transcendent excellencies, and correspondent habits of complacency in, and dependence upon him; habits of reverence and gratitude to God, and habits of love and compassion to our fellow men; and habits of temperance, recollection, and self-government, will afford us a real and substantial pleasure. We may then exult in a consciousness of the favor of God, and the prospect of everlasting felicity.

(WJA II 20)

(14 June 1756)

From a sense of the government of God, and regard to the laws established by his Providence, should all our actions for ourselves or for other men primarily originate; and this master passion in a good man's soul, like the larger fishes of prey, will swallow up and destroy all the rest.

(WJA II 22-23)

(14 August 1756)

The situation that I am in, and the advantages that I enjoy, are thought to be the best for me by Him who alone is competent to judge of fitness and propriety. Shall I then complain? Oh! madness, pride, impiety!

(WJA II 30)

(August 1765)
Comments on the settlers of the American colonies.

Religious to some degree of enthusiasm it may be admitted they were; but this can be no peculiar derogation from their character; because it was at that time almost the universal character not only of England, but of Christendom. Had this, however, been otherwise, their enthusiasm, considering the principles on which it was founded and the ends to which it was directed, far from being a reproach to them, was greatly to their honor; for I believe it will be found universally true, that no great enterprise for the honor or happiness of mankind was ever achieved without a large mixture of that noble infirmity.

(WJA III 452)

(1774)

The designs of Providence are inscrutable. It affords conjunctures, favorable for their designs, to bad men, as well as to good.

(WJA IV 22)

(4 July 1774)

[We] took our horses to meeting in the afternoon and heard the minister again upon "Seek first the kingdom of God and his right-eousness, and all these things shall be added unto you." There is great pleasure in hearing sermons so serious, so clear, so sensible and instructive as these.

(FL 10)

(28 August 1774)

Resignation to the will of Heaven is our only resource in such dangerous times.

(FL 27)

(8 May 1774)

I pray for you all, and hope to be prayed for. Certainly there is a Providence; certainly we must depend upon Providence, or we fail; certainly the sincere prayers of good men avail much. But resignation is our duty in all events.

(FL 55)

(11 June 1774)

I have been this morning to hear Mr. Duffield, a preacher . . . whose principles, prayers, and sermons more nearly resemble those of our New England clergy than any that I have heard. His discourse was a kind of exposition on the thirty-fifth chapter of Isaiah. America was the wilderness, and the solitary place, and he said it would be glad, "rejoice and blossom as the rose." He la-bored "to strengthen the weak hands and confirm the feeble knees." He "said to them that were of a fearful hear, Be strong, fear not. Behold, your God will come with vengeance, even God with a recompense; he will come and save you," "No lion shall be there, nor any ravenous beast shall go up thereon, but the redeemed shall walk there," etc. He applied the whole prophecy to this country, and gave us as animating an entertainment as I ever heard. He filled and swelled the bosom of every hearer.

(FL 65)

(9 October 1774)

Went, in the afternoon, to the Romish chapel [in Philadelphia], and heard a good discourse upon the duty of parents to their children, founded in justice and charity. The scenery and the music are so calculated to take in mankind, that I wonder the Reformation ever succeeded.

(WJA II 395)

(30 July 1775)

This day I have heard my parish priest, Mr. Duffield, from 2 Chronicles 15 1–2. This gentleman never fails to adapt his discourse to the times. He pressed upon his audience the necessity of piety and virtue, in the present times of adversity, and held up to their view the army before Boston as an example.

(FL 90)

(17 September 1775)

Mixing the sacred character with that of the statesman, as it is quite unnecessary at this time of day, in these colonies, is not attended with any good effects. The clergy are too little acquainted with the world and the modes of business, to engage in civil affairs with any advantage. Besides, those of them who are really men of learning, have conversed with books so much more than men as to be too much loaded with vanity to be good politicians.

(FL 99)

(18 April 1776)

Not a sparrow falls, nor a hair is lost, but by the direction of infinite wisdom.

(FL 160)

(21 June 1776)

Statesmen . . . may plan and speculate for liberty, but it is religion and morality alone, which can establish the principles upon which freedom can securely stand.

(WJA IX 401)

(22 June 1776)

I am for the most liberal toleration of all denominations of religionists, but I hope that Congress will never meddle with religion further than to say their own prayers, and to fast and give thanks once a year. Let every colony have its own religion without molestation.

(WJA IX 402)

(8 October 1776)

The spirit of venality . . . is the most dreadful and alarming enemy America has to oppose. . . . This predominant avarice will ruin America, if she is ever ruined. If God Almighty does not interfere by his grace to control this universal idolatry to the mammon of unrighteousness, we shall be given up to the chastisements of his judgments. I am ashamed of the age I live in.

(FL 232)

(7 March 1777)

More than one half of the inhabitants [of Philadelphia] have removed into the country, as it was their wisdom to do. The remainder are chiefly Quakers, as dull as beetles. From these neither good is to be expected nor evil to be apprehended. They are a kind of neutral tribe, or the race of the insipids.

(FL 249)

(2 June 1778)

How is it possible that the children can have any just sense of the sacred obligations of morality or religion, if, from their earliest infancy, they learn that their mothers live in habitual infidelity to their fathers, and their fathers in as constant infidelity to their mothers? Besides, the Catholic doctrine is, that the contract of marriage is not only a civil and moral engagement, but a sacrament; one of the most solemn vows and oaths of religious devotion. Can they then believe religion, and morality too, anything more than a veil, a cloak, a hypocritical pretext, for political purposes of decency and conveniency?

(WJA III 172)

(13 February 1779)

There is no such thing as human wisdom; all is the Providence of God.

(WJA III 191)

(October 1779)
Article III of the Massachusetts Constitution as proposed by Adams, dropped by the Convention of 1779.

Good morals being necessary to the preservation of civil society; and the knowledge and belief of the being of God, His providential government of the world, and of a future state of rewards and punishment, being the only true foundation of morality, the legislature hath, therefore, a right, and ought to provide, at the expense of the subject, if necessary, a suitable religion and morals; and to enjoin upon the subjects an attendance upon their instructions at stated times and seasons; provided there be any such teacher on whose ministry they can conscientiously and conveniently attend.

(WJA IV 221)

(27 July 1780)
Description of the St. Michael cathedral in Brussels, then part of the kingdom of the Netherlands.

Went to the cathedral,—a great feast, an infinite crowd. The church more splendidly ornamented than any that I had seen, hung with tapestry. The church music here is in the Italian style. A picture in tapestry was hung up, of a number of Jews stabbing the wafer, the *bon Dieu,* and blood gushing in streams from the bread. This insufferable piece of pious villainy shocked me beyond measure; but thousands were before it, on their knees, adoring. I could not help cursing the knavery of the priesthood and the brutal ignorance of the people; yet, perhaps, I was rash and unreasonable, and that it is as much virtue and wisdom in them to adore, as in me to detest and despise.

(WJA III 267–68)

(8 April 1783)

When all men of all religions consistent with morals and property, shall enjoy equal liberty, property, or rather security of property, and an equal chance for honors and power, and when government shall be considered as having in it nothing more mysterious or divine than other arts or sciences, we may expect that improvements will be made in the human character and the state of society. But at what an immense distance is that period!

(WJA VIII 232)

(17 July 1789)

The duration of our president is neither perpetual nor for life; it is only for four years. . . . I know of no first magistrate in any republican government, excepting England and Neuchâtel [Switzerland], who possesses a constitutional dignity, authority, and power comparable to his. The power of sending and receiving ambassadors, of raising and commanding armies and navies, of nominating and appointing and commissioning all officers, of managing the treasures, the internal and external affairs of the nation; nay, the whole executive power, coextensive with the Legislative power, is vested in him, and he has the right, and his is the duty, to take care that the laws be faithfully executed.

(WJA VI 430)

(26 July 1796)
Comment made while reading the book Apology for the Bible, *a refutation of Thomas Paine's* Age of Reason.

The Christian religion, is, above all the religions that ever prevailed or existed in ancient or modern times, the religion of wisdom, virtue, equity, and humanity, let the blackguard Paine say what he will; it is resignation to God, it is goodness itself to man.

(WJA III 421)

(14 August 1796)

One great advantage of the Christian religion is, that it brings the great principle of the law of nature and nations,—Love your neighbor as yourself, and do to others as you would that others should do to you,—to the knowledge, belief, and veneration of the whole people. Children, servants, women, and men, are all professors in the science of public and private morality. No other institution for education, no kind of political discipline, could diffuse this kind of necessary information, so universally among all ranks and descriptions of citizens. The duties and rights of the man and the citizen are thus taught from early infancy to every creature. The sanctions of a future life are thus added to the observance of civil and political, as well as domestic and private duties. Prudence, justice, temperance, and fortitude, are thus taught to be the means and conditions of future as well as present happiness.

(WJA III 424)

(23 March 1798)
Adams's presidential proclamation for a national day of fasting.

I hereby recommend, that Wednesday, the 9th of May next, be observed throughout the United States, as a day of solemn humiliation, fasting and prayer; that the citizens of these States, abstaining on that day from their customary worldly occupations, offer their devout addresses to the Father of mercies, . . . acknowledge before God the manifold sins and transgressions with which we are justly chargeable as individuals and as a nation; beseeching Him at the same time, of his infinite grace, through the Redeemer of the world, freely to remit all our offences, and to incline us, by his Holy Spirit, to that sincere repentance and refor-

mation which may afford us reason to hope for his inestimable
favor and heavenly benediction. . . .

(WJA IX 169-70)

(3 July 1799)
On the need for chaplains in the American navy.

Enclosed is a letter from the president and professor of divinity of
our university [Harvard], recommending William Frothingham
to be a chaplain on board of some frigate. I know not whether the
commanders of our ships have given much attention to this subject; but in my humble opinion we shall be very unskillful politicians, as well as bad Christians and unwise men, if we neglect this
important office in our infant navy.

(WJA VIII 661–62)

(11 March 1801)

Long have I been led to think our planet a mere bedlam, and the
uncommonly extravagant ravings of our own times, especially
for a few years past, and still in the highest rant, have greatly increased and confirmed that opinion. Look round our whirling
globe, my friend, where you will, east, west, north, or south,
where is the spot in which are not many thousands of these mad
lunatics? But not a few strong symptoms seem now loudly to pro-
claim that this terrible, catching epidemic cannot be far from its
crisis; and when arrived there, our all knowing, unerring
Physician, always mercifully producing good from evil, and setting to rights the mad, destructive freaks of mortals, will, it is to
be hoped, in the present forlorn distresses interfere, and give such
a favorable turn to the crisis, as to make this bedlam-commitment
end in the cure of all its miserable captives. More and more
happy, I bless God, do I every day feel myself to find that my passage over this life's Atlantic is almost gained, having been in
soundings for some time, not far from my wished-for port, waiting only for a favorable breeze from our kind Savior to waft me to
that pleasing and expected land for which I cheerfully and
humbly hope.

(WJA IX 579–80)

(1801)

I think there is nothing upon this earth more sublime and affecting than the idea of a great nation all on their knees at once before their God, acknowledging their faults and imploring his blessing and protection, when the prospect before them threatens great danger and calamity.

(WJA IX 291)

(3 March 1804)

In the wisdom, power, and goodness of our Maker is all the security we have against roasting in volcanoes and writhing with the tortures of gout, stone, colic, and cancers; sinking under the burdens of dray-horses and hackney coach-horses to all eternity. Nature produces all these evils, and if she does it by chance, she may assign them all to us, whether we behave well or ill, and the poor hag will not know what she does.

(WJA IX 589)

(12 April 1809)
To Benjamin Rush.

In short, I have every reason to acknowledge the protecting Providence of God, from my birth, and especially through my public life. I have gone through life with much more safety and felicity than I ever expected. With devout gratitude I acknowledge the divine favor in many instances, and among others for giving me a friend in you, who, though you would never follow me as a disciple, have always been my friend.

(WJA IX 619)

(21 January 1810)

The Christian religion, as I understand it, is the brightness of the glory and the express portrait of the character of the eternal, self-existent, independent, benevolent, all powerful and all merciful creator, preserver, and father of the universe, the first good, first perfect, and first fair. It will last as long as the world. Neither savage nor civilized man, without a revelation, could ever have discovered or invented it. Ask me not, then, whether I am a Catholic or Protestant, Calvinist or Arminian. As far as they are Christians, I wish to be a fellow-disciple with them all.

(WJA IX 627)

(28 August 1811)

If I should recommend the sanctification of the Sabbath, like a divine, or even only a regular attendance on public worship, as a means of moral instruction and social improvement, like a philosopher or statesman, I should be charged with vain ostentation again, and a selfish desire to revive the remembrance of my own punctuality in this respect; for it is notorious enough that I have been a church-going animal for seventy-six years, from the cradle. And this has been alleged as one proof of my hypocrisy.

(WJA IX 637)

(28 June 1812)

I am weary of contemplating nations from the lowest and most beastly degradations of human life to the highest refinement of civilization. I am weary of philosophers, theologians, politicians, and historians. They are immense masses of absurdities, vices, and lies. Montesquieu had sense enough to say in jest, that all our knowledge might be comprehended in twelve pages in duodecimo; and I believe him in earnest. I could express my faith in shorter terms. He who loves the Workman and his work, and does what he can to preserve and improve it, shall be accepted of him.

(WJA X 19)

(14 September 1813)

My adoration of the Author of the universe is too profound and too sincere. The love of God and his creation—delight, joy, triumph, exultation in my own existence—though but an atom, a *molécule organique* in the universe—are my religion.

(WJA X 67)

(14 September 1813)

It has been long, very long, a settled opinion in my mind, that there is now, ever will be, and ever was, but one Being who can understand the universe, and that it is not only vain but wicked for insects to pretend to comprehend it.

(WJA X 69)

(15 September 1813)

No mind but one can see through the immeasurable system.

(WJA X 69)

(25 December 1813)

Philosophy, which is the result of reason, is the first, the original revelation of the Creator to his creature, man. When this revelation is clear and certain, by intuition or necessary inductions, no subsequent revelation, supported by prophecies or miracles, can supersede it. Philosophy is not only the love of wisdom, but the science of the universe and its cause. There is, there was, and there will be but one master of philosophy in the universe.

(WJA X 85)

(25 December 1813)

I have examined all, as well as my narrow sphere, my straitened means, and my busy life would allow me; and the result is, that the Bible is the best book in the world. It contains more of my little philosophy than all the libraries I have seen; and such parts of it as I cannot reconcile to my little philosophy, I postpone for future investigation.

(WJA X 85)

(13 July 1815)

For this whole period I have searched after truth by every means and by every opportunity in my power, and with a sincerity and impartiality, for which I can appeal to God, my adored Maker. My religion is founded on the love of God and my neighbor; on the hope of pardon for my offenses; upon contrition; upon the duty as well as necessity of supporting with patience the inevitable evils of life; in the duty of doing no wrong, but all the good I can, to the creation, of which I am but an infinitesimal part.

(WJA X 170)

(26 November 1815)

Awakenings and revivals of religion always attend the most cruel extremities of anarchy, despotism, and civil war. They have brought again the Pope and all his train of Jesuits, Inquisitions, Sorbonnes, massacres, etc. The pendulum swings as far on one side as on the other.

(WJA X 181)

(2 March 1816)

Why, then, should we abhor the word *God*, and fall in love with the word *fate*? We know there exists energy and intellect enough to produce such a world as this, which is a sublime and beautiful one, and a very benevolent one, notwithstanding all our snarling; and a happy one, if it is not made otherwise by our own fault.

(WJA X 212)

(3 May 1816)
To Thomas Jefferson.

I admire your navigation, and should like to sail with you either in your bark or in my own, alongside with yours. Hope, with her gay ensigns displayed at the prow; fear, with her hobgoblins behind the stern. Hope remains. What pleasure? I mean, take away fear, and what pain remains? Ninety-nine hundredths of the pleasures and pains of life are nothing but hopes and fears. The Maker of the universe, the cause of all things, whether we call it fate, or chance, or God, has inspired this hope. If it is a fraud, we shall never know it; we shall never resent the imposition, be grateful for the illusion, nor grieve for the disappointment; we shall be no more.

(WJA 215)

(6 May 1816)

Grief drives men into habits of serious reflection, sharpens the understanding, and softens the heart; it compels them to rouse their reason, to assert its empire over their passions, propensities and prejudices, to elevate them to a superiority over all human events . . . in short, to make them stoics and Christians. . . . Though stoical apathy is impossible, yet patience, and resignation, and tranquility may be acquired, by consideration, in a great degree, very much for the happiness of life.

(WJA X 218)

(6 May 1816)

I have lately read Pascal's letters over again, and four volumes of the History of the Jesuits. If ever any congregation of men could merit eternal perdition on earth and in hell, according to these historians, though, like Pascal, true Catholics, it is this company of Loyola. Our system, however, of religious liberty must afford them an asylum; but if they do not put the purity of our elections to a severe trial, it will be a wonder.

(WJA X 218)

(26 May 1816)

Resignation is our own affair. What good does it do to God? Prudence dictates to us to make the best we can of inevitable evils. We may fret and fume and peeve, and scold and rave, but what good does this do? It hurts ourselves, and may hurt our neighbors by the weak, silly, foolish example, but does no good in the universe that we can imagine.

(WJA X 220)

(9 August 1816)

Promise me eternal life, free from pain, though in all other respects no better than our present terrestrial existence, I know not how many thousand Smithfield fires I would not endure to obtain it. In fine, without the supposition of a future state, mankind and this globe appear to me the most sublime and beautiful bubble and bauble that imagination can conceive. Let us, then, wish for immortality at all hazards, and trust the ruler with his skies. I do, and earnestly wish for his commands, which, to the utmost of my power, shall be implicitly and piously obeyed.

(WJA X 225)

(4 November 1816)

The Ten Commandments and the Sermon on the Mount contain my religion.

(WJA X 229)

(27 December 1816)

Jesus is benevolence personified, an example for all men.

(WJA X 234)

(27 December 1816)

As I understand the Christian religion, it was, and is, a revelation. But how has it happened that millions of fables, tales, legends, have been blended with both Jewish and Christian revelation that have made them the most bloody religion that ever existed? How has it happened that all the fine arts, architecture, painting, sculpture, statuary, music, poetry, and oratory, have been prostituted, from the creation of the world, to the sordid and detestable purposes of superstition and fraud?

(WJA X 235)

(27 December 1816)

Let it once be revealed or demonstrated that there is no future state, and my advice to every man, woman, and child would be, as our existence would be in our own power, to take opium.

(WJA X 235)

(19 April 1817)

Twenty times, in the course of my late reading, have I been on the point of breaking out, "this would be the best of all possible worlds, if there was no religion in it!!!" But in this exclamation, I should have been as fanatical as Bryant or Cleverly. Without religion, this world would be something not fit to be mentioned in polite company—I mean Hell.

(WJA X 254)

(23 September 1818)

The Indians are as bigoted to their religion as the Mohammedans are to their Koran, the Hindus to their Shaster, the Chinese to Confucius, the Romans to their saints and angels, or the Jews to Moses and the Prophets. It is a principle of religion, at bottom, which inspires the Indians with such an invincible aversion both to civilization and Christianity. The same principle has excited their perpetual hostilities against the colonists and the independent Americans.

(WJA X 361–62)

(8 December 1818)

I know not how to prove, physically, that we shall meet and know each other in a future state; nor does revelation, as I can find, give us any positive assurance of such a felicity. My reasons for believing it, as I do most undoubtedly, are that I cannot conceive such a being could make such a species as the human, merely to live and die upon this earth. If I did not believe in a future state, I should believe in no God.

(WJA X 363)

(17 January 1820)

When we say God is a spirit, we know what we mean, as well as we do when we say that the pyramids of Egypt are matter. Let us be content, therefore, to believe him to be a spirit, that is, an essence that we know nothing of, in which originally and necessarily reside all energy, all power, all capacity, all activity, all wisdom, all goodness.

(WJA X 388)

(7 March 1820)

I never delighted much in contemplating commas and colons, or in spelling or measuring syllables; but now, while reading Cato, if I attempt to look at these little objects, I find my imagination, in spite of all my exertions, roaming in the Milky Way, among the nebulae, those mighty orbs, and stupendous orbits of suns, planets, satellites, and comets, which compose this incomprehensible universe; and, if I do not sink into nothing in my own estimation, I feel an irresistible impulse to fall on my knees, in adoration of the power that moves, the wisdom that directs, and the benevolence that sanctifies this wonderful whole.

(WJA X 389)

(8 July 1820)

I must be a very unnatural son to entertain any prejudices against the Calvinists, or Calvinism . . . for my father and mother, my uncles and aunts, and all my predecessors, from our common ancestor, who landed in this country two hundred years ago . . . were of that persuasion. Indeed, I have never known any better people than the Calvinists. Nevertheless, I must acknowledge that I cannot class myself under that denomination. My opinions, indeed, on religious subjects ought not to be of any consequence to any but myself.

(WJA X 389)

(8 July 1820)

I have been overwhelmed with sorrow to see the natural love and fear of that Being wrought upon by politicians to produce the most horrid cruelties, superstitions, and hypocrisy, from the sacrifices to Moloch down to those of Juggernaut, and the sacrifices of the kings of Whidah and Ashantee. The great result of all my researches has been a most diffusive and comprehensive charity. I believe with Justin Martyr, that all good men are Christians, and I believe there have been, and are, good men in all nations, sincere and conscientious.

(WJA X 390)

(22 May 1821)

I am not tormented with the fear of death, nor, though suffering under many infirmities, and agitated by many afflictions, weary of life. I have a better opinion of this world and of its Ruler than some people seem to have. A kind Providence has preserved and supported me for eighty-five years and seven months, through many dangers and difficulties, though in great weakness, and I am not afraid to trust in its goodness to all eternity. I have a numerous posterity, to whom my continuance may be of some importance, and I am willing to await the order of the Supreme Power.

(WJA X 399)

(23 January 1825)

The substance and essence of Christianity, as I understand it, is eternal and unchangeable, and will bear examination forever, but it has been mixed with extraneous ingredients, which I think will not bear examination, and they ought to be separated.

(WJA X 416)

7

LETTERS TO ABIGAIL

(1807)
From Adams's Autobiography.

I passed the summer of 1764 in attending courts and pursuing my studies, with some amusement on my little farm, to which I was frequently making additions, until the fall, when, on the 25th of October, I was married to Miss Smith, second daughter of the Rev. William Smith, minister of Weymouth, granddaughter of the Honorable John Quincy of Braintree, a connection which has been the source of all my felicity, although a sense of duty, which forced me away from her and my children for so many years, produced all the griefs of my heart, and all that I esteem real afflictions in life.

(WJA II 145)

(2 May 1774)
While Adams involved himself with law and politics in Boston, Abigail and the children stayed in Braintree and tended to the farm.

I am often concerned for you and our dear babes, surrounded, as you are, by people who are too timorous and too much susceptible of alarms. Many fears and jealousies and imaginary dangers will be suggested to you, but I hope you will not be impressed by them. In case of real danger, of which you cannot fail to have previous intimations, fly to the woods with our children.

(FL 52)

(12 May 1774)

We live, my dear soul, in an age of trial. What will be the consequences, I know not.

(FL 2)

(29 June 1774)

My life has been a continual scene of fatigue, vexation, labor, and
anxiety. I have four children. I had a pretty estate from my father;
I have been assisted by your father; I have done the greatest business in the province; I have had the very richest clients in the
province. Yet I am poor, in comparison with others.

(FL 3–4)

(29 June 1774)

Let frugality and industry be our virtues. And above all cares of
this life, let our ardent anxiety be to mold the minds and manners
of our children. Let us teach them not only to do virtuously, but to
excel. To excel, they must be taught to be steady, active, and industrious.

(FL 4)

(1 July 1774)

I must entreat you, my dear partner in all the joys and sorrows,
prosperity and adversity of my life, to take a part with me in the
struggle. I pray God for your health: entreat you to rouse your
whole attention to the family, the stock, the farm, the dairy. Let
every article of expense which can possibly be spared be re-
trenched; keep the hands attentive to their business, and the most
prudent measures of every kind be adopted and pursued with
alacrity and spirit.

(FL 8)

(2 July 1774)

I write you this tittle-tattle, my dear, in confidence. You must keep
these letters to yourself, and communicate them with great cau-

tion and reserve. I should advise you to put them up safe and preserve them. They may exhibit to our posterity a kind of picture of
the manners, opinions, and principles of these times of perplexity,
danger, and distress.

(FL 9)

(28 August 1774)

The education of our children is never out of my mind. Train
them to virtue. Habituate them to industry, activity, and spirit.
Make them consider every vice as shameful and unmanly. Fire
them with ambition to be useful. Make them disdain to be desti-
tute of any useful knowledge or accomplishment. Fix their ambition upon great and solid objects, and their contempt upon little,
frivolous, and useless ones. It is time, my dear, to teach them
French. Every decency, grace, and honesty should be inculcated
upon them.

(FL 28)

(20 September 1774)
*In September and October, Adams was in Philadelphia as a delegate to the
First Continental Congress.*

Frugality, my dear, frugality, economy, parsimony, must be our
refuge. I hope the ladies are every day diminishing their ornaments, and the gentlemen, too. Let us eat potatoes and drink
water; let us wear canvas, and undressed sheepskins, rather than
submit to the unrighteous and ignominious domination that is
prepared for us.

(FL 40-41)

(10 June 1775)
*On May 10, the Second Continental Congress began deliberations in
Philadelphia.*

My health and life ought to be hazarded in the cause of my country, as well as yours, and all my friends.

(FL 61)

(7 July 1775)
The Battle of Bunker's Hill was fought on June 17, and was watched by Abigail and John Quincy from a hill beside their home.

It gives me more pleasure than I can express, to learn that you sustain with so much fortitude the shocks and terrors of the times. You are really brave, my dear. You are a heroine, and you have reason to be. For the worst that can happen can do you no harm. A soul as pure, as benevolent, as virtuous and pious as yours, has nothing to fear, but everything to hope and expect from the last of human evils.

(FL 77)

(7 July 1775)

Your description of the distresses of the worthy inhabitants of Boston and the other seaport towns is enough to melt a heart of stone. Our consolation must be this, my dear, that cities may be rebuilt, and a people reduced to poverty may acquire fresh property. But a constitution of government, once changed from freedom, can never be restored. Liberty, once lost, is lost forever. When the people once surrender their share in the legislature, and their right of defending the limitations upon the Government, and of resisting every encroachment upon them, they can never regain it.

(FL 76)

(1 October 1775)

At this distance I can do no good to you or yours. I pray God to support you. I hope our friends and neighbors are kind as usual. I feel for them in the general calamity. I am so far from thinking you melancholy, that I am charmed with that admirable fortitude and that divine spirit of resignation which appear in your letters. I cannot express the satisfaction it gives me, nor how much it contributes to support me.

(FL 100)

(13 October 1775)

You and I, my dear, have reason, if ever mortals had to be thought-ful; to look forward beyond the transitory scene. Whatever is preparing for us, let us be prepared to receive. It is time for us to subdue our passions of every kind. The prospect before us is an ocean of uncertainties, in which no pleasing objects appear.

(FL 109)

(19 October 1775)

Really, it is very painful to be four hundred miles from one's fam-ily and friends, when we know they are in affliction. It seems as if it would be a joy to me to fly home, even to share with you your burdens and misfortunes. Surely, if I were with you, it would be my study to allay your griefs, to mitigate your pains, and to di-vert your melancholy thoughts.

(FL 110)

(29 October 1775)

The benevolence, charity, capacity, and industry which, exerted in private life, would make a family, a parish, or a town happy, em-ployed upon a larger scale, in support of the great principles of virtue and freedom of political regulations, might secure whole nations and generations from misery, want, and contempt. Public virtues and political qualities, therefore, should be incessantly cherished in our children.

(FL 118)

(3 December 1775)

My best friend—I wish I could write you every day, more than once, for although I have a number of friends and many relations who are very dear to me, yet all the friendship I have for others is far unequal to that which warms my heart for you. The most agreeable time that I spend here is in writing to you, and convers-ing with you, when I am alone. But the call of friendship and of private affection must give place to that of duty and honor. Even private friendship and affections require it.

(FL 126–7)

(18 February 1776)

I wish I understood French as well as you . . . I feel the want of education every day, particularly of that language. I pray, my dear, that you would not suffer your sons or your daughter ever to feel a similar pain. It is in your power to teach them French, and I every day see more and more that it will become a necessary accomplishment of an American gentleman or lady.

(FL 136)

(14 April 1776)

Your letter was the first intimation that another tribe [women], more numerous than all the rest, were grown discontented. This is rather too coarse a compliment, but you are so saucy, I won't blot it out. Depend on it, we know better than to repeal our masculine systems. Although they are in full force, you know they are little more than theory. We dare not exert our power in its full latitude. We are obliged to go fair and softly, and, in practice, you know we are the subjects. We have only the name of masters, and rather than give up this, which would completely subject us to the despotism of the petticoat, I hope General Washington and all our brave heroes would fight.

(FL 155)

(15 April 1776)
The education of the children was a frequent topic of discussion.

John has genius, and so has Charles. Take care that they don't go astray. Cultivate their minds, inspire their little hearts, raise their wishes. Fix their attention upon great and glorious objects. Root out every little thing. Weed out every meanness. Make them great and manly. Teach them to scorn injustice, ingratitude, cowardice, and falsehood. Let them revere nothing but religion, morality, and liberty.

(FL 159)

(28 April 1776)

It gives me concern to think of the many cares you must have upon your mind. Your reputation as a farmer, or anything else you undertake, I dare answer for. Your partner's character as a statesman is much more problematical.

(FL 165)

(28 April 1776)

Is there no way for two friendly souls to converse together although the bodies are four hundred miles off? Yes, by letter. But I want a better communication. I want to hear you think or to see your thoughts. The conclusion of your letter makes my heart throb more than a cannonade would. You bid me burn your letters. But I must forget you first.

(FL 166)

(15 May 1776)

In one or two of your letters, you remind me to think of you as I ought. Be assured, there is not an hour of the day in which I don't think of you as I ought, that is, with every sentiment of tenderness, esteem, and admiration.

(FL 175)

(22 May 1776)

Among all the disappointments and perplexities which have fallen to my share in life, nothing has contributed so much to support my mind as the choice blessing of a wife whose capacity enabled her to comprehend, and whose virtue obliged her to approve, the views of her husband. This has been the cheering consolation of my heart in my most solitary, gloomy, and disconsolate hours. In this remote situation, I am deprived in a great measure of this comfort. Yet I read and read again your charming letters, and they serve me, in some faint degree, as a substitute for the company and conversation of the writer. I want to take a walk with you in the garden, to go over to the common, the plain, the meadow. I want to take Charles in one hand and Tom in the other, and walk with you, Abby on your right hand and John upon my left, to view the cornfields, the orchards, etc.

Alas, poor imagination! How faintly and imperfectly do you supply the want of originality and reality. But instead of these pleasing scenes of domestic life, I hope you will not be disturbed with the alarms of war. I hope, yet I fear.

(FL 176)

(27 May 1776)

I think you shine as a stateswoman of late, as well as a farmeress. Pray, where do you get your maxims of state? They are very apropos.

(FL 177)

(7 July 1776)

Early youth is the time to learn the arts and sciences, and especially to correct the ear and the imagination, by forming a style. I wish you would think of forming the taste and judgment of your children now, before any unchaste sounds have fastened on their ears, and before any affectation or vanity is settled upon their minds, upon the pure principles of nature. Music is a great advantage; for style depends, in part, upon a delicate ear. The faculty of writing is attainable by art, practice, and habit only. The sooner, therefore, the practice begins, the more likely it will be to succeed. Have no mercy upon an affected phrase, any more than an affected air, gait, dress, or manners.

(FL 197)

(9 January 1777)
After a three-month recess, Congress reconvened in Baltimore, where it had been moved due to fears of a British attack on Philadelphia.

It was cruel parting this morning. My heart was most deeply affected, although I had the presence of mind to appear composed. May God Almighty's providence protect you, my dear, and all our little ones. My good genius, my guardian angel, whispers me that we shall see happier days, and that I shall live to enjoy the felicities of domestic life with her whom my heart esteems above all earthly blessings.

(FL 233)

(25 April 1778)
Elected as a commissioner to France with Benjamin Franklin and Arthur Lee, Adams, together with his son John Quincy, sailed across the Atlantic in February.

To tell you the truth, I admire the ladies here in France. Don't be jealous. They are handsome and very well educated. Their accomplishments are exceedingly brilliant, and their knowledge of letters and arts exceeds that of the English ladies, I believe.

(FL 330)

(9 February 1779)
Letters from France were often intercepted by British or French officials.

The character and situation in which I am here, and the situation of public affairs, absolutely forbid my writing freely. I must be excused. So many vessels are taken, and there are so many persons indiscreet and so many others inquisitive, that I may not write. God knows how much I suffer for want of writing to you. It used to be a cordial to my spirits.

(FL 353–54)

(9 February 1779)
The relationship between the commissioners in Paris grew very strained, especially between Adams and Franklin.

This much I can say with perfect sincerity, that I have found nothing to disgust me, or in any manner disturb me, in the French nation. My evils here arise altogether from the Americans.

(FL 354)

(20 February 1779)

For God's sake never reproach me again with not writing or with writing scrips. Your wounds are too deep. You know not, you feel not the dangers that surround me nor those that may be brought upon our country. Millions would not tempt me to write you as I used. I have no security that every letter I write you will not be broken open, and copied, and transmitted to Congress and to English newspapers.

(FL 357)

(1780)

In the summer of 1779, Adams and his son sailed back to Boston after learning that Congress had made Franklin the sole diplomatic representative in France. Shortly after his return, Congress appointed Adams to begin peace negotiations with the British minister in Paris. Adams sailed again across the Atlantic with his sons John Quincy and Charles, arriving in Paris in February 1780 after an arduous journey on foot through Spain.

There is everything here that can inform the understanding or refine the taste, and indeed, one would think, purify the heart. Yet it must be remembered there is everything here, too, which can seduce, betray, deceive, deprave, corrupt, and debauch it. Hercules marches here in full view of the steeps of virtue on one hand and the flowery paths of pleasure on the other, and there are few who make the choice of Hercules. That my children may follow his example is my earnest prayer; but I sometimes tremble when I hear the siren song of sloth, lest they should be captivated with her bewitching charms and her soft, insinuating music.

(FL 380)

(17 June 1780)

May Heaven permit you and me to enjoy the cool evening of life in tranquility, undisturbed by the cares of politics or war, and above all, with the sweetest of reflections, that neither ambition nor vanity nor avarice nor malice nor envy nor revenge nor fear nor any base motive or sordid passion, through the whole course of this mighty revolution, and the rapid, impetuous course of great and terrible events that have attended it, have drawn us aside from the line of our duty and the dictates of our consciences.

(FL 383)

(2 December 1781)

Adams traveled to the Netherlands in August 1780, after being directed by Congress to raise loans there for the war effort.

What a fine affair it would be, if we could flit across the Atlantic as they say the angels do from planet to planet! I would dart to Penn's hill and bring you over on my wings; but, alas, we must keep house separately for some time. But one thing I am determined on. If God should please to restore me once more to your fireside, I will never again leave it without your ladyship's company—no, not even to go to Congress to Philadelphia, and there I am determined to go, if I can make interest enough to get chosen, whenever I return.

(FL 398)

(4 December 1782)

Your proposal of coming to Europe has long and tenderly affected me. The dangers and inconveniences are such, and a European life would be so disagreeable to you, that I have suffered a great deal of anxiety in reflecting upon it. And upon the whole, I think it will be most for the happiness of my family, and most for the honor of my country, that I should come home. I have, therefore, this day written to Congress a resignation of all my employments, and as soon as I shall receive their acceptance of it, I will embark for America, which will be in the spring or beginning of summer.

(FL 410)

(28 December 1782)

My children, I hope, will once at length discover they have a father who is not unmindful of their welfare. They have had too much reason to think themselves forgotten, although I know that an anxiety for their happiness has corroded me every day of my life.

With a tenderness which words cannot express, I am theirs and yours forever.

(FL 413)

(18 February 1783)

Despite the promise contained in this letter, diplomatic responsibilities prevented Adams from returning home. Abigail, who had grown quite concerned over the illnesses that her husband had suffered, sailed across the Atlantic with her daughter Abby. Reconciled after being apart for over two years, they spent the next four years in France, England, and Holland before returning to the United States.

I shall certainly return home in the spring. With or without leave, resignation accepted or not, home I will come, so you have nothing to do but wait to receive your old friend.

(FL 413)

Part III

THE PUBLIC ADAMS

8

The Presidency

(July 1789)

In the first election following the ratification of the Constitution, George Washington was elected as president, and Adams, with the second-highest number of votes, became vice president. Adams was appalled at the degree of resistance to presidential authority.

The president's own officers, in a thousand instances, will oppose his just and constitutional exertions, and screen themselves under the wings of their patrons and party in the legislature.

(WJA VI 435)

(30 August 1789)

No man, I believe, has influence with the President. He seeks information from all quarters, and judges more independently than any man I ever knew. It is of such importance to the public that he should preserve this superiority, that I hope I shall never see the time that any man will have influence with him beyond the powers of reason and argument.

(WJA IX 561)

(1 September 1789)

As the vice president, Adams was asked what he thought of the possibility of being made president in case of Washington's death.

That I look up to that goal sometimes, is very probable, because it is not far above me, only one step, and it is directly before my eyes, so that I must be blind not to see it. I am forced to look up to it, and bound by duty to do so, because there is only the breath of one mortal between it. There was lately cause enough to look up to it, as I did with horror, when that breath was in some danger of expiring.

(WJA VIII 494)

(31 October 1789)

The worst evil that can happen in any government is a divided executive; and, as a plural executive must, from the nature of men, be forever divided, this is a demonstration that a plural executive is a great evil, and incompatible with liberty.

(WJA VIII 560)

(19 April 1794)

Pretexts are never wanting to ingenious men; but the views of all the principal parties are always directed to the election of the first magistrate.

(WJA I 472)

(20 January 1796)
On the prospect of being nominated for the presidency.

I am . . . quite a favorite . . . I am heir apparent, you know, and a succession is soon to take place. . . . All these hints must be secrets. It is not a subject of conversation as yet. I have a pious and philosophical resignation to the voice of the people in this case, which is the voice of God. I have no very ardent desire to be the butt of party malevolence. Having tasted of that cup, I find it bitter, nauseous, and unwholesome.

(WJA I 485)

(1 March 1796)
With Abigail's encouragement, Adams started warming up to the idea of being elected president.

The only question that labors in my mind is, whether I shall retire with [President Washington]. I hate to live in Philadelphia in summer, and I hate still more to relinquish my farm. I hate speeches, messages, addresses and answers, proclamations, and such affected, studied, constrained things. I hate levees and drawing-rooms. I hate to speak to a thousand people to whom I have nothing to say. Yet all this I can do.

(WJA I 487)

(13 March 1796)
Thomas Jefferson was the other frontrunner during the presidential election of 1796.

If Mr. Jefferson should be President, I believe I must put up as a candidate for the House. But this is my vanity. I feel sometimes as if I could speechify among them; but, alas, alas, alas, I am too old!

(WJA I 489)

(1 April 1796)
It was hoped by many that Washington would serve another four-year term.

One good effect of a persevering opposition in the House would be that we should preserve the President [Washington] for another four years. For I presume he will have sufficient spirit to hold the helm till he has steered the ship through this storm, unless the people should remove him, which most certainly they will not.

(WJA I 489–90)

(12 December 1796)
Letter to Abigail Adams quoting William Branch Giles, senator from Virginia, announcing the result of the presidential election. Adams had won by three votes over Jefferson, who became his vice president.

Giles says "the point is settled. The V.P. will be President. He is undoubtedly chosen. The old man will make a good President, too."

(WJA I 495)

(5 March 1797)
The day after his election, Adams expressed his concern in this imaginary comment from George Washington.

Methought I heard him say: "Ay! I am fairly out, and you fairly in! See which of us will be happiest."

(WJA I 506)

(15 June 1798)
The XYZ Affair, in which French Foreign Minister Talleyrand demanded bribes from American negotiators, was revealed by President Adams to Congress in April. War preparations were under way.

If the object of France, in her revolution, ever was liberty, it was a liberty very ill defined and never understood. She now aims at dominion such as never has before prevailed in Europe. If with the principles, maxims, and systems of her present leaders she is to become the model and arbiter of nations, the liberties of the world will be in danger.

(WJA IX 201)

(21 June 1798)
Message to Congress during the crisis brought on by the XYZ Affair.

I will never send another minister to France, without assurances that he will be received, respected, and honored as the representative of a great, free, powerful, and independent nation.

(WJA IX 159)

(8 December 1798)
Against the backdrop of war preparations, Adams tried to keep open the possibility of peace.

I give a pledge to France and to the world that the executive authority of this country still adheres to the humane and pacific policy which has invariably governed its proceedings, in conformity with the wishes of the other branches of the government, and the people of the United States. But considering the late manifestations of her policy towards foreign nations, I deem it a duty deliberately and solemnly to declare my opinion, that, whether we negotiate with her or not, vigorous preparations for war will be alike indispensable. These alone will give us an equal treaty and insure its observance.

(WJA I 537)

(19 February 1799)

Tranquility upon just and honorable terms, is undoubtedly the ardent desire of the friends of this country, and I wish the babyish and womanly blubbering for peace may not necessitate the conclusion of a treaty that will not be just nor very honorable. I do not intend, however, that they shall. There is not much sincerity in the cant about peace; those who snivel for it now, were hot for war against Britain a few months ago, and would be now, if they saw a chance. In elective governments, peace or war are alike embraced by parties, when they think they can employ either for electioneering purposes.

(WJA VIII 625–26)

(27 December 1799)
To Martha Washington, after George Washington's death on December 14.

In conformity with the desire of Congress ... assuring you of the profound respect Congress will ever bear to your person and character, and of their condolence on this afflicting dispensation of Providence. In pursuance of the same desire, I entreat your assent to the interment of the remains of the General under the marble monument to be erected in the capital, at the city of Washington, to commemorate the great events of his military and political life.

(WJA IX 45)

(22 February 1799)

I have no idea that I shall be chosen President a second time; though this is not to be talked of. The business of the office is so oppressive that I shall hardly support it two years longer.

(WJA I 544–45)

(13 May 1799)
Letter from his home in Quincy, where President Adams stayed when Congress was not in session.

Mrs. Adams, it is true, is better; but she is still in a state so delicate, and has such returns of that dreadful disorder, which kept her on the brink of the grave almost all the last summer, that it would be a presumptuous imprudence, little less criminal than deliberate suicide, for her to attempt to go one hundred miles south of this latitude, before the violent heat of summer shall be passed.

(WJA VIII 646)

(16 May 1800)
Adams signed the Alien and Sedition Acts in response to the perceived threat of French spies in America, and to counteract malicious political and personal attacks in newspapers.

I transmit you a copy of the resolution of the Senate of the United States, passed in Congress on the 14th of this month, by which I am requested to instruct the proper law officers to commence and carry on a prosecution against William Duane, editor of a newspaper called the Aurora, for certain false, defamatory, scandalous, and malicious publications in the said newspaper of the 19th of February last past, tending to defame the Senate of the United States, and to bring them into contempt and disrepute, and to excite against them the hatred of the good people of the United States.

(WJA IX 56)

(27 August 1800)
Having endured almost continual attempts by members of his cabinet to undermine his presidential authority, Adams finally dismissed Secretary of State Timothy Pickering for trying to stall the peace mission to France.

If a President of the United States has not authority enough to change his own Secretaries, he is no longer fit for his office. If he must enter into a controversy in pamphlets and newspapers, in vindication of his measures, he would have employment enough for his whole life, and must neglect the duties and business of his station.

(WJA IX 79)

(22 November 1800)
From the Fourth Annual Message to Congress.

As one of the grand community of nations, our attention is irresistibly drawn to the important scenes which surround us. If they have exhibited an uncommon portion of calamity, it is the province of humanity to deplore, and of wisdom to avoid the causes which may have produced it. If, turning our eyes homeward, we find reason to rejoice at the prospect which presents itself; if we perceive the interior of our country prosperous, free and happy; if all enjoy in safety, under the protection of laws emanating only from the general will, the fruits of their own labor, we ought to fortify and cling to those institutions which have been the source of much real felicity, and resist with unabating perseverance the progress of those dangerous innovations which may diminish their influence.

(WJA I 592)

(22 November 1800)
From the fourth Annual Message to Congress.

The manufacture of arms within the United States still invites the attention of the national legislature. At a considerable expense to the public this manufacture has been brought to such a state of maturity as, with continued encouragement, will supersede the necessity of future importations from foreign countries.

(WJA IX 146)

(24 January 1801)
Opinion on slavery, to Quakers George Churchman and Jacob Lindley.

Although I have never sought popularity by any animated speeches or inflammatory publications against the slavery of the blacks, my opinion against it has always been known, and my practice has been so conformable to my sentiments that I have always employed freemen, both as domestics and laborers, and never in my life did I own a slave. The abolition of slavery must be gradual, and accomplished with much caution and circumspection. Violent means and measures would produce greater violations of justice and humanity than the continuance of the practice. Neither Mr. Mifflin nor yourselves, I presume, would be willing to venture on exertions which would probably excite insurrections among the blacks to rise against their masters, and imbue their hands in innocent blood.

(WJA IX 92)

(26 January 1801)
After narrowly losing the bitterly fought presidential election of 1800,
Adams was eager to return home.

The remainder of my days will probably be spent in the labors of
agriculture, and the amusements of literature, in both of which I
have always taken more delight than in any public office, whatever rank.

(WJA IX 94)

(31 January 1801)
In one of his last actions as president, Adams appointed Federalist John
Marshall Chief Justice of the Supreme Court. Marshall would become one of
the most influential men to ever fill the position.

I hereby authorize and request you to execute the office of
Secretary of State so far as to affix the seal of the United States to
the enclosed commission to the present Secretary of State, John
Marshall, of Virginia, to be Chief Justice of the United States.

(WJA IX 95–6)

(16 April 1801)
One month after retiring to his home in Quincy.

The only consolation I shall want will be that of employment.
Ennui, when it rains on a man in large drops, is worse than one of
our north-east storms; but the labors of agriculture and amusement of letters will shelter me. My greatest grief is that I cannot
return to the bar. There I should forget in a moment that I was
ever a member of Congress, a foreign minister, or President of the
United States.

(WJA IX 585)

(1809)
In his retirement, Adams began publishing a long series of letters in the
Boston Patriot.

It may be thought presumption in me to impute errors to the nation; but . . . I hope to be excused if I suggest, that the general sen-

timent in most parts of the continent, that all the danger to liberty arises from the executive power, and that the President's office cannot be too much restrained, is an error.

(WJA IX 302)

(10 June 1809)
To the Boston Patriot, *recounting the internal dissension in the peace negotiations with France during the Quasi-War.*

When I look back on the opposition and embarrassments I had to overcome, from the faction of British subjects, from that large body of Americans who revere the English and abhor the French, from some of the heads of departments, from so many gentlemen in Senate, and so many more in the House of Representatives, and from the insidious and dark intrigues as well as open remonstrances of Mr. Hamilton, I am astonished at the event.

(WJA IX 310)

(10 June 1809)

In some of my jocular moments I have compared myself to an animal I have seen take hold of the end of a cord with his teeth, and be drawn slowly up by pulleys, through a storm of squibs, crackers, and rockets, flashing and blazing round him every moment; and though the scorching flames made him groan, and mourn, and roar, he would not let go his hold till he had reached the ceiling of a lofty theater, where he hung some time, still suffering a flight of rockets, and at last descended through another storm of burning powder, and never let go till his four feet were safely landed on the floor.

(WJA IX 310)

(18 February 1811)

The President has, or ought to have, the whole nation before him, and he ought to select the men best qualified and most meritorious for offices at his own responsibility, without being shackled by any check by law, constitution, or institution. Without this unrestrained liberty, he is not a check upon the legislative power nor either branch of it. Indeed, he must be the slave of the party that brought him in. He never can be independent or impartial.

(WJA IX 634)

(14 June 1813)
Adams tried to get Thomas Jefferson to acknowledge some responsibility for the Alien and Sedition Acts. One of the first actions by President Jefferson was to free everyone jailed under its provisions.

As your name is subscribed to that law, as Vice-President, and mine as President, I know not why you are not as responsible for it as I am. Neither of us was concerned in the formation of it. We were then at war with France. French spies then swarmed in our cities and our country; some of them were intolerably impudent, turbulent, and seditious. To check these, was the design of this law. Was there ever a government which had not authority to defend itself against spies in its own bosom—spies of an enemy at war?

(WJA X 42)

(January 1815)
Regarding the negotiations that ended the Quasi-War with France.

I . . . will defend my missions to France, as long as I have an eye to direct my hand, or a finger to hold my pen. They were the most disinterested and meritorious actions of my life. I reflect upon them with so much satisfaction, that I desire no other inscription over my gravestone than: "Here lies John Adams, who took upon himself the responsibility of the peace with France in 1800."

(WJA X 111)

(30 March 1815)

It was impossible not to perceive a profound and artful plot hatching in England, France, Spain, South and North America, to draw me into a decided instead of a *quasi* war with France, Spain, Holland, and all the enemies of England, and a perpetual alliance, offensive and defensive, with Great Britain; or in other words, to entangle us forever in all the wars of Europe. This plot I was determined to resist and defeat, if I could; and accordingly I embraced the first overtures from France to make peace with her upon terms honorable and advantageous to the United States.

(WJA X 151)

(31 March 1815)
During the Quasi-War, Adams rebuilt the American navy.

I purchased navy yards, which would now sell for double their cost with compound interest. I built frigates, manned a navy, and selected officers with great anxiety and care, who perfectly protected our commerce, and gained virgin victories over the French, and who afterwards acquired such laurels in the Mediterranean, and who have lately emblazoned themselves and their country with a naval glory, which I tremble to think of.

(WJA X 152–53)

(31 March 1815)

I was engaged in the most earnest, sedulous, and, I must own, expensive exertions to preserve peace with the Indians, and prepare them for agriculture and civilization, through the whole of my administration. I had the inexpressible satisfaction of complete success. Not a hatchet was lifted in my time; and the single battle of Tippecanoe has since cost the United States a hundred times more money than it cost me to maintain universal and perpetual peace.

(WJA X 153)

(31 March 1815)
Adams was denounced by many when he gave a presidential pardon to John Fries and his followers, who had launched a short-lived insurrection in Pennsylvania.

My judgment was clear, that their crime did not amount to treason. They had been guilty of a high-handed riot and rescue, attended with circumstances hot, rash, violent, and dangerous, but all these did not amount to treason. And I thought the officers of the law had been injudicious in indicting them for any crime higher than riot, aggravated by rescue.

(WJA X 154)

(31 March 1815)

As I had been intimately connected with Mr. Jefferson in friendship and affection for five-and-twenty years, I well knew his crude and visionary notions of government as well as his learning, taste, and talent in other arts and sciences. I expected his reign would be very nearly what it has been. I regretted it, but could not help it. At the same time, I thought it would be better than following the fools who were intriguing to plunge us into an alliance with England, an endless war with all the rest of the world, and wild expeditions to South America and St. Domingo; and, what was worse than all the rest, a civil war, which I knew would be the consequence of the measures the heads of that party wished to pursue.

(WJA X 154–55)

(14 May 1821)

The legislative and executive authorities are too much blended together. While the Senate of the United States have a negative on all appointments to office, we can never have a national President. In spite of his own judgment, he must be the President, not to say the tool, of a party.

(WJA X 397)

(22 January 1825)
To Thomas Jefferson on the election of his son, John Quincy Adams, to the presidency.

The Presidential election has given me less anxiety than I myself could have imagined. The next administration will be a troubled one, to whomsoever it falls, and our John has been too much worn to contend much longer with contending factions.

(WJA X 414)

9

GOVERNMENT

(29 August 1763)

The steady management of a good government is the most anxious, arduous, and hazardous vocation on this side of the grave.

(WJA III 437)

(August 1765)

The poor people, it is true, have been much less successful than the great. They have seldom found either leisure or opportunity to form a union and exert their strength; ignorant as they were of arts and letters, they have seldom been able to frame and support a regular opposition. This, however, has been known by the great to be the temper of mankind; and they have accordingly labored, in all ages, to wrest from the populace, as they are contemptuously called, the knowledge of their rights and wrongs, and the power to assert the former or redress the latter. I say RIGHTS, for such they have, undoubtedly, antecedent to all earthly government,—*Rights,* that cannot be repealed or restrained by human laws,—*Rights,* derived from the great Legislator of the universe.

(WJA III 448–49)

(August 1765)

Rulers are no more than attorneys, agents, and trustees, for the people; and if the cause, the interest and trust, is insidiously betrayed, or wantonly trifled away, the people have a right to revoke the authority that they themselves have deputed, and to constitute abler and better agents, attorneys, and trustees.

(WJA III 457)

(July 1770)

The good of the governed is the end, and rewards and punishments are the means, of all government.

(WJA II 250)

(July 1770)

In times of simplicity and innocence, ability and integrity will be the principal recommendations to the public service, and the sole title to those honors and emoluments which are in the power of the public to bestow. But when elegance, luxury, and effeminacy begin to be established, these rewards will begin to be distributed to vanity and folly; but when a government becomes totally corrupted, the system of God Almighty in the government of the world, and the rules of all good government upon the earth, will be reversed, and virtue, integrity, and ability, will become the objects of the malice, hatred, and revenge of the men in power, and folly, vice, and villainy will be cherished and supported.

(WJA II 251)

(12 February 1771)

Of the legislature, the people constitute one essential branch; and, while they hold this power unlimited, and exercise it frequently, as they ought, no law can be made, and continue long in force, that is inconvenient, hurtful, or disagreeable to the mass of society.

(WJA II 253)

(17 June 1775)

America is a great, unwieldy body. Its progress must be slow. It is like a large fleet sailing under convoy. The fleetest sailors must wait for the dullest and slowest. Like a coach and six, the swiftest horses must be slackened, and slowest quickened, that all may keep an even pace.

(FL 66)

(15 November 1775)

A legislative, an executive, and a judicial power comprehend the whole of what is meant and understood by government. It is by balancing each of these powers against the other two, that the efforts in human nature towards tyranny can alone be checked and restrained, and any degree of freedom preserved in the constitution.

(WJA IV 186)

(1775)
Adams's draft of "A Proclamation by the Great and General Court of the Colony of Massachusetts Bay" was ordered by the legislature to be read aloud at every court and town meeting throughout the province.

As the happiness of the people is the sole end of government, so the consent of the people is the only foundation of it, in reason, morality, and the natural fitness of things. And, therefore, every act of government, every exercise of sovereignty, against or without the consent of the people, is injustice, usurpation, and tyranny.

It is a maxim, that in every government there must exist somewhere a supreme, sovereign, absolute, and uncontrollable power; but this power resides always in the body of the people; the great creator having never given to men a right to vest others with authority over them unlimited either in duration or degree.

When kings, ministers, governors, or legislators, therefore, instead of exercising the powers entrusted with them according to the principles, forms, and proportions stated by the constitution, and established by the original compact, prostitute those powers to the purposes of oppression; to subvert, instead of preserving the lives, liberties, and properties of the people; they are no longer to be deemed magistrates vested with a sacred character, but become public enemies, and ought to be resisted.

(WJA I 193)

(1775)

The present generation . . . may be congratulated on the acquisition of a form of government more immediately in all its branches under the influence and control of the people, and therefore, more free and happy than was enjoyed by their ancestors. But as a government so popular can be supported only by universal knowledge and virtue, in the body of the people, it is the duty of all ranks to promote the means of education for the rising generation, as well as true religion, purity of manners, and integrity of life among all orders and degrees.

(WJA I 195)

(April 1776)
Adams wrote Thoughts on Government *in response to an inquiry from George Wythe, a fellow delegate from Virginia to the First Continental Congress. Wythe questioned how existing colonial governments would have to change once independence was declared.*

We ought to consider what is the end of government, before we determine which is the best form. Upon this point all speculative politicians will agree, that the happiness of society is the end of government, as all divines and moral philosophers will agree that the happiness of the individual is the end of man.

(WJA IV 193)

(April 1776)
Thoughts on government.

The foundation of every government is some principle or passion in the minds of the people. The noblest principles and most generous affections in our nature, then, have the fairest chance to support the noblest and most generous models of government.

(WJA IV 194)

(April 1776)
Thoughts on government.

As good government is an empire of laws, how shall your laws be made? In a large society, inhabiting an extensive country, it is impossible that the whole should assemble to make laws. The first necessary step, then, is to depute power from the many to a few of the most wise and good. But by what rules shall you choose your representatives? Agree upon the number and qualifications of persons who shall have the benefit of choosing, or annex this privilege to the inhabitants of a certain extent of ground.

The principle difficulty lies, and the greatest care should be employed, in constituting this representative assembly. It should be in miniature an exact portrait of the people at large. It should think, feel, reason, and act like them. That it may be the interest of this assembly to do strict justice at all times, it should be an equal representation, or, in other words, equal interests among the people should have equal interests in it. Great care should be taken to effect this, and to prevent unfair, partial, and corrupt elections.

(WJA IV 194–95)

(April 1776)
Thoughts on government.

I think a people cannot be long free, nor ever happy, whose government is in one assembly.

(WJA IV 195)

(April 1776)
Thoughts on government.

If the colonies should assume governments separately, they should be left entirely to their own choice of the forms; and if a continental constitution should be formed, it should be a congress, containing a fair and adequate representation of the colonies, and its authority should sacredly be confined to these cases, namely, war, trade, disputes between colony and colony, the post-office, and the unappropriated lands of the crown, as they used to be called.

(WJA IV 200)

(April 1776)
Thoughts on government.

How few of the human race have ever enjoyed an opportunity of making an election of government, more than of air, soil, or climate, for themselves or their children! When, before the present epoch, had three millions of people full power and a fair opportunity to form and establish the wisest and happiest government that human wisdom can contrive?

(WJA IV 200)

(23 March 1776)

The success of this war depends on a skilful steerage of the political vessel. The difficulty lies in forming particular constitutions for particular colonies, and a continental constitution for the whole. Each colony should establish its own government, and then a league should be formed between them all. This can be done only on popular principles and axioms, which are so abhorrent to the inclinations of the barons of the south, and the proprietary interests in the Middle States, as well as to that avarice of land which has made on this continent so many votaries to mammon, that I sometimes dread the consequences.

(WJA I 207)

(17 May 1776)

There is something very unnatural and odious in a government a thousand leagues off. A whole government of our own choice, managed by persons whom we love, revere, and can confide in, has charms in it for which men will fight.

(FL 174)

(25 August 1776)

We have been apt to flatter ourselves with gay prospects of happiness to the people, prosperity to the State, and glory to our arms, from those free kinds of governments which are to be created in America. And it is very true that no people ever had a finer opportunity to settle things upon the best foundations. But yet I fear that human nature will be found to be the same in America as it has been in Europe, and that the true principles of liberty will not be sufficiently attended to.

(WJA IX 434)

(25 August 1776)

A popular government is the worst curse to which human nature can be devoted, when it is thoroughly corrupted. Despotism is better. A sober, conscientious habit of electing for the public good alone must be introduced, and every appearance of interest, favor, and partiality reprobated, or you will very soon make wise and honest men wish for monarchy again; nay, you will make them introduce it into America.

(WJA IX 435)

(25 August 1776)

Equality of representation in the legislature is a first principle of liberty, and the moment the least departure from such equality takes place, that moment an inroad is made upon liberty. Yet, this essential principle is disregarded in many places in several of these republics. Every county is to have an equal voice, although some counties are six times more numerous and twelve times more wealthy. The same iniquity will be established in Congress. Rhode Island will have an equal weight with the Massachusetts, the Delaware government with Pennsylvania, and Georgia with Virginia. Thus we are sowing the seeds of ignorance, corruption, and injustice in the fairest field of liberty that ever appeared upon earth, even in the first attempts to cultivate it.

(WJA IX 435)

(6 December 1777)

Every man's liberty and life are equally dear to him; every man, therefore, ought to be taxed equally for the defense of his life and liberty. That is, the poll-tax should be equal. Every man's property is equally dear both to himself and to the public: every man's property ought to be taxed for the defense of the public in proportion to the quantity of it. These are fundamental maxims of sound policy.

(WJA IX 470)

(5 August 1778)

The confederation is an important object, and nothing is more wished for in Europe than its completion, and the finishing of the separate governments. The eagerness to complete the American code, and the strains of panegyric in which they speak and write of those parts of it, which have been published in Europe, are very remarkable, and seem to indicate a general revolution in the sentiments of mankind upon the subject of government.

(DC IV 263)

(5 September 1780)

As eloquence is cultivated with more care in free republics than in other governments, it has been found by constant experience that such republics have produced the greatest purity, copiousness, and perfection of language. It is not to be disputed that the form of government has an influence upon language, and language in its turn influences not only the form of government, but the temper, the sentiments, and manners of the people. The admirable models which have been transmitted through the world, and continued down to these days, so as to form an essential part of the education of mankind from generation to generation, by those two ancient towns, Athens and Rome, would be sufficient, without any other argument, to show the United States the importance to their liberty, prosperity, and glory, of an early attention to the subject of eloquence and language.

(WJA VII 249)

(2 October 1780)
While attempting to secure loans in Holland, Adams met Hendrik Calkoen, a Dutch lawyer who expressed a keen interest in the foundations of the American Revolution. As Calkoen did not speak English, Adams agreed to put his replies in writing. These letters were later bound and published as Letters from a Distinguished American.

There is nothing which I dread so much as a division of the republic into two great parties, each arranged under its leader, and concerting measures in opposition to each other. This, in my humble apprehension, is to be dreaded as the greatest political evil under our constitution.

(WJA IX 511)

(October 1780)
Letters from a Distinguished American.

The true profit of America is the continual augmentation of the price and value of land. Improvement in land is her principal employment, her best policy, and the principal source of her growing wealth.

(WJA VII 294)

(October 1780)
Letters from a Distinguished American.

Agriculture ever was, and ever will be, the dominant interest in America.

(WJA VII 309)

(21 May 1782)

I have the honor and consolation to be a republican on principle; that is to say, I esteem that form of government the best of which human nature is capable.

(WJA VII 593)

(18 July 1783)

If the union of the States is not preserved, and even their unity, in many great points, instead of being the happiest people under the sun, I do not know but we may be the most miserable. We shall find our foreign affairs the most difficult to manage of any of our interests; we shall see and feel them disturbed by invisible agents and causes, by secret intrigues, by dark and mysterious insinuations, by concealed corruptions of a thousand sorts.

(WJA VIII 108)

(18 July 1783)

I may be thought gloomy, but this ought not to discourage me from laying before Congress my apprehensions. The dependence of those who have designs upon us, upon our want of affection to each other, and of authority over one another, is so great, that, in my opinion, if the United States do not soon show to the world a proof that they can command a common revenue, to satisfy their creditors at home and abroad that they can act as one people, as one nation, as one man, in their transactions with foreign nations, we shall be soon so far despised, that it will be but a few years, perhaps but a few months only, before we are involved in another war.

(WJA VIII 108)

(27 July 1783)

The philosophers are speculating upon our constitutions, and, I hope, will throw out hints which will be of use to our countrymen. The science of government, as it is founded upon the genuine principles of society, is many centuries behind that of most other sciences, that of the fine arts, as well as that of trades and manufactures. As it is the first in importance, it is to be hoped it may overtake the rest, and that mankind may find their account in it.

(WJA VIII 208)

(24 November 1785)

There is no question more frequently asked me by the foreign ministers, than what can be the reason of such frequent divisions of States in America, and of the disposition to crumble into little separate societies, whereby there seems to be danger of multiplying the members of the confederation without end, or of setting up petty republics, unacknowledged by the confederacy, and refusing obedience to its laws. In the infancy of societies, men have generally been too little informed in their understandings, and too much given up to the government of their passions, to associate in large communities; but experience has shown them the ill effects of too many divisions.

(WJA VIII 347–48)

(3 February 1786)

It has ever been my hobby-horse to see rising in America an empire of liberty, and a prospect of two or three hundred millions of freemen, without one noble or one king among them.

(WJA IX 546)

(20 July 1786)

The sovereign power is constituted to defend individuals against the tyranny of others.

(WJA III 400)

(8 May 1787)

The settlement of so many great controversies, such as those between the Massachusetts and New York, Pennsylvania and Connecticut, New York and Vermont, etc., shows that the union has great weight in the minds of the people. It is, indeed, an object of such magnitude, that great sacrifices ought to be made to its preservation. The consequences of a division of the continent cannot be foreseen fully, by any man; but the most shortsighted must perceive such manifest danger, both from foreign powers and from one another, as cannot be looked upon without terror.

(WJA VIII 439)

(23 September 1787)

O fortunate Americans, if you did but know your own felicity! Instead of trampling on the laws, the rights, the generous plans of power delivered down from your remote forefathers, you should cherish and fortify those noble institutions with filial and religious reverence. Instead of envying the rights of others, every American citizen has cause to rejoice in his own. . . . What would have become of American liberty, if there had not been more faith, honor, and justice in the minds of their common citizens, than are found in the common people in Europe? . . . If the common people in America lose their integrity, they will soon set up tyrants of their own, or court a foreign.

(WJA VIII 454–55)

(1 January, 1787)
From the preface to A Defense of the Constitutions of Government, *which Adams wrote in response to an attack on American theories of government by the French economist Turgot.*

Representations, instead of collections, of the people; a total separation of the executive from the legislative power, and of the judicial from both; and a balance in the legislature, by three independent, equal branches, are perhaps the only three discoveries in the constitution of a free government, since the institution of Lycurgus. Even these have been so unfortunate, that they have never spread: the first has been given up by all the nations, excepting one, which had once adopted it; and the other two, reduced to practice, if not invented, by the English nation, have never been imitated by any other, except their own descendants in America.

(WJA IV 284)

(1 January 1787)
A Defense of the Constitutions of Government.

The United States are large and populous nations, in comparison with the Grecian commonwealths, or even the Swiss cantons; and they are growing every day more disproportionate, and therefore less capable of being held together by simple governments. Countries that increase in population so rapidly as the States of America did, even during such an impoverishing and destructive war as the last was, are not to be long bound with silken threads; lions, young or old, will not be bound by cobwebs.

(WJA IV 287)

(1 January 1787)
A Defense of the Constitutions of Government.

Democracy, simple democracy, never had a patron among men of letters.

(WJA IV 289)

(1 January 1787)
A Defense of the Constitutions of Government.

If there is one certain truth to be collected from the history of all ages, it is this; that the people's rights and liberties, and the democratic mixture in a constitution, can never be preserved without a strong executive, or, in other words, without separating the executive from the Legislative power. If the executive power, or any considerable part of it, is left in the hands either of an aristocratic or a democratic assembly, it will corrupt the legislature as necessarily as rust corrupts iron, or as arsenic poisons the human body; and when the legislature is corrupted, the people are undone.

(WJA IV 290)

(1 January 1787)
A Defense of the Constitutions of Government.

The rich, the wellborn, and the able, acquire an influence among the people that will soon be too much for simple honesty and plain sense, in a house of representatives. The most illustrious of them must, therefore, be separated from the mass, and placed by themselves in a senate; this is, to all honest and useful intents, an ostracism.

(WJA IV 290)

(1 January 1787)
A Defense of the Constitutions of Government.

The English nation, for their improvements in the theory of government, has, at least, more merit with the human race than any other among the moderns. The late most beautiful and liberal speculations of many writers, in various parts of Europe, are manifestly derived from English sources. Americans, too, ought forever to acknowledge their obligations to English writers, or rather have as good a right to indulge a pride in the recollection of them as the inhabitants of the three kingdoms. The original plantation of our country was occasioned, her continual growth has been promoted, and her present liberties have been established by these generous theories.

(WJA VI 3)

(1 January 1787)
A Defense of the Constitutions of Government.

It is for the young to make themselves masters of what their predecessors have been able to comprehend and accomplish but imperfectly.

(WJA VI 218)

(1 January 1787)
A Defense of the Constitutions of Government.

When we recollect that the wisdom or the folly, the virtue or the vice, the liberty or servitude, of those millions now beheld by us, only as Columbus saw these times in vision, are certainly to be influenced, perhaps decided, by the manners, examples, principles, and political institutions of the present generation, that mind must be hardened into stone that is not melted into reverence and awe.

(WJA VI 218)

(1 January 1787)
A Defense of the Constitutions of Government.

The best republics will be virtuous, and have been so; but we may hazard a conjecture, that the virtues have been the effect of the well-ordered constitution, rather than the cause.

(WJA VI 219)

(6 December 1787)
Letter to Thomas Jefferson discussing the Constitution, which had been drafted earlier in the year.

You are afraid of the one, I, of the few. We agree perfectly that the many should have a full, fair, and perfect representation. You are apprehensive of monarchy, I, of aristocracy. I would, therefore, have given more power to the president, and less to the senate. The nomination and appointment to all offices, I would have given to the president, assisted only by a privy council of his own creation; but not a vote or voice would I have given to the senate or any senator unless he were of the privy council. Faction and distraction are the sure and certain consequence of giving to a senate, a vote in the distribution of offices. You are apprehensive that the president, when once chosen, will be chosen again and again as long as he lives. So much the better, as it appears to me. You are apprehensive of foreign interference, intrigue, and influence. So am I. But as often as elections happen, the danger of foreign influence renews. The less frequently they happen, the less danger; and if the same man may be chosen again, it is possible he will be, and the danger of foreign influence will be less. Foreigners, seeing little prospect, will have less courage for enterprise. Elections, my dear sir, to offices which are a great object of ambition, I look at with terror. Experiments of this kind have been so often tried, and so universally found productive of horrors, that there is great reason to dread them.

(WJA VIII 464–65)

(16 December 1787)
More thoughts about the proposed Constitution.

The public mind cannot be occupied about a nobler object than the proposed plan of government. It appears to be admirably calculated to cement all America in affection and interest, as one great nation. A result of accommodation and compromise cannot be supposed perfectly to coincide with everyone's ideas of perfection. But, as all the great principles necessary to order, liberty, and safety, are respected in it, and provision is made for corrections and amendments, as they may be found necessary, I confess I hope to hear of its adoption by all the States.

(WJA VIII 467)

(21 April 1789)
On April 21, Adams became vice president under George Washington.

It is with satisfaction that I congratulate the people of America on the formation of a national Constitution, and the fair prospect of a

consistent administration of a government of laws; on the acquisition of a House of Representatives, chosen by themselves; of a
Senate, thus composed by their own State legislatures; and on the
prospect of an executive authority, in the hands of one, whose
portrait I shall not presume to draw.

(WJA VIII 486)

(21 April 1789)
Vice president's speech to Congress.

A trust of the greatest magnitude is committed to this legislature,
and the eyes of the world are upon you. Your country expects, from
the results of your deliberations, in concurrence with the other
branches of government, consideration abroad and contentment at
home, prosperity, order, justice, peace, and liberty. And may God
Almighty's Providence assist you to answer their just expectations.

(WJA VIII 487)

(July 1789)

The Constitution should guard against a possibility of its subver-
sion; but we may take stronger ground, and assert that it is a
probable such cases will happen, and that the Constitution will,
in fact, be subverted in this way. Nay, I go further, and say, that
from the constitution of human nature, and the constant course of
human affairs, it is certain that our Constitution will be subverted, if not amended, and that in a very short time, merely for
want of a decisive negative in the executive.

(WJA VI 432)

(18 August 1789)

After a generous contest for liberty, of twenty years' continuance,
Americans forgot wherein liberty consisted. After a bloody war in
defense of property, they forgot that property was sacred. After
an arduous struggle for the freedom of commerce, they voluntarily shackled it with arbitrary trammels. After fighting for justice
as the end of government, they seemed determined to banish that
virtue from the earth.

(WJA IX 560)

(25 September 1789)

Union, peace and liberty to North America, are the objects to which I have devoted my life. . . . I reckon among my friends all who are in the communion of such sentiments, though they may differ in their opinion of the means of obtaining those ends. I will not say that an energetic government is the only means; but I will hazard an opinion, that a well-ordered, a well-balanced, a judiciously-limited government, is indispensably necessary to the preservation of all or either of those blessings. If the poor are to domineer over the rich, or the rich over the poor, we shall never enjoy the happiness of good government; and without an intermediate power, sufficiently elevated and independent to oversee the contending parties in its excesses, one or the other will forever tyrannize.

(WJA VIII 495–96)

(1 June 1790)

I know not how it is, but mankind have an aversion to the study of the science of government. Is it because the subject is dry? To me, no romance is more entertaining.

(WJA IX 567)

(11 June 1790)

My fundamental maxim of government is, never to trust the lamb to the custody of the wolf.

(WJA IX 571)

(18 October 1790)

It is a fixed principle with me, that all good government is and must be republican. But, at the same time, your candor will agree with me, that there is not in lexicography a more fraudulent word. Whenever I use the word *republic* with approbation, I mean a government in which the people have collectively, or by representation, an essential share in the sovereignty.

(WJA VI 415)

(18 October 1790)

The numbers of men in all ages have preferred ease, slumber, and good cheer to liberty, when they have been in competition. We must not then depend alone upon the love of liberty in the soul of man for its preservation. Some political institutions must be prepared, to assist this love against its enemies. Without these, the struggle will ever end only in a change of impostors.

(WJA VI 418)

(23 January 1791)

The rivalry between the State governments and the national government, is growing daily more active and ardent. Thirteen strong men, embracing thirteen pillars at once, and bowing themselves in concert, will easily pull down a frail edifice. If the superiority of the national government is not more clearly acknowledged, we shall soon be in a confusion which we shall not get out of for twenty years. There was never more occasion for firmness in all who wish in sincerity for peace, liberty, or safety.

(WJA IX 573)

(23 January 1791)
Regarding the vice presidency.

For myself, I find the office I hold, though laborious, so wholly insignificant, and, from the blind policy of that part of the world from whence I came, so stupidly pinched and betrayed that I wish myself again at the bar, old as I am. My own situation is almost the only one in the world, in which firmness and patience are useless.

(WJA IX 573)

(1790–91)
From 1790–91, Vice President Adams published a series of articles in the Gazette of the United States, *which were later collected as* Discourses on Davila.

The desire of the esteem of others is as real a want of nature as hunger; and the neglect and contempt of the world as severe a pain as the gout or stone. It sooner and oftener produces despair, and a detestation of existence; of equal importance to individuals, to families, and to nations. It is a principal end of government to regulate this passion, which in its turn becomes a principal means of government. It is the only adequate instrument of order and subordination in society, and alone commands effectual obedience to laws, since without it neither human reason, nor standing armies, would ever produce that great effect.

(WJA VI 234)

(1790–91)
Discourses on Davila.

That world, for the regulation of whose prejudices, passions, imaginations, and interests, governments are instituted, is so unjust, that neither religion, natural or revealed, nor anything, but a well-ordered and well-balanced government, has ever been able to correct it, and that but imperfectly.

(WJA VI 263)

(1790–91)
Discourses on Davila.

In a well-balanced government, reason, conscience, truth, and virtue, must be respected by all parties, and exerted for the public good.

(WJA VI 277)

(1790–91)
Discourses on Davila.

Property must be secured, or liberty cannot exist.

(WJA VI 280)

(1790–91)
Discourses on Davila.

The essence of a free government consists in an effectual control of rivalries. The executive and the legislative powers are natural rivals; and if each has not an effectual control over the other, the weaker will ever be the lamb in the paws of the wolf.

(WJA VI 280)

(1790–91)
Discourses on Davila.

The haughty, arrogant insolence of aristocracy, and the feeble, timorous patience and humility of democracy, are apparent in this and all other history. But when democracy gets the upper hand, it seems to be conscious that its power will be short, and makes haste to glut its vengeance by a plentiful harvest of blood and cruelty, murder, massacre, and devastation. Hence despotism! Hence Napoleon! Hence Caesar! Hence Cromwell! Hence Charles XII! Hence Genghis! Hence Tamerlane! Hence Kouli Khan!

O man! Art thou a rational, a moral, a social animal?

(WJA VI 312)

(1790–91)
Discourses on Davila.

Let the rich and poor unite in the bands of mutual affection, be mutually sensible of each other's ignorance, weakness, and error, and unite in concerting measures for their mutual defense against each other's vices and follies, by supporting an impartial mediator.

(WJA VI 396)

(1790–91)
Closing paragraph of Adams's Discourses on Davila.

It has been said, that it is extremely difficult to preserve a balance. This is no more than to say that it is extremely difficult to preserve liberty. To this truth all ages and nations attest. It is so difficult, that the very appearance of it is lost over the whole earth, excepting one island and North America. How long it will be before she returns to her native skies, and leaves the whole human race in slavery, will depend on the intelligence and virtue of the people. A balance, with all its difficulty, must be preserved, or liberty is lost forever. Perhaps a perfect balance, if it ever existed, has not been long maintained in its perfection; yet, such a balance as has been sufficient to liberty, has been supported in some nations for many centuries together; and we must come as near as we can to a perfect equilibrium, or all is lost. When it is once widely departed from, the departure increases rapidly, till the whole is lost. If the people have not understanding and public virtue enough, and will not be persuaded of the necessity of supporting an independent executive authority, an independent Senate, and an independent judiciary power, as well as an independent House of Representatives, all pretensions to a balance are lost, and with them all hopes of security to our dearest interests, all hopes of liberty.

(WJA VI 399)

(29 July 1791)
Thomas Jefferson frequently claimed that Adams was a monarchist at heart.

I know not what your idea is of the best form of government. You and I have never had a serious conversation together, that I can recollect, concerning the nature of government. The very transient hints that have ever passed between us have been jocular and superficial, without ever coming to an explanation. If you suppose that I have, or ever had, a design or desire of attempting to introduce a government of King, Lords, and Commons, or in other words, a hereditary executive, or a hereditary senate, either into the government of the United States or that of any individual State, you are wholly mistaken. There is not such a thought expressed or intimated in any public writing or private letter, and I may safely challenge all mankind to produce such a passage, and quote the chapter and verse. If you have ever put such a construction on anything of mine, I beg you would mention it to me, and I will undertake to convince you that it has no such mention.

(WJA VIII 508)

(5 May 1794)

The ways and means before the House of Representatives is a very important and a very difficult system. While I confess the necessity of it, and see its importance in giving strength to our government at home and consideration to our country abroad, I lament the introduction of taxes and expenses which will accumulate a perpetual debt and lead to future revolutions.

(WJA I 473)

(4 March 1797)
From Adams's first Inaugural Speech.

Employed in the service of my country abroad, during the whole course of these transactions, I first saw the Constitution of the United States in a foreign country. Irritated by no literary altercation, animated by no public debate, heated by no party animosity, I read it with great satisfaction, as a result of good heads, prompted by good hearts; as an experiment better adapted to the genius, character, situation, and relations of this nation and country, than any which had ever been proposed or suggested.

(WJA IX 106)

(4 March 1797)
First Inaugural Speech.

Returning to the bosom of my country, after a painful separation from it for ten years, I had the honor to be elected to a station under the new order of things, and I have repeatedly laid myself under the most serious obligations to support the Constitution. The operation of it has equaled the most sanguine expectations of its friends; and, from a habitual attention to it, satisfaction in its administration, and delight in its effect upon the peace, order, prosperity, and happiness of the nation, I have acquired a habitual attachment to it, and veneration for it.

What other form of government, indeed, can so well deserve our esteem and love?

(WJA IX 107)

(16 May 1797)

It must not be permitted to be doubted, whether the people of the United States will support the government established by their voluntary consent, and appointed by their free choice; or whether, by surrendering themselves to the direction of foreign and domestic factions, in opposition to their own government, they will forfeit the honorable station they have hitherto maintained.

(WJA IX 118)

(3 December 1799)
Announcement that the federal capital would move to Washington in 1800.

The act of Congress, relative to the seat of the government of the United States, requiring that on the first Monday of December next, it should be transferred from Philadelphia to the district chosen for its permanent seat, it is proper for me to inform you, that the commissioners appointed to provide suitable buildings for the accommodation of Congress, and of the President, and of the public offices of the government, have made a report of the state of the buildings designed for those purposes in the city of Washington; from which they conclude that the removal of the seat of government to that place, at the time required, will be practicable, and the accommodation satisfactory.

(WJA IX 139)

(17 May 1799)

Mankind will not learn wisdom by experience in matters of government.

(WJA VIII 649)

(22 November 1800)
Speech to Congress during the first session held in Washington.

It would be unbecoming the representatives of this nation to assemble, for the first time, in this solemn temple, without looking up to the Supreme Ruler of the universe, and imploring his blessing.

May this territory be the residence of virtue and happiness! In this city may that piety and virtue, that wisdom and magnanimity, that constancy and self-government, which adorned the great character whose name it bears, be forever held in veneration! Here and throughout our country, may simple manners, pure morals, and true religion, flourish forever!

(WJA IX 143–44)

(5 February 1805)

Such is the nature of the people, and such the construction of our
government, that about once in a dozen years there will be an entire change in the administration. I lived twelve years as President
and Vice-President; Jefferson may possibly last sixteen; but New
York and Pennsylvania cannot remain longer than that period in
their present unnatural attachment to the southern States, nor
will the natural inconstancy of the people allow them to persevere longer in their present career. Our government will be a
game of leap-frog, of factions leaping over one another's backs
about once in twelve years, according to my computation.

(WJA IX 590)

(8 March 1805)

I had read Harrington, Sidney, Hobbes, Nedham, and Locke, but
with very little application to any particular views, till these debates in Congress [1775], and the interrogatories in public and
private, turned my thoughts to these researches, which produced
the "Thoughts on Government," the Constitution of Massachusetts, and at length the "Defense of the Constitutions of the
United States," and the "Discourses on Davila," writings which
have never done any good to me, though some of them undoubtedly contributed to produce the Constitution of New York, the
Constitution of the United States, and the last constitutions of
Pennsylvania and Georgia. They undoubtedly, also, contributed
to the writings of Publius, called the Federalist, which were all
written after the publication of my work in Philadelphia, New
York, and Boston. Whether the people will permit any of these
constitutions to stand upon their pedestals, or whether they will
throw them all down, I know not. Appearances at present are un-
favorable and threatening. I have done all in my power according
to what I thought my duty. I can do no more.

(WJA III 23)

(1805)

The truth is, that neither [in 1778], nor at any former time, since I
had attained any maturity in age, reading, and reflection, had I

imbibed any general prejudice against, or in favor of kings. It appeared to me then, as it has done ever since, that there is a state of society in which a republican government is the best, and, in America, the only one which ought to be adopted or thought of, because the morals of the people, and circumstances of the country, not only can bear it, but require it.

(WJA III 154)

(27 September 1808)

When public virtue is gone, when the national spirit is fled, when a party is substituted for the nation and faction for a party, when venality lurks and skulks in secret, and, much more, when it impudently braves the public censure, whether it be sent in the form of emissaries from foreign powers, or is employed by ambitious and intriguing domestic citizens, the republic is lost in essence, though it may still exist in form.

(WJA IX 603)

(1810)

The executive powers lodged in the Senate are the most dangerous to the Constitution, and to liberty, of all the powers in it.

(WJA IX 302)

(9 February 1811)

Prophecies of division have been familiar in my ears for six-and-thirty years. They have been incessant, but have had no other effect than to increase the attachment of the people to the Union. However lightly we may think of the voice of the people sometimes, they not infrequently see farther than you or I, in many great fundamental questions; and you may depend upon it, they see, in a partition of the Union, more danger to American liberty than poor [Fisher] Ames's distempered imaginations conceived, and a total loss of independence for both fragments, or all the fragments, of the Union.

(WJA IX 631)

(9 February 1811)

The Constitution, it is true, must speak for itself, and be interpreted by its own phraseology; yet the history and state of things at the time may be consulted to elucidate the meaning of words, and determine the bona fide intention of the Convention.

(WJA IX 631–2)

(18 February 1811)

No law, no constitution that human wit or wisdom can devise, can ever prevent senators or representatives from soliciting offices and favors for their friends.

(WJA IX 634)

(28 August 1811)

Funds and banks I never approved, or was satisfied with our funding system; it was founded in no consistent principle; it was contrived to enrich particular individuals at the public expense. Our whole banking system I ever abhorred, I continue to abhor, and shall die abhorring.

(WJA IX 638)

(21 June 1812)
On the French Revolution.

I acknowledge that the most unaccountable phenomenon ever beheld, in the seventy-seven years, almost, that I have lived, was to see men of the most extensive knowledge and deepest reflection entertain for a moment an opinion that a democratical republic could be erected in a nation of five-and-twenty millions of people, four-and-twenty millions and five hundred thousand of whom could neither read nor write.

(WJA X 16)

(1814–24)
In 1814, Adams began writing a series of letters to John Taylor to counter his attack on Adams's Defense of the Constitutions of the United States.

There is but one element of government, and that is, the people.

(WJA VI 474)

(1814–24)
Letter to John Taylor.

Democracy must be respected; democracy must be honored; democracy must be cherished; democracy must be an essential, an integral part of the sovereignty, and have a control over the whole government, or moral liberty cannot exist, or any other liberty. I have been always grieved by the gross abuses of this respectable word. One party speak of it as the most amiable, venerable, indeed, as the sole object of its adoration; the other, as the sole object of its scorn, abhorrence, and execration. Neither party, in my opinion, know what they say. Some of them care not what they say, provided they can accomplish their own selfish purposes. These ought not to be forgiven.

(WJA VI 477–78)

(1814–24)
Letter to John Taylor.

Mankind do not love to read anything upon any theory of government. Very few read anything but libels. Theoretical books upon government will not sell. Booksellers and printers, far from purchasing the manuscript, will not accept it as a gift. For example, no printer would publish these remarks at his own risk; and if I should print them at mine, they would fall dead from the press. I should never sell ten copies of them.

(WJA VI 482)

(1814–24)
Letter to John Taylor.

Remember, democracy never lasts long. It soon wastes, exhausts, and murders itself. There never was a democracy yet that did not commit suicide. It is vain to say that democracy is less vain, less

proud, less selfish, less ambitious, or less avaricious than aristocracy or monarchy.

(WJA VI 484)

(1814–24)
Letter to John Taylor.

Property makes a permanent distinction between aristocrats and
democrats. There are many more persons in the world who have
no property, than there are who have any; and, therefore, the
democracy is, and will be, more numerous than the aristocracy.

(WJA VI 512)

(1814–24)
Letter to John Taylor.

It does not appear that democracy has ever distinguished itself
more than aristocracy, in zeal or exertion for the promotion of science, literature, the fine arts, or mechanic arts, not even the art of
printing.

(WJA VI 514)

(1814–24)
Letter to John Taylor.

Remember always, as we go along, that by democrats I mean ex-
clusively those who are simple units, who have but one vote in
society.

(WJA VI 515)

(1814–24)
Letter to John Taylor.

Depend upon it, unless you give a share in the sovereignty to the
democrats, the more you increase knowledge in the nation, the
more you will grind and gripe the democrats, till you reduce
them to the calculations concerning West India negroes, Scottish
and English coal-heavers, Dutch turf-lifters, and the street-walking

girls of the night in Paris and London. For knowledge will forever be monopolized by the aristocracy. The moment you give knowledge to a democrat, you make him an aristocrat. If you give more than a share in the sovereignty to the democrats, that is, if you give them the command or preponderance in the sovereignty, that is, the legislature, they will vote all property out of the hands of you aristocrats, and if they let you escape with your lives, it will be more humanity, consideration, and generosity than any triumphant democracy ever displayed since the creation. And what will follow? The aristocracy among the democrats will take your places, and treat their fellows as severely and sternly as you have treated them.

(WJA VI 515–16)

(1814–24)
Letter to John Taylor.

I hope it will be no offense to say, that public opinion is often formed upon imperfect, partial, and false information from the press.

(WJA VI 518)

(16 July 1814)

Government has never been much studied by mankind; but their attention has been drawn to it in the latter part of the last century and the beginning of this, more than at any former period, and the vast variety of experiments which have been made of constitutions in America, in France, in Holland, in Geneva, in Switzerland, and even in Spain and South America, can never be forgotten. They will be studied, and their immediate and remote effects and final catastrophes noted. The result in time will be improvements; and I have no doubt that the horrors we have experienced for the last forty years will ultimately terminate in the advancement of civil and religious liberty, and amelioration in the condition of mankind.

(WJA X 100–01)

(1 June 1818)
Comment on James Otis's view that slaves and white colonists were born equally free.

Not a Quaker in Philadelphia, or Mr. Jefferson, of Virginia, ever asserted the rights of negroes in stronger terms. Young as I was, and ignorant as I was, I shuddered at the doctrine that he taught; and I have all my lifetime shuddered, and still shudder, at the consequences that may be drawn from such premises. Shall we say, that the rights of masters and servants clash, and can be decided only by force? I adore the idea of gradual abolitions! But who shall decide how fast or how slowly these abolitions shall be made?

(WJA X 315)

(17 June 1817)

The questions concerning universal suffrage, and those concerning the necessary limitations of the power of suffrage, are among the most difficult. It is hard to say that every man has not an equal right; but, admit this equal right and equal power, and an immediate revolution would ensue.

(WJA X 267–68)

(12 March 1819)

I have never had but one opinion concerning banking, from the institution of the first, in Philadelphia, by Mr. Robert Morris and Mr. Gouvernor Morris, and that opinion has uniformly been that the banks have done more injury to the religion, morality, tranquility, prosperity, and even wealth of the nation, than they can have done or ever will do good. They are like party spirit, the delusion of the many for the interest of a few.

(WJA X 375)

(30 April 1819)

Of republics, the varieties are infinite, or at least as numerous as the tunes and changes that can be rung upon a complete set of bells. Of all the varieties, a democracy is the most natural, the most ancient, and the most fundamental and essential.

(WJA X 378)

(8 June 1819)

The turpitude, the inhumanity, the cruelty, and the infamy of the African commerce in slaves, have been so impressively represented to the public by the highest powers of eloquence, that nothing that I can say would increase the just odium in which it is and ought to be held. If, however, humanity dictates the duty of adopting the most prudent measures for accomplishing so excellent a purpose, the same humanity requires, that we should not inflict severer calamities on the objects of our commiseration than those which they at present endure, by reducing them to despair, or the necessity of robbery, plunder, assassination, and massacre, to preserve their lives, some provision for furnishing them employment, or some means of supplying them with the necessary comforts of life. The same humanity requires that we should not by any rash or violent measures expose the lives and property of those of our fellow citizens, who are so unfortunate as to be surrounded with these fellow creatures, by hereditary descent, or by any other means without their own fault. I have, through my whole life, held the practice of slavery in such abhorrence, that I have lived for many years in times, when the practice was not disgraceful, when the best men in my vicinity thought it not inconsistent with their character, and when it has cost me thousands of dollars for the labor and subsistence of free men, which I might have saved by the purchase of negroes at times when they were very cheap.

(WJA X 379–80)

(3 November 1820)

I have great reason to rejoice in the happiness of my country, which has fully equaled, though not exceeded, the sanguine anticipation of my youth. God prosper long our glorious country, and make it a pattern for the world!

(WJA X 393)

(14 May 1821)

The probability is, that the fabrication of constitutions will be the occupation or the sport, the tragedy, comedy, or farce, for the entertainment of the world for a century to come.

(WJA X 397)

(14 May 1821)

Straight is the gate and narrow is the way that leads to liberty, and few nations, if any, have found it.

(WJA X 397)

(19 May 1821)

I may refine too much, I may be an enthusiast, but I think a free government is a complicated piece of machinery, the nice and exact adjustment of whose springs, wheels, and weights, is not yet well comprehended by the artists of the age, and still less by the people.

(WJA X 398)

(22 May 1821)

We shall leave the world with many consolations. It is better than we found it. Superstition, persecution, and bigotry are somewhat abated; governments are a little ameliorated; science and literature are greatly improved, and more widely spread. Our country has brilliant and exhilarating prospects before it, instead of that solemn gloom in which many of the former parts of our lives have been obscured.

(WJA X 399)

(15 August 1823)

I am no king killer, merely because they are kings. Poor creatures! They know no better; they sincerely and conscientiously believe that God made them to rule the world. I would not, therefore, behead them, or send them to St. Helena to be treated like Napoleon; but I would shut them up like the man in the mask, feed them well, and give them as much finery as they please, until they could be converted to right reason and common sense.

(WJA X 409)

(17 September 1823)

It is melancholy to contemplate the cruel wars, desolations of countries, and oceans of blood, which must occur before rational principles and rational systems of government can prevail and be established; but as these are inevitable, we must content ourselves with the consolations which you from sound and sure reasons so clearly suggest. These hopes are as well founded as our fears of the contrary evils. On the whole, the prospect is cheering.

(WJA X 410)

(7 June 1826)
One month before the fiftieth anniversary of the Declaration of Independence.

The present feeble state of my health will not permit me to indulge the hope of participating with more than my best wishes in the joys and festivities and solemn services of that day, on which will be completed the fiftieth year from the birth of the independence of these United States. A memorable epoch in the annals of the human race; destined in future history to form the brightest or the blackest page, according to the use or the abuse of those political institutions by which they shall in time to come be shaped by the *human mind.*

(WJA X 417)

(10 June 1826)
To a celebration committee in New York, less than one month before Adams's death.

Visions of future bliss in prospect, for the better condition of the human race, resulting from this unparalleled event, might be indulged, but sufficient unto the day be the glory thereof; and while you, gentlemen of the committee, indulge with your fellow citi-

zens of the city of New York in demonstrations of joy and effu-
sions of hilarity worthy the occasion, the wonderful growth of the
State, whose capital you represent, within the lapse of half a century, cannot fail to convince you that the indulgence of enthusiastic views of the future must be stamped with any epithet other
than visionary.

(WJA X 418)

10

POLITICS, FACTIONS, AND PARTIES

(29 August 1763)

The favorites of parties, although they have always some virtues, have always many imperfections. Many of the ablest tongues and pens have, in every age, been employed in the foolish, deluded, and pernicious flattery of one set of partisans, and in furious, prostitute invectives against another; but such kinds of oratory never had any charms for me; and if I must do one or the other, I would quarrel with both parties and with every individual of each, before I would subjugate my understanding, or prostitute my tongue or pen to either.

(WJA III 432)

(29 August 1763)

If engagements to a party are necessary to make a fortune, I had rather make none at all; and spend the remainder of my days like my favorite author, that ancient and immortal husbandman, philosopher, politician, and general, Xenophon, in his retreat, considering kings and princes as shepherds, and their people and subjects like flocks and herds, or as mere objects of contemplation and parts of a curious machine in which I had no interest, than to wound my own mind by engaging in any party, and spreading prejudices, vices, or follies.

(WJA III 433)

(29 August 1763)

Let not writers nor statesmen deceive themselves. The springs of their own conduct and opinions are not always so clear and pure, nor are those of their antagonists in politics always so polluted and corrupted, as they believe, and would have the world believe too. Mere readers and private persons can see virtues and talents on each side; and to their sorrow they have not yet seen any side altogether free from atrocious vices, extreme ignorance, and most lamentable folly.

(WJA III 436)

(25 June 1774)

Politics are an ordeal path among red-hot plowshares. Who, then, would be a politician, for the pleasure of running about barefoot among them? Yet somebody must.

(WJA I 149)

(6 July 1774)

These bickerings of opposite parties, and their mutual reproaches, their declamations, their singsong, their triumphs and defiances, their dismals and prophecies, are all delusions.

(FL 16)

(14 September 1774)

A Tory here is the most despicable animal in the creation. Spiders, toads, snakes are their only proper emblems.

(FL 32)

(29 September 1774)

I shall be killed with kindness in this place. We go to Congress at nine, and there we stay, most earnestly engaged in debates upon the most abstruse mysteries of state, until three in the afternoon; then we adjourn, and go to dine with some of the nobles of

Pennsylvania at four o'clock, and feast upon ten thousand delicacies, and sit drinking Madeira, Claret, and Burgundy, till six or seven, and then go home fatigued to death with business, company, and care. Yet I hold out surprisingly.

(FL 43)

(9 October 1774)

I am wearied to death with the life I lead. The business of the Congress is tedious beyond expression. This assembly is like no other that ever existed. Every man in it is a great man, an orator, a critic, a statesman; and therefore every man upon every question must show his oratory, his criticism, and his political abilities. The consequence of this is that business is drawn and spun out to an immeasurable length. I believe if it was moved and seconded that we should come to a resolution that three and two make five, we should be entertained with logic and rhetoric, law, history, politics, and mathematics, and then—we should pass the resolution unanimously in the affirmative. The perpetual round of feasting, too, which we are obliged to submit to, makes the pilgrimage more tedious to me.

(FL 45-46)

(10 October 1774)
During the First Continental Congress.

The deliberations of the Congress are spun out to an immeasurable length. There is so much wit, sense, learning, acuteness, subtlety, eloquence, etc. among fifty gentlemen, each of whom has been habituated to lead and guide in his own Province, that an immensity of time is spent unnecessarily.

(WJA II 395)

(24 October 1774)

In Congress, nibbling and quibbling as usual. There is no greater mortification than to sit with half a dozen wits, deliberating upon a petition, address, or memorial. These great wits, these subtle critics, these refined geniuses, these learned lawyers, these wise statesmen, are so fond of showing their parts and powers, as to make their consultations very tedious.

(WJA II 401)

(23 March 1776)
During the Second Continental Congress.

In politics, the middle way is none at all. If we finally fail in this great and glorious contest, it will be by bewildering ourselves in groping after this middle way.

(WJA I 207)

(26 May 1776)

Such is the frailty of the human heart, that very few men who have no property, have any judgment of their own. They talk and vote as they are directed by some man of property, who has attached their minds to his interest.

(WJA IX 376)

(26 May 1776)
Adams read the works of many political philosophers, including the seventeenth-century English author James Harrington.

Harrington has shown that power always follows property. This I believe to be as infallible a maxim in politics, as that action and re-action are equal, is in mechanics. Nay, I believe we may advance one step farther, and affirm that the balance of power in a society, accompanies the balance of property in land. The only possible way, then, of preserving the balance of power on the side of equal liberty and public virtue, is to make the acquisition of land easy to every member of society; to make a division of the land into small quantities, so that the multitude may be possessed of landed estates. If the multitude is possessed of the balance of real estate, the multitude will have the balance of power, and in that case the multitude will take care of the liberty, virtue, and interest of the multitude, in all acts of government.

(WJA IX 376–77)

(26 May 1776)
The subject of voting rights in the proposed union of states was hotly debated.

Depend on it . . . it is dangerous to open so fruitful a source of controversy and altercation as would be opened by attempting to alter the qualifications of voters; there will be no end of it. New claims will arise; women will demand a vote; lads from twelve to twenty-one will think their rights not enough attended to; and every man who has not a farthing, will demand an equal voice with any other, in all acts of state. It tends to confound and destroy all distinctions, and prostrate all ranks to one common level.

(WJA IX 378)

(12 June 1776)

Let me recommend to you an observation that one of my colleagues is very fond of, "The first virtue of a politician is patience; the second is patience; and the third is patience!" as Demosthenes observed that action was the first, second, and third quality of an orator. You will experience in public life such violent, sudden, and unexpected provocations and disappointments, that if you are not now possessed of all the patience of Job, I would advise you to acquire it as soon as possible.

(WJA IX 394)

(4 October 1776)

We live in an age of political experiments. Among many that will fail, some, I hope, will succeed.

(FL 231)

(28 July 1778)

In order to continue the war, or at least that we may do any good in the common cause, the credit of our currency must be supported. But how? Taxes, my dear Sir, taxes. Pray let our countrymen consider and be wise; every farthing they pay in taxes is a farthing's worth of wealth and good policy.

(DC IV 258)

(4 August 1779)

The State which is poor and in debt has no political stability.

(WJA VII 104)

(20 July 1780)

We have no need of such aids as political lies.

(WJA VII 231)

(13 May 1782)

I shall be plagued with piddling politicians as long as I live; at least, until I retire from the political career to the blue hills.

(WJA VII 584)

(17 June 1782)

What is to become of an independent statesman, one who will bow the knee to no idol, who will worship nothing as a divinity but truth, virtue, and his country? I will tell you; he will be regarded more by posterity than those who worship hounds and horses; and although he will not make his own fortune, he will make the fortune of his country.

(WJA IX 512)

(18 November 1782)
While negotiating the peace treaty with Great Britain, Adams often conversed with British ambassador Richard Oswald.

In another part of the conversation, I said, that when I was young, and addicted to reading, I had heard about dancing on the points of metaphysical needles; but, by mixing in the world, I had found the points of political needles finer and sharper than the metaphysical ones.

(WJA III 315)

(23 January 1783)

I have lived long enough, and had experience enough of the conduct of governments and people, nations and courts, to be convinced that gratitude, friendship, unsuspecting confidence, and all the most amiable passions in human nature, are the most dangerous guides in politics.

(WJA VIII 27)

(1 May 1783)
During the ongoing peace negotiations in Paris, Adams began thinking of his political future.

I do not intend to decline taking a seat in Congress, if any State in the confederation should think it worthwhile to offer me one. I am grown very ambitious of being a limb of that sovereign. I had rather be master than servant, on the same principle that men swear at Highgate,—never to kiss the maid when they can kiss the mistress.

(WJA VIII 56–57)

(10 May 1783)

In general, it is now sufficient to say, that private interest, party spirit, factions, cabals, and slanders have obstructed, perplexed, and tortured our loan in Holland, as well as all our other affairs, foreign and domestic.

(WJA VIII 59)

(23 June 1783)

Wise statesmen, like able artists of every kind, study nature, and their works are perfect in proportion as they conform to her laws.

(WJA VIII 74)

(21 August 1785)

We are so fond of being seen and talked of, we have such a passion for the esteem and confidence of our fellow-men, that wherever applications for office are permitted by the laws and manners, there will be many to apply, whether the profits are large or small, or none at all. If the profits are none, all the rich will apply, that is to say, all who can live upon their own incomes; all others will be excluded, because, if they labor for the public, themselves and families must starve. By this means an aristocracy or oligarchy of the rich will be formed, which will soon put an end by their arts and craft to this self-denying system. If many apply, all applications should be forbidden, or, if they are permitted, a choice should be made of such out of the multitude as will be contented with legal profits, without making advantage of patronage and perquisites.

(WJA IX 534)

(21 August 1785)

Every public man should be honestly paid for his services; then justice is done to him. But he should be restrained from every perquisite not known by the laws, and he should make no claims upon the gratitude of the public, nor ever confer an office within his patronage, upon a son, a brother, a friend, upon pretense that he is not paid for his services by the profits of his office.

(WJA IX 535)

(10 September 1785)

An office without profits, without salary, fees, perquisites, or any kind of emolument, is sought for with servility, faction, and corruption, from ambition, as often as an office of profit is sought from avarice. And this is the way in which corruption is constantly introduced into society. It constantly begins with the people, in their elections. Indeed, the first step of corruption is this dishonest disposition in the people, an unwillingness to pay their representatives. The moment they require of a candidate that he serve them gratis, they establish an aristocracy by excluding from a possibility of serving them, all who are poor and unambitious, and by confining their suffrages to a few rich men. When this point is once gained of the people, which is easily gained, because their own avarice pleads for it, tyranny has made a gigantic stride.

(WJA IX 538)

(22 September 1787)
While Adams was in Holland, the Constitutional Convention began deliberating in Philadelphia.

The convention of Philadelphia is composed of heroes, sages, and demigods, to be sure, who want no assistance from me in forming the best possible plan; but they may have occasion for under-laborers, to make it accepted by the people, or, at least, to make them unanimous in it and contented in it. One of these under-workmen, in a cool retreat, it shall be my ambition to become.

(WJA VIII 452)

(3 December 1788)

The constancy of the people in a course of annual elections has discarded from their confidence almost all the old, staunch, firm patriots, who conducted the revolution in all the civil depart-ments, and has called to the helm pilots much more selfish and much less skilful.

(WJA IX 557)

(July 1789)
As vice president, Adams was very active in the Senate and often cast the deciding vote in contentious issues.

We shall very soon have parties formed; a court and country party, and these parties will have names given them. One party in the House of Representatives will support the president and his measures and ministers; the other will oppose them. A similar party will be in the Senate; these parties will study with all their arts, perhaps with intrigue, perhaps with corruption, at every election to increase their own friends and diminish their op-posers. Suppose such parties formed in the Senate, and then con-sider what factious divisions we shall have there upon every nomination.

(WJA VI 435)

(31 October 1789)

The worst evil that can happen in any government is a divided executive; and, as a plural executive must, from the nature of men, be forever divided, this is a demonstration that a plural ex-ecutive is a great evil, and incompatible with liberty. That emula-tion in the human heart, which produces rivalries of men, cities, and nations, which produces almost all the good in human life, produces, also, almost all the evil. This is my philosophy of government. The great art lies in managing this emulation. It is the only defense against its own excesses. The emulation of the Legislative and executive powers should be made to control each other. The emulation between the rich and the poor among the people, should be made to check itself by balancing the two houses in the legislature, which represent these two classes of society, so invidious at all times against each other.

(WJA VIII 560)

(18 April 1790)

I wish very heartily that a change of Vice President could be made tomorrow. I have been too ill-used in the office to be fond of it;— if I had not been introduced into it in a manner that made it a disgrace. I will never serve in it again upon such terms.

(WJA IX 567)

(19 September 1793)

My country has in its wisdom contrived for me the most insignificant office that ever the invention of man contrived or his imagination conceived.

(WJA I 460)

(2 January 1794)

Cabal, intrigue, maneuver, as bad as any species of corruption, we have already seen in our elections; and when and where will they stop?

(WJA I 461)

(10 May 1794)

We go on as usual, Congress resolving one thing, and the democratical societies resolving the contrary; the President doing what is right, and clubs and mobs resolving it to be all wrong.

(WJA I 473)

(10 May 1794)

It is interesting to note the comment upon the introduction of the practice of voting with printed ballots, which has since become universal. The effect of it, in increasing the force of associated action, and diminishing the individual power of choice between candidates, has never yet been sufficiently set forth.

(WJA I 474)

(7 January 1796)

The expenses of living at the seat of government are so exorbitant, so far beyond all proportion to the salaries, and the sure reward of integrity in the discharge of public functions is such obloquy, contempt, and insult, that no man of any feeling is willing to renounce his home, forsake his property and profession for the sake of removing to Philadelphia, where he is almost sure of disgrace and ruin.

(WJA I 483)

(8 July 1797)

There will ever be parties and divisions in all nations; but our people will support their government, and so will the French theirs. Not to expect divisions in a free country, would be an absurdity.

(WJA VIII 548)

(10 March 1800)

When I came into office, it was my determination to make as few removals as possible—not one from party considerations. This resolution I have invariably observed.

(WJA IX 47)

(10 September 1800)
Newspaper writers were merciless in their attacks on the policies of president Adams.

Porcupine's gazette, and Fenno's gazette, from the moment of the mission to France, aided, countenanced, and encouraged by *soi-*

disant Federalists in Boston, New York, and Philadelphia, have done more to shuffle the cards into the hands of the Jacobin leaders, than all the acts of administration, and all the policy of the opposition, from the commencement of the government.

(WJA IX 83)

(31 March 1801)
Victory in the 1801 election for Democratic-Republican Thomas Jefferson caused a crisis among Adams's party.

We Federalists are much in the situation of the party of Bolingbroke and Harley, after the treaty of Utrecht, completely and totally routed and defeated. We are not yet attainted by act of Congress, and, I hope, shall not fly out into rebellion. No party, that ever existed, knew itself so little, or so vainly overrated its own influence and popularity, as ours. None ever understood so ill the causes of its own power, or so wantonly destroyed them.

(WJA IX 582)

(1810)

I have great reason to believe, that Mr. Jefferson came into office with the same spirit that I did, that is, with a sincere desire of conciliating parties, as far as he possibly could, consistently with his principles. But he soon found, as I did, that the Senate had a decided majority of Republicans, five or six to one, a much greater majority than there was in my time of Federalists, which was never more than two to one.

(WJA IX 302)

(6 August 1812)

There are two tyrants in human life who domineer in all nations, in Indians and Negroes, in Tartars and Arabs, in Hindus and Chinese, in Greeks and Romans, in Britons and Gauls, as well as in our simple, youthful, and beloved United States of America. These two tyrants are fashion and party. They are sometimes at variance, and I know not whether their mutual hostility is not the only security of human happiness. But they are forever struggling for an alliance with each other; and, when they are united, truth, reason, honor, justice, gratitude, and humanity itself in combination are no match for the coalition. Upon the maturest reflection of a long experience, I am much inclined to believe that fashion is the worst of all tyrants, because he is the original source, cause, preserver, and supporter of all the others.

(WJA X 21)

(25 November 1812)
On political divisions.

Alas! They began with human nature; they have existed in America from its first plantation. In every colony, divisions always prevailed. In New York, Pennsylvania, Virginia, Massachusetts, and all the rest, a court and country party have always contended. Whig and Tory disputed very sharply before the revolution, and in every step during the revolution. Every measure of Congress, from 1774 to 1787 inclusively, was disputed with acrimony, and decided by as small majorities as any question is decided in these days.

(WJA X 23)

(25 November 1812)

When I was exerting every nerve to vindicate the honor, and demand a redress of the wrongs of the nation against the tyranny of France, the arm of the nation was palsied by one party. Now Mr. Madison is acting the same part, for the same ends, against Great Britain, the arm of the nation is palsied by the opposite party. And so it will always be while we feel like colonists, dependent for protection on France and England; while we have so little national public opinion, so little national principle, national feeling, national patriotism; while we have no sentiment of our own strength, power, and resources.

(WJA X 23–24)

(3 March 1813)

The political and literary world are much indebted for the invention of the new word Ideology. Our English words, Idiocy or Idiotism, express not the force of meaning of it. It is presumed its proper definition is the science of Idiocy. And a very profound, abstruse, and mysterious science it is. You must descend deeper than the divers in the Dunciad to make any discoveries, and after all you will find no bottom. It is the bathos, the theory, the art, the skill of diving and sinking in government. It was taught in the school of folly; but, alas! Franklin, Turgot, Rochefoucauld, and Condorcet, under Tom Paine, were the great masters of that academy!

(WJA VI 403)

(30 June 1813)

The real terrors of both parties have always been, and now are, the fear that they shall lose elections, and, consequently, the loaves and fishes, and that their antagonists will get them. Both parties have excited artificial terrorism, and, if I were summoned as a witness to say, upon oath, which party had excited the most terror, and which had really felt the most, I could not give a more sincere answer than in the vulgar style, "put them in a bag and shake them, and then see which will come out first."

(WJA X 48)

(14 March 1814)

I dare not look beyond my nose into futurity. Our money, our commerce, our religion, our national and state constitutions, even our arts and sciences, are so many seed-plots of division, faction, sedition, and rebellion. Everything is transmuted into an instrument of electioneering. Election is the Grand Brahma, the immortal Lama, I had almost said the Juggernaut; for wives are almost ready to burn upon the pile, and children to be thrown under the wheel.

(WJA X 90–91)

(16 July 1814)

Our hopes . . . of sudden tranquility ought not to be too sanguine. Fanaticism and superstition will still be selfish, subtle, intriguing, and, at times, furious. Despotism will still struggle for domination; monarchy will still study to rival nobility in popularity; aristocracy will continue to envy all above it, and despise and oppress all below it; democracy will envy all, contend with all, endeavor to pull down all, and when by chance it happens to get the upper hand for a short time, it will be revengeful, bloody, and cruel. These and other elements of fanaticism and anarchy will yet for a long time continue a fermentation, which will excite alarms and require vigilance.

(WJA X 101)

(11 February 1815)

Each party is deliberately and studiously kept in ignorance of the other. Have naked truth and honest candor a fair hearing or impartial reading in this or any other country? Have not narrow bigotry, the most envious malignity, the most base, vulgar, sordid, fishwoman scurrility, and the most palpable lies, a plenary indulgence, and an unbounded licentiousness? If there is ever to be an amelioration of the condition of mankind, philosophers, theologians, legislators, politicians and moralists will find that the regulation of the press is the most difficult, dangerous, and important problem they have to resolve. Mankind cannot now be governed without it, nor at present with it.

(WJA X 117)

(11 February 1815)

Parties in politics, like sects in religion, will not read, indeed they are not permitted by their leaders to read, anything against their own creed, nor indeed to converse with any but their own club.

(WJA X 117)

(24 April 1815)

But is it not wonderful that one party should now found their arguments in favor of union, principally on the authority of Washington, and that the other party, in his name, and under the pretense of his authority, should intrigue and cabal the destruction of the Union? Good God! Is there a man or woman in the United

States, of common sense and information, who wants the authority of Washington to prove the necessity of Union?

(WJA X 165)

(13 November 1815)

The fundamental article of my political creed is, that despotism,
or unlimited sovereignty, or absolute power, is the same in a majority of a popular assembly, an aristocratical council, an oli-
garchical junto, and a single emperor. Equally arbitrary, cruel,
bloody, and in every respect diabolical.

(WJA X 174)

(4 February 1817)

There is an overweening fondness for representing this country
as a scene of liberty, equality, fraternity, union, harmony, and
benevolence. But let not your sons or mine deceive themselves.
This country, like all others, has been a theater of parties and
feuds for near two hundred years.

(WJA X 242)

11

FOREIGN POLICY

(28 July 1778)
In February, Adams arrived in France as a joint commissioner to the French court with his son John Quincy.

It is not much to the honor of human nature, but the fact is certain, that neighboring nations are never friends in reality. In the times of the most perfect peace between them, their hearts and their passions are hostile, and this will certainly be the case forever between the thirteen United States and the English colonies.

(DC IV 257)

(4 August 1778)

America will grow with astonishing rapidity, and England, France, and every other nation in Europe will be the better for her prosperity. Peace, which is her dear delight, will be her wealth and her glory, for I cannot see the seed of a war with any part of the world in future, but with Great Britain, and such States as may be weak enough, if any such there should be, to become her allies.

(DC IV 262)

(25 September 1778)
Fishing rights on the Grand Banks off Newfoundland were often negotiated.

The fishery was a source of luxury and vanity that did us much injury; yet this was the fault of the management, not of the fishery. One part of our fish went to the West India Islands for rum, and molasses to distill into rum, which injured our health and our morals; the other part went to Spain and Portugal for gold and silver, almost the whole of which went to London, sometimes for valuable articles of clothing, but too often for lace and ribbons. If, therefore, the cessation of the fishery, for twenty years to come, was to introduce the culture of flax and wool, which it certainly would do so far as would be necessary for the purposes of decency and comfort, if a loss of wealth should be the consequence of it, the acquisition of morals and of wisdom would perhaps make us gainers in the end.

(WJA VII 47–48)

(27 February 1779)

The great source of danger and unhappiness to the States, then, probably will be a depreciating currency. The prospect of a loan in Europe, after every measure that has been or could be taken, I think it my duty to say frankly to Congress, is very unpromising.

(WJA VII 87)

(4 August 1779)

In the opinion of some, the power with which we shall one day have a relation the most immediate, next to that of France, is Great Britain. But it ought to be considered that this power loses every day her consideration, and runs towards her ruin. Her riches, in which her power consisted, she has lost with us, and never can regain. . . . I think that every citizen, in the present circumstances, who respects his country and the engagements she has taken, ought to abstain from the foresight of a return of friendship between us and the English, and act as if it never was to be.

(WJA VII 103)

(4 August 1779)

The similitude of manners, of religion, and, in some respects, of constitution, the analogy between the means by which the two republics arrived at independency, but, above all, the attractions of commercial interest, will infallibly bring [the United States and Holland] together.

(WJA VII 104)

(18 February 1780)

Whether it is, that the art of political lying is better understood in England than in any other country, or whether it is more practiced there than elsewhere, or whether it is accidental that they have more success in making their fictions gain credit in the world, I know not. But it is certain, that every winter since the commencement of the present war with America, and indeed for some years before, they sent out large quantities of this manufacture over all Europe, and throughout all America, and what is astonishing is, that they should still find numbers in every country ready to take them off their hands.

(DC IV 370)

(19 February 1780)

There are two reflections, which the English cannot bear, one is that of losing the domination of the colonies as indispensable to the support of their naval superiority over France and Spain, or either of them, in possession of a powerful fleet at the peace. Their maxim is to make themselves terrible at sea to all nations, and they are convinced that if they make a peace leaving America independent, and France and Spain powerful at sea, they shall never again be terrible to any maritime power. These reasons convince me, that Great Britain will hazard all rather than make peace at present.

(DC IV 375)

(28 February 1780)

Instead of wishing and hoping for peace, my dear countrymen must qualify themselves for war, and learn the value of liberty by the dearness of its purchase. The foundations of lasting prosperity are laid in great military talents and virtues. Every sigh for peace, until it can be obtained with honor, is unmanly. If our enemies can be obstinate and desperate in a wicked and disgraceful cause, surely we can be determined and persevering in the most just, the most honorable, and the most glorious cause, that was ever undertaken by men.

(DC IV 392)

(12 March 1780)

The events of war are uncertain at sea, more than even by land; but America has resources for the final defense of her liberty, which Britain will never be able to exhaust, though she should exhaust France and Spain, and it may not impossibly be our hard fate, but it will be our unfading glory finally to turn the scale of the war, to humble the pride, which is so terrible to the commercial nations of Europe, and to produce a balance of power on the seas. To this end Americans must be soldiers and seamen.

(DC IV 405)

(18 April 1780)

The longer this war is continued in America, the more Americans become habituated to the characters of the soldier and the marine. Military virtues and talents and passions will gain strength and additional activity every year while the war lasts; and the more these virtues, talents, and passions are multiplied, the deeper will the foundations of American power be laid, and the more dangerous will it become to some or other of the powers of Europe; to France, as likely as to any other power, because it will be more likely to be ambitious and enterprising, and to aspire at conquests by sea and land.

(WJA VII 151)

(18 April 1780)

Let us, above all things, avoid as much as possible entangling ourselves with their war or politics. Our business with them, and theirs with us, is commerce, not politics, much less war. America has been the sport of European wars and politics long enough.

(WJA VII 151)

(17 May 1780)

If a peace should unhappily be made, leaving England in possession of Canada, Nova Scotia, the Floridas, or any one spot of
ground in America, they will be perpetually encroaching upon
the States of America; whereas, France, having renounced all ter-
ritorial jurisdiction in America, will have no room for controversy.

(WJA VII 175)

(13 July 1780)

The United States of America are a great and powerful people,
whatever European statesmen may think of them. If we take into
our estimate the numbers and the character of her people, the extent, variety, and fertility of her soil, her commerce, and her skill
and materials for shipbuilding, and her seamen, excepting France,
Spain, England, Germany, and Russia, there is not a state in Europe
so powerful. Breaking off such a nation as this from the English so
suddenly, and uniting it so closely with France, is one of the most
extraordinary events that ever happened among mankind.

(WJA VII 226–27)

(5 September 1780)
In August, John and John Quincy arrived in Holland.

English is destined to be in the next and succeeding centuries
more generally the language of the world than Latin was in the
last or French is in the present age. The reason of this is obvious,
because the increasing population in America, and their universal
connection and correspondence with all nations will, aided by the
influence of England in the world, whether great or small, force
their language into general use, in spite of all the obstacles that
may be thrown in their way, if any such there should be.

(WJA VII 250)

(7 October 1780)

All the men-of-war in Europe would not be sufficient to block up a
seacoast of two thousand miles in extent, varied as that of America

is by such an innumerable multitude of ports, bays, harbors, rivers, creeks, inlets, and islands; with a coast so tempestuous, that there are many occasions in the course of the year when merchant vessels can push out and in, although men-of-war cannot cruise.

(WJA VII 274–75)

(7 October 1780)

America is, most undoubtedly, capable of being the most independent country upon earth. It produces everything for the necessity, comfort, and conveniency of life, and many of the luxuries too. So that, if there were an eternal separation between Europe and America, the inhabitants of America would not only live but multiply, and, for what I know, be wiser, better, and happier than they will be as it is.

(WJA VII 275)

(23 April 1782)

Etiquette, when it becomes too glaring by affectation, imposes no longer either upon the populace or upon the courtiers, but becomes ridiculous to all. This will soon be the case everywhere with respect to American ministers.

(WJA VII 574)

(17 June 1782)

It is a pretty amusement to play a game with nations as if they were fox and geese, or coins upon a checker board, or the personages at chess, is it not? It is, however, the real employment of a statesman to play such a game sometimes; a sublime one, truly; enough to make a man serious, however addicted to sport. Politics are the divine science, after all.

(WJA IX 512)

(13 August 1782)
Congress deferred to the French ministry in European affairs, and to Adams's dismay, in peace negotiations with Great Britain.

Either Congress should recall all their ministers from Europe, and leave all negotiations to the French ministry, or they must support their ministers against all insinuations. If Congress will see with their own eyes, I can assure them, without fear of being contradicted, that neither the color, figure, nor magnitude of objects will always appear to them exactly as they do to their allies. To send ministers to Europe, who are supposed by the people of America to see for themselves, while in effect they see, or pretend to see nothing, but what appears through the glass of a French minister, is to betray the just expectations of that people.

(WJA VII 631)

(8 November 1782)

Ranks, titles, and etiquettes, and every species of punctilios, even down to the visits of cards, are of infinitely more importance in Europe than in America, and therefore Congress cannot be too tender of disgracing their ministers abroad in any of these things, nor too determined not to disgrace themselves.

(WJA VIII 3)

(8 November 1782)

History shows that nations have generally had as much difficulty to arrange their affairs with their allies as with their enemies.

(WJA VIII 8)

(8 November 1782)

America has been long enough involved in the wars of Europe. She has been a football between contending nations from the beginning, and it is easy to foresee, that France and England both will endeavor to involve us in their future wars. It is our interest and duty to avoid them as much as possible, and to be completely independent, and to have nothing to do with either of them, but in commerce. My poor thoughts and feeble efforts have been from the beginning constantly employed to arrange all our European connections to this end, and will continue to be so employed, whether they succeed or not.

(WJA VIII 9)

(4 December 1782)
Throughout his time in Paris, there was bitter infighting among the American negotiators.

I hope it will be permitted to me, or to some other who can do it better, some ten or fifteen years hence, to collect together in one view my little negotiations in Europe. Fifty years hence it may be published, perhaps twenty. I will venture to say, however feebly I may have acted my part, or whatever mistakes I may have committed, yet the situations I have been in, between angry nations and more angry factions, have been some of the most singular and interesting that ever happened to any man. The fury of enemies as well as of elements, the subtlety and arrogance of allies, and, what has been worse than all the jealousy, envy, and little pranks of friends and copatriots, would form one of the most instructive lessons in morals and politics that ever was committed to paper.

(WJA III 343)

(5 February 1783)
Adams dutifully reported to Congress on all matters, including these suggested qualifications for foreign ministers.

And if it should not be thought too presumptuous, I would beg leave to add, what is my idea of the qualifications necessary for an American foreign minister in general, and particularly and above all to the Court of St. James [Great Britain].

In the first place, he should have had an education in classical learning, and in the knowledge of general history, ancient and modern, and particularly the history of France, England, Holland, and America. He should be well versed in the principles of ethics, of the law of nature and nations, of legislation and government, of the civil Roman law, of the laws of England and the United States, of the public law of Europe, and in the letters, memoirs, and histories of those great men, who have heretofore shone in the diplomatic order, and conducted the affairs of nations, and the world. He should be of an age to possess a maturity of judgment, arising from experience in business. He should be active, attentive, and industrious; and above all, he should possess an upright heart and an independent spirit, and should be one who decidedly makes the interest of his country, not the policy of any other nation, nor his own private ambition or interest, or those of his family, friends, and connections, the rule of his conduct.

(WJA VIII 38)

(3 July 1783)

The first maxim of a statesman, as well as that of a [sculptor] or a painter, should be to study nature; to cast his eyes round about his country, and see what advantages nature has given it. This was well attended to in the boundary between the United States and Canada, and in the fisheries. The commerce of the West India Islands falls necessarily into the natural system of the commerce of the United States. We are necessary to them, and they to us; and there will be a commerce between us. If the governments forbid it, it will be carried on clandestinely.

(WJA VIII 79)

(11 July 1783)

The thirteen States, in relation to the discharge of the debts of Congress, must consider themselves as one body, animated by one soul. The stability of our confederation at home, our reputation abroad, our power of defense, the confidence and affection of the people of one State towards those of another, all depend upon it.

(WJA VIII 92–3)

(14 July 1783)

Let us bind ourselves to nothing, but reserve a right of making navigation acts when we please, if we find them necessary or useful.

(WJA VIII 99)

(16 July 1783)

The politics of Europe are such a labyrinth of profound mysteries, that the more one sees of them, the more causes of uncertainty and anxiety he discovers.

(WJA VIII 103)

(18 July 1783)
Negotiations over the core provisions of the peace treaty with Great Britain dragged on for months.

The present ministers in England have very bad advisers; the refugees, and emissaries of various other sorts; and we have nobody to watch, to counteract, to correct or prevent anything. The United States will soon see the necessity of uniting in measures to counteract their enemies, and even their friends. What powers Congress should have for governing the trade of the whole, for making or recommending prohibitions or imposts, deserves the serious consideration of every man in America.

(WJA VIII 107)

(5 September 1783)
Two days after the Treaty of Paris was signed between the United States and Great Britain.

Our country has but lately been a dependent one, and our people, although enlightened and virtuous, have had their minds and hearts habitually filled with all the passions of a dependent and subordinate people; that is to say, with fear, with diffidence, and distrust of themselves, with admiration of foreigners, etc. Now, I say, that it is one of the most necessary and one of the most difficult branches of the policy of Congress to eradicate from the American mind every remaining fiber of this fear and self-diffidence on one hand, and of this excessive admiration of foreigners on the other.

(WJA VIII 144)

(3 May 1785)
Remarks made after Adams was appointed the first United States ambassador to Great Britain.

One of the foreign ambassadors said to me, "You have been often in England." "Never, but once in November and December, 1783." "You have relations in England, no doubt." "None at all." "None, how can that be? You are of English extraction?" "Neither my father or mother, grandfather or grandmother, great grandfather or great grandmother, nor any other relation that I know of, or care a farthing for, has been in England these one hundred and fifty years; so that you see I have not one drop of blood in my veins but what is American." "Ay, we have seen," said he, "proof enough of that." This flattered me, no doubt, and I was vain enough to be pleased with it.

(WJA III 392)

(8 May 1785)

It behooves the United States, then, to knit themselves together in the bands of affection and mutual confidence, search their own resources to the bottom, form their foreign commerce into a system, and encourage their own navigation and seamen, and to those ends their carrying trade; and I am much afraid we shall never be able to do this, unless Congress are vested with full power, under the limitations prescribed of fifteen years, and the concurrence of nine States, of forming treaties of commerce with foreign powers.

(WJA VIII 246)

(6 August 1785)

Britain has ventured to begin commercial hostilities. I call them hostilities, because their direct object is not so much the increase of their own wealth, ships, or sailors, as the diminution of ours. A jealousy of our naval power is the true motive, the real passion which actuates them; they consider the United States as their rival, and the most dangerous rival they have in the world.

(WJA VIII 290–91)

(30 August 1785)

I hope the States will be cool, and do nothing precipitately; but, I hope, they will be firm and wise. Confining our exports to our own ships, and laying on heavy duties upon all foreign luxuries, and encouraging our own manufactures, appear to me to be our only resource, although I am very sensible of the many difficulties in the way, and of the danger of their bringing on, in the course of a few years, another war.

(WJA VIII 313)

(3 December 1785)
After the Treaty of Paris, the British still had forts located on the frontiers of
the United States.

The posts upon our frontier give me great uneasiness. The ministers and people are so assured of peace with all their neighbors in
Europe, that they hold all we can do in indifference. They think
that if we should raise an army and take these posts, as we have a
right to do, it would not oblige them to go to war with us; but, if
we should march an army to Quebec, and take it, and another to
Nova Scotia, and take that, it would be no great harm to them; if
we should fit out privateers against their trade, they could easily
send a line of frigates along our coast, that would do us more
harm. So that they are quite easy. But they rely upon it, that we
shall not raise an army to take the posts. The expense and difficulty they know will be great, and, therefore, they think they may
play with us as long as they please.

(WJA VIII 354)

(6 December 1785)

If all intercourse between Europe and America could be cut off
forever, if every ship we have were burnt, and the keel of another
never to be laid, we might still be the happiest people upon earth,
and, in fifty years, the most powerful. The luxuries we import
from Europe, instead of promoting our prosperity, only enfeeble
our race of men and retard the increase of population. But the
character of our people must be taken into consideration. They
are as aquatic as the tortoises and sea-fowl, and the love of commerce, with its conveniences and pleasures, is a habit in them as
unalterable as their natures. It is in vain, then, to amuse ourselves
with the thoughts of annihilating commerce, unless as philosophical speculations. We are to consider who our constituents are,
and what they expect of us. Upon this principle we shall find that
we must have connections with Europe, Asia, and Africa; and,
therefore, the sooner we form those connections into a judicious
system, the better it will be for us and our children.

(WJA VIII 357)

(2 March 1786)
Written while in London.

The United States are willing to throw wide open every port in their dominions to British ships and merchants and merchandizes, and I am ready, in their behalf, to pledge their faith in a treaty to this effect, upon the reciprocal stipulation of this nation that her ports shall be equally open to our ships, merchants, and produce. But the United States must repel monopolies with monopolies, and answer prohibitions by prohibitions.

(WJA VIII 383)

(2 March 1786)

The Americans are, at this day, a great people, and are not to be trifled with. Their numbers have increased fifty percent since 1774. A people that can multiply at this rate, amidst all the calamities of such a war of eight years, will, in twenty years more, be too respectable to want friends.

(WJA VIII 385)

(9 May 1786)
Algerian pirates preyed on American shipping in the Mediterranean and, without a large navy, bribes were seen as the only way to stop the aggression.

Peace with the Turks, comprehending, under this term, Constantinople, Tunis, Tripoli, Algiers, and Morocco, is essential to our navigation and commerce, and political consideration in Europe. Two or three hundred thousand guineas, and nothing less, will obtain it. It will be miserable policy and economy to lose two or three millions in trade, insurance, etc. etc., and still worse, to add two or three millions more in fitting out a navy to fight them, in order to save that sum in customary presents.

(WJA VIII 390)

(27 October 1786)

The present appearances of friendship are forced and feigned. The time may not be far distant, however, when we may see a combination of England and the house of Bourbon against the United States. It is not in gloomy moments only, but in the utmost gayety of heart, I cannot get rid of the persuasion that the fair plant of liberty in America must be watered in blood.

(WJA VIII 416)

(1 June 1790)

I know by experience that in revolutions the most fiery spirits and flighty geniuses frequently obtain more influence than men of sense and judgment, and the weakest men may carry foolish measures in opposition to wise ones proposed by the ablest. France is in great danger from this quarter.

(WJA IX 568)

(29 August 1790)

A pacific character, in opposition to a warlike temper, a spirit of conquest, or a disposition to military enterprise, is of great importance to us to preserve in Europe; and, therefore, we should not engage, even in defensive war, until the necessity of it should become apparent, or, at least, until we have it in our power to make it manifest in Europe as well as at home.

(WJA VIII 498)

(9 January 1794)
At the height of the French Revolution, Louis XVI and his wife, Marie Antoinette, were beheaded.

The news of this evening is, that the Queen of France is no more. When will savages be satiated with blood? No prospect of peace in Europe, and therefore none of internal harmony in America.

(WJA I 461)

(7 April 1794)
In April, President Washington assigned Chief Justice John Jay to negotiate a peace treaty with Great Britain. Unresolved provisions of the Treaty of Paris had led to escalating tensions, culminating in the seizure by the British of some American vessels in the West Indies.

One firebrand is scarcely quenched before another is thrown in; and if the sound part of the community is not uncommonly active and attentive to support us, we shall be drawn off from our neutral ground, and involved in incomprehensible evils. In danger of a war that will be unnecessary, if not unjust; that has no public object in view; that must be carried on with allies the most dangerous that ever existed, my situation is as disagreeable as any I ever knew. I should have no fear of an honest war; but a knavish one would fill me with disgust and abhorrence.

(WJA I 470–71)

(15 April 1794)

We are ill-treated by Britain, and you and I know it is owing to a national insolence against us. If they force us into a war, it is my firm faith they will be chastised for it a second time worse than the first.

(WJA I 472)

(16 May 1797)

However we may consider ourselves, the maritime and commercial powers of the world will consider the United States of America as forming a weight in that balance of power in Europe, which never can be forgotten or neglected. It would not only be against our interest, but it would be doing wrong to one half of Europe at least, if we should voluntarily throw ourselves into either scale.

(WJA IX 117)

(23 November 1797)
Adams continually pushed for a strong American navy as a protection against foreign aggression.

The world has furnished no example of a flourishing commerce, without a maritime protection; and a moderate knowledge of man and his history will convince anyone that no such prodigy ever can arise.

(WJA IX 127)

(4 September 1799)
During the Quasi-War, Adams desperately worked to keep the United States out of another altercation.

France has always been a pendulum. The extremest vibration to the left has always been suddenly followed by the extemest vibration to the right.

(WJA IX 20)

(5 January 1813)

Nothing but a navy under Heaven can secure, protect, or defend us.

(WJA X 25)

(30 May 1814)

We must hold Europe at arm's length, do them justice, treat them with civility, and set their envy, jealousy, malice, retaliation, and revenge at defiance.

(WJA X 98)

(January 1815)

National defense is one of the cardinal duties of a statesman.

(WJA X 111)

(12 March 1815)
The War of 1812 had just ended with the Treaty of Ghent.

I wish I could amalgamate oil and water; I wish I could reconcile the interests, passions, prejudices, and even the caprices of Britons and Americans. But I have despaired of it more than sixty years, and despair of it still.

(WJA X 138)

(29 March 1815)

For full forty years, three points have been settled in my mind after mature deliberation.

1. That neutrality in the wars of Europe is our truest policy; and to preserve this, alliances ought to be avoided as much and as long as possible.

But, if we should be driven to the necessity of an alliance,

2. Then France is our natural ally; and
3. That Great Britain is the last power, to which we should, in any, the last extremity, resort for any alliance, political or military.

(WJA X 147)

(5 April 1815)

The ocean and its treasures are common property of all men, and we have a natural right to navigate the ocean and to fish in it, whenever and wherever we please. Upon this broad and deep and strong foundation do I build, and with this cogent and irresistible argument do I fortify our rights and liberties in the fisheries on the coasts as well as on the banks, namely, the gift and grant of God Almighty in his creation of man, and his land and water; and, with resignation only to the eternal counsels of his Providence, they never will and never shall be surrendered to any human authority or anything but divine power.

(WJA X 160)

(14 December 1819)

I am old enough to remember the war of 1745, and its end; the war of 1755, and its close; the war of 1775, and its termination; the war of 1812, and its pacification. Every one of these wars has been followed by a general distress; embarrassment on commerce, destruction of manufactures, fall of the price of produce and of lands, similar to those we feel at the present day, and all produced by the same causes. I have wondered that so much experience has not taught us more caution. The British merchants and manufacturers, immediately after the peace, disgorged upon us all their stores of merchandise and manufactures, not only without profit, but at certain loss for a time, with the express purpose of annihilating all our manufacturers, and ruining all our manufactories.

The cheapness of these articles allures us into extravagance and luxury, involves us in debt, exhausts our resources, and at length produces universal complaint.

(WJA X 384)

(14 December 1819)

What would be the consequence of the abolition of all restrictive, exclusive, and monopolizing laws, if adopted by all the nations of the earth, I pretend not to say. But while all the nations, with whom we have intercourse, persevere in cherishing such laws, I know not how we can do ourselves justice without introducing, with great prudence and discretion, however, some portions of the same system.

(WJA X 384)

(18 December 1819)
Reflecting on the proposal to admit Missouri into the Union as a slave state.

The Missouri question, I hope, will follow other waves under the ship, and do no harm. I know it is high treason to express a doubt of the perpetual duration of our vast American empire and our free institutions ... but I am sometimes Cassandra enough to dream that another Hamilton, another Burr, might rend this mighty fabric in twain, or, perhaps, into a leash, and a few more choice spirits of the same stamp might produce as many nations in North America as there are in Europe.

(WJA X 386)

12

LAW AND JUSTICE

(18 November 1755)
Adams considered becoming a preacher before deciding on law.

Necessity drove me to [decide to study law], but my inclination, I think, was to preach. However, that would not do. But I set out with firm resolutions, I think, never to commit any meanness or injustice in the practice of law. The study and practice of law, I am sure, does not dissolve the obligations of morality or of religion.

(WJA I 32)

(19 October 1756)

The students in the law are very numerous, and some of them youths of which no country, no age, would need to be ashamed. And if I can gain the honor of treading in the rear, and silently admiring the noble air and gallant achievements of the foremost rank, I shall think myself worthy of a louder triumph than if I had headed the whole army of orthodox preachers.

(WJA I 37)

(3 January 1759)
Adams frequently exhorted himself to study harder, as in this diary entry.

Labor to get distinct ideas of law, right, wrong, justice, equity; search for them in your own mind, in Roman, Grecian, French, English treatises of natural, civil, common, statute law; aim at an exact knowledge of nature, end, and means of government; compare the different forms of it with each other, and each of them with their effects on public and private happiness.

(WJA II 59)

(1761)

Multitudes of needless matters, and some that are nonsensical, it must be confessed, have in the course of ages crept into the law. But I beg to know what art or science can be found in the whole circle, that has not been taught by silly, senseless pedants, and is not stuffed with their crudities and jargon.

(WJA II 115)

(1761)

If the grandeur and importance of a subject have any share in the pleasure it communicates, I am sure the law has by far the advantage of most other sciences. Nothing less than the preservation of the health and properties, lives and tranquility, morals and liberties of millions of the human species, is the object and design of the law; and a comparison of several constitutions of government invented for those purposes, and examination of the great causes of their danger, as well as those of their safety, must be as agreeable an employment as can exercise the mind.

(WJA II 115)

(1 August 1763)

The great distinction between savage nations and polite ones, lies in this,—that among the former every individual is his own judge and executioner; but among the latter all pretensions to judgment and punishment are resigned to tribunals erected by the public; a resignation which savages are not, without infinite difficulty, persuaded to make, as it is of a right and privilege extremely dear and tender to an uncultivated nature.

(WJA III 429)

(5 September 1763)

Resistance to sudden violence, for the preservation not only of my person, my limbs and life, but of my property, is an indisputable right of nature which I never surrendered to the public by the compact of society, and which, perhaps, I could not surrender if I would.

(WJA III 438)

(5 September 1763)

Such is the wisdom and humanity of English law; upon so thorough a knowledge of human nature is it founded, and so well is it calculated to preserve the lives and limbs of men and the interior tranquility of societies!

(WJA III 440)

(August 1765)

Since the promulgation of Christianity, the two greatest systems of tyranny that have sprung from this original, are the canon and the feudal law. The desire of dominion, that great principle by which we have attempted to account for so much good and so much evil, is, when properly restrained, a very useful and noble movement in the human mind. But when such restraints are taken off, it becomes an encroaching, grasping, restless, and ungovernable power. Numberless have been the systems of iniquity contrived by the great for the gratification of this passion in themselves; but in none of them were they ever more successful than in the invention and establishment of the canon and the feudal law.

(WJA III 449)

(1765)

By the laws of England, justice flows with an uninterrupted stream! In that music the law knows of neither rests nor pauses. Nothing but violence, invasion, or rebellion, can obstruct the river or untune the instrument.

(WJA II 164)

(1770)

Facts are stubborn things, and whatever may be our wishes, our inclinations, or the dictates of our passions, they cannot alter the state of facts and evidence.

(WJA I 113)

(23 July 1771)

Of all that I have heard from judges, lawyers, jurors, clients, clerks, I cannot recollect a word, a sentence, worth committing to writing.

(WJA II 289)

(5 March 1773)
Adams successfully defended the British soldiers who were charged in the Boston Massacre.

The part I took in defense of Captain Preston and the soldiers procured me anxiety and obloquy enough. It was, however, one of the most gallant, generous, manly, and disinterested actions of my whole life, and one of the best pieces of service I ever rendered my country. Judgment of death against those soldiers would have been as foul a stain upon this country as the executions of the Quakers or witches anciently. As the evidence was, the verdict of the jury was exactly right.

(WJA II 317)

(7 July 1774)
Adams deplored the rioting that broke out in Boston in response to British policies.

If popular commotions can be justified in opposition to attacks upon the constitution, it can only when fundamentals are invaded, nor then unless for absolute necessity, and with great caution. But these tarrings and featherings, this breaking open houses by rude and insolent rabble in resentment for private wrongs, or in pursuance of private prejudices and passions, must

be discountenanced. It cannot be even excused upon any principle which can be entertained by a good citizen, a worthy member
of society.

(WJA)

(January 1776)

The dignity and stability of government in all its branches, the
morals of the people, and every blessing of society depend so
much upon an upright and skilful administration of justice, that
the judicial power ought to be distinct from both the legislative
and executive, and independent upon both, that so it may be a
check upon both, as both should be checks upon that. The judges,
therefore, should be always men of learning and experience in the
laws, of exemplary morals, great patience, calmness, coolness,
and attention. Their minds should not be distracted with jarring
interests; they should not be dependent upon any man, or body of
men. To these ends, they should hold estates for life in their offices; or, in other words, their commissions should be during
good behavior, and their salaries ascertained and established by
law.

(WJA IV 198)

(18 July 1776)
To John Mason, who became a student in Adams's law office.

To attain the real knowledge which is necessary for a lawyer, requires the whole time and thoughts of a man in his youth, and it
will do him no good to dissipate his mind among the confused
objects of a camp.

(WJA IX 423)

(16 February 1778)

Few things have ever given me greater pleasure than the tuition
of youth to the bar, and the advancement of merit.

(WJA III 97)

(4 November 1779)

I think there ought to be an article in the declaration of rights of every State, securing freedom of speech, impartiality, and independence at the bar. There is nothing on which the rights of every member of society more depend.

(WJA IX 507)

(4 November 1779)

There is no man so bad but he ought to have a fair trial, and an equal chance to obtain the ablest counsel, or the advocate of his choice, to see that he has fair play, and the benefit of truth and law.

(WJA IX 507)

(11 July 1783)

Without a sacred regard to public justice, no society can exist; it is the only tie which can unite men's minds and hearts in pursuit of the common interest.

(WJA VIII 93)

(20 July 1786)

Crimes are acts of tyranny of one or more on another or more. A murderer, a thief, a robber, a burglar, is a tyrant. Perjury, slander, are tyranny too, when they hurt anyone.

(WJA III 400)

(23 September 1787)

Laws alone, and those political institutions which are the guardians of them, and a sacred administration of justice, can preserve honor, virtue, and integrity in the minds of men.

(WJA VIII 455)

(22 November 1800)
Presidential speech to both houses of Congress.

It is in every point of view of such primary importance to carry the laws into prompt and faithful execution, and to render that part of the administration of justice which the Constitution and laws devolve on the federal courts, as convenient to the people as may consist with their present circumstances, that I cannot omit once more to recommend to your serious consideration the judiciary system of the United States. No subject is more interesting than this to the public happiness, and to none can those improvements which may have been suggested by experience, be more beneficially applied.

(WJA IX 144)

(6 August 1812)

Integrity and skill at the bar, are better supporters of independence than any fortune, talents, or eloquence elsewhere. A man of genius, talents, eloquence, integrity, and judgment at the bar, is the most independent man in society. Presidents, governors, senators, judges, have not so much honest liberty; but it ought always to be regulated by prudence, and never abused.

(WJA X 21–22)

(5 June 1813)

In former parts of my life I have known somewhat of the thing called a *bar*—a significant word, and an important thing.

By all that I can remember of the history of England, the British Constitution has been preserved by *the bar*. In all civil contests and political struggles, the lawyers have been divided; some have advocated the prerogatives of the crown, and some the rights of the people. All, or at least a majority, have united, at last, in restoring and improving the Constitution.

(WJA X 38)

(18 December 1816)

When courts of justice dare not speak in open air, nor see the daylight, where is life, liberty, or property?

(WJA X 234)

13

EDUCATION

(15 March 1756)
Written during his short stint as a grammar school teacher.

I had rather sit in school and consider which of my pupils will
turn out in his future life a hero, and which a rake, which a
philosopher, and which a parasite, than change breasts with
[rakes and fools], though possessed of twenty laced waistcoats
and a thousand pounds a year.

(WJA II 10)

(1761)

No man will be an adept in grammar or rhetoric, or poetry, or
music, or architecture, without laboring through a vast deal of
nonsense and impertinence; in short, nonsense seems an unalienable property of human affairs; and it is as idle to expect that any
author should write well upon any subject, without intermin-
gling some proportion of it, as it is to expect that a rapid torrent
should descend from the mountains without washing some dirt
and earth along with it.

(WJA II 115)

(1761)

No man, either king or subject, clergyman or layman, has any
right to dictate to me the person I shall choose for my legislator
and ruler. I must judge for myself. But how can I judge, how can

212

any man judge, unless his mind has been opened and enlarged by reading?

(WJA II 131)

(August 1765)

Be it remembered . . . that liberty must at all hazards be supported. We have a right to it, derived from our Maker. But if we had not, our fathers have earned and bought it for us, at the expense of their ease, their estates, their pleasure, and their blood. And liberty cannot be preserved without a general knowledge among the people, who have a right, from the frame of their nature, to knowledge, as their great Creator, who does nothing in vain, has given them understandings, and a desire to know; but besides this, they have a right, an indisputable, unalienable, indefeasible, divine right to that most dreaded and envied kind of knowledge, I mean, of the characters and conduct of their rulers.

(WJA III 456)

(August 1765)

Let us tenderly and kindly cherish, therefore, the means of knowledge. Let us dare to read, think, speak, and write. Let every order and degree among the people rouse their attention and animate their resolution. Let them all become attentive to the grounds and principles of government, ecclesiastical and civil. Let us study the law of nature; search into the spirit of the British constitution; read the histories of ancient ages; contemplate the great examples of Greece and Rome; set before us the conduct of our own British ancestors, who have defended for us the inherent rights of mankind against foreign and domestic tyrants and usurpers, against arbitrary kings and cruel priests, in short, against the gates of earth and hell.

(WJA III 462)

(August 1765)

The preservation of the means of knowledge among the lowest ranks, is of more importance to the public than all the property of all the rich men in the country. It is even of more consequence to the rich themselves, and to their posterity. The only question is, whether it is a public emolument; and if it is, the rich ought undoubtedly to contribute, in the same proportion as to all other public burdens,—that is, in proportion to their wealth, which is secured by public expenses.

(WJA III 457)

(22 July 1771)

I would not ... conclude peremptorily against sending sons or daughters to dancing, or fencing, or music, but had much rather they should be ignorant of them all than fond of any of them.

(WJA II 289)

(1 July 1774)

I sometimes think I must come to this: to be the foreman upon my own farm and the schoolmaster to my own children.

(FL 7)

(29 October 1775)

Human nature, with all its infirmities and deprivation, is still capable of great things. It is capable of attaining to degrees of wisdom and of goodness which, we have reason to believe, appear respectable in the estimation of superior intelligences. Education makes a greater difference between man and man, than nature has made between man and brute. The virtues and powers to which men may be trained, by early education and constant discipline, are truly sublime and astonishing.

(FL 119)

(January 1776)

Laws for the liberal education of youth, especially of the lower class of people, are so extremely wise and useful, that, to a humane and generous mind, no expense for this purpose would be thought extravagant.

(WJA IV 199)

(25 August 1776)

Knowledge is among the most essential foundations of liberty.

(WJA IX 434)

(2 June 1778)

The foundations of national morality must be laid in private families. In vain are schools, academies, and universities, instituted, if loose principles and licentious habits are impressed upon children in their earliest years. The mothers are the earliest and most important instructors of youth. The vices and examples of the parents cannot be concealed from the children.

(WJA III 172)

(October 1779)
From the Massachusetts constitution, which Adams wrote between his diplomatic missions to Europe.

Wisdom and knowledge, as well as virtue, diffused generally among the body of the people, being necessary for the preservation of their rights and liberties, and as these depend on spreading the opportunities and advantages of education in the various parts of the country, and among the different orders of the people, it shall be the duty of legislators and magistrates, in all future periods of this commonwealth, to cherish the interests of literature and sciences, and all seminaries of them; especially the university at Cambridge [Harvard], public schools and grammar schools in the towns; to encourage private societies and public institutions, rewards and immunities for the promotion of agriculture, arts, sciences, commerce, trades, manufactures, and a natural history of the country; to countenance and inculcate the principles of humanity and general benevolence, public and private charity, industry and frugality, honesty and punctuality in their dealings, sincerity, good humor, and all social affections and generous sentiments among the people.

(WJA IV 259)

(1780)

The science of government it is my duty to study, more than all the other sciences; the arts of legislation and administration and negotiation ought to take place of, indeed to exclude, in a manner all other arts. I must study mathematics and philosophy. My sons ought to study mathematics, philosophy, geography, natural history and naval architecture, navigation, commerce, and agriculture, in order to give their children a right to study painting, poetry, music, architecture, statuary, tapestry, and porcelain.

(FL 381)

(23 September 1780)

You must know I have undertaken to prophecy that English will be the most respectable language in the world, and the most universally read and spoken, in the next century, if not before the close of this. American population will in the next age produce a greater number of persons who will speak English than any other language, and these persons will have more general acquaintance and conversation with all other nations than any other people, which will naturally introduce their language everywhere, as the general medium of correspondence and conversation among the learned of all nations, and among all travelers and strangers, as Latin was in the last century, and French has been in this. Let us, then, encourage and advise everybody to study English.

(WJA IX 509–10)

(10 September 1785)

The social science will never be much improved, until the people unanimously know and consider themselves as the fountain of power, and until they shall know how to manage it wisely and honestly. Reformation must begin with the body of the people, which can be done only, to effect, in their educations. The whole people must take upon themselves the education of the whole people, and must be willing to bear the expenses of it. There should not be a district of one mile square, without a school in it, not founded by a charitable individual, but maintained at the expense of the people themselves. They must be taught to reverence themselves, instead of adoring their servants, their generals, admirals, bishops, and statesmen. . . . Instead of adoring a Washington, mankind should applaud the nation which educated him.

(WJA IX 540)

(1790–91)

The terror of punishment, by forcing attention, may compel a child to perform a task, but can never infuse that ardor for study, which alone can arrive at great attainments.

(WJA VI 246)

(1790–91)

Leisure for study must ever be a portion of a few.

(WJA VI 280)

(17 May 1798)
To the Young Men of Philadelphia.

Without wishing to damp the ardor of curiosity, or influence the freedom of inquiry, I will hazard a prediction, that, after the most industrious and impartial researches, the longest liver of you all will find no principles, institutions, or systems of education more fit, in general, to be transmitted to your posterity, than those you have received from your ancestors.

(WJA IX 188)

(11 March 1809)

At college, next to the ordinary routine of classical studies, mathematics and natural philosophy were my favorite pursuits. When I began to study law, I found ethics, the law of nations, the civil law, the common law, a field too vast to admit of many other inquiries. Classics, history, and philosophy have, however, never been wholly neglected to this day.

(WJA IX 613)

(28 August 1811)

Free schools, and all schools, colleges, academies and seminaries
of learning, I can recommend from my heart; but I dare not say
that a suffrage should never be permitted to a man who cannot
read and write.

(WJA IX 639)

(28 August 1811)

Borrowed eloquence, if it contains as good stuff, is as good as
own eloquence.

(WJA IX 639)

(31 August 1813)

Can you account for the apathy, the antipathy of this nation to
their own history? Is there not a repugnance to the thought of
looking back? While thousands of frivolous novels are read with
eagerness and got by heart, the history of our own native country
is not only neglected, but despised and abhorred.

(WJA X 62)

(1814)

My humble opinion is, that knowledge, upon the whole, pro-
motes virtue and happiness. I therefore hope that . . . gentlemen
of property, education, and reputation will exert [their] utmost influence in establishing schools, colleges, academies, and universities, and employ every means and opportunity to spread
information, even to the lowest dregs of the people.

(WJA VI 519)

(16 July 1814)
Adams and Thomas Jefferson frequently discussed the education of youth.

Education! O education! the greatest grief of my heart, and the
greatest affliction of my life! To my mortification I must confess

that I have never closely thought or deliberately reflected upon the subject, which never occurs to me now without producing a deep sigh, a heavy groan, and sometimes tears. My cruel destiny separated me from my children almost continually from their birth to their manhood. I was compelled to leave them to the ordinary routine of reading, writing, and Latin school, academy, and college. John [Quincy Adams] was much with me, and he, but occasionally.

(JA 19 104)

(16 July 1814)
Thoughts on structuring academic courses at Jefferson's planned University of Virginia.

Grammar, rhetoric, logic, ethics, mathematics, cannot be neglected. Classics . . . I must think indispensable. Natural history, mechanics, and experimental philosophy, chemistry, etc., at least their rudiments, cannot be forgotten. Geography, astronomy, and even history and chronology. . . . Theology I would leave to Ray, Durham, Nieuwentyt, and Paley, rather than to Luther, Zinzendorf, Swedenborg, Wesley, or Whitefield, or Thomas Aquinas, or Wollebius. Metaphysics I would leave in the clouds with the materialists and spiritualists, with Leibnitz, Berkeley, Priestley, and Edwards, and, I might add, Hume and Reed. Or, if permitted to be read, it should be with romances and novels. What shall I say of music, drawing, fencing, dancing, and gymnastic exercises? What of languages, oriental or occidental? Of French, Italian, German, or Russian, Sanskrit, or Chinese? The task you have prescribed to me of grouping these sciences or arts, under professors, within the views of an enlightened economy, is far beyond my forces.

(WJA X 105)

(4 March 1815)

I have little faith in history. I read it as I do romance, believing what is probable and rejecting what I must. Thucydides, Tacitus, Livy, Hume, Robertson, Gibbon, Raynal, and Voltaire, are all alike. Our American history for the last fifty years is already as much corrupted as any half century of ecclesiastical history, from the Council of Nice to the restoration of the Inquisition in 1814.

(WJA X 133)

(2 March 1816)
To Thomas Jefferson on a curriculum for his University of Virginia.

When you asked my opinion of a university, it would have been easy to advise mathematics, experimental philosophy, natural history, chemistry, and astronomy, geography, and the fine arts, to the exclusion of ontology, metaphysics, and theology. But knowing the eager impatience of the human mind to search into eternity and infinity, the first cause and last end of all things, as I have been these fifty years, that there is but one being of the universe who comprehends it, and our last resource is resignation.

(WJA 213)

(23 January 1818)

Oratory . . . as it consists in expressions of the countenance, graces of attitude and motion, and intonation of voice, although it is altogether superficial and ornamental, will always command admiration; yet it deserves little veneration. Flashes of wit, coruscations of imagination, and gay pictures, what are they? Strict truth, rapid reason, and pure integrity are the only essential ingredients in sound oratory.

(WJA X 279)

(29 May 1818)
To Thomas Jefferson on his love of reading.

I congratulate you upon your "canine appetite" for reading. I have been equally voracious for several years, and it has kept me alive.

(WJA X 313)

(1 June 1818)

Young men should be taught to honor merit, but not to adore it.

(WJA X 317)

(7 March 1819)

"Proper words in proper places." ... Hume, Robertson, and Gibbon, owed more their fame to this than to their accuracy or impartiality; woe to the writer in this age of the world, who is rash enough to despise or neglect it!

(WJA X 375)

(22 January 1825)
To Thomas Jefferson, whose University of Virginia would open in March.

Your university is a noble employment in your old age, and your ardor for its success does you honor; but I do not approve of your sending to Europe for tutors and professors. I do believe there are sufficient scholars in America, to fill your professorships and tutorships with more active ingenuity and independent minds than you can bring from Europe. The Europeans are deeply tainted with prejudices, both ecclesiastical and temporal, which they can never be rid of. They are all infected with Episcopal and Presbyterian creeds, and confessions of faith. They all believe that great Principle which has produced this boundless universe, Newton's universe and Herschell's universe, came down to this little a ball, to be spit upon by Jews. And until this awful blasphemy is got rid of, there never will be any liberal science in the world.

(WJA X 415)

Part IV

PEOPLE AND PLACES

14

Character Sketches

(14 June 1776)
To Samuel Chase, Maryland delegate to Congress and fellow signer of the Declaration of Independence.

I have no objection to writing you facts, but I would not meddle with characters for the world. A burnt child dreads the fire. I have smarted too severely for a few crude expressions written in a pet to a bosom friend, to venture on such boldnesses again. Besides, if I were to tell you all that I think of all characters, I should appear so ill natured and censorious that I should detest myself. By my soul, I think very heinously, I cannot think of a better word, of some people. They think as badly of me, I suppose; and neither of us care a farthing for that. So the account is balanced, and perhaps, after all, both sides may be deceived, both may be very honest men.

(WJA IX 396)

Abigail Adams (1744–1818)

Daughter of Rev. William Smith and Elizabeth Quincy, who married John Adams in 1764. She had four children: John Quincy, Thomas, Charles, and Abigail. Although she did not benefit from a formal education, she was very well read and frequently quoted long passages of poetry from memory in her correspondence. Her letters to friends and family are still highly regarded today for their vivid imagery and descriptive qualities. She died of typhoid fever.

(15 December 1809)
To F. A. Vanderkemp.

It is little remarkable that you never heard the literary character of
my consort. There have been few ladies in the world of a more
correct or elegant taste. A collection of her letters, for the forty-
five years that we have been married, would be worth ten times
more than Madame de Sévigné's, though not so perfectly mea-
sured in syllables and letters, and would, or at least ought to put
to the blush Lady Mary Wortley Montagu and all her admirers. So
much you will say, for conjugal complaisance. So much, I say, for
simple justice to her merit.

(WJA IX 625)

Samuel Adams (1722–1803)

*Revolutionary statesman and one of the foremost agitators for American in-
dependence. Adams became a member of the Massachusetts House of
Representatives in 1765, where he quickly distinguished himself, becoming
its leader in the years leading up to the Revolution. He became the Governor
of Massachusetts in 1793. John and Samuel Adams were second cousins,
and the two men corresponded until Samuel's death.*

(1768)

Adams, I believe, has the most thorough understanding of liberty
and her resources in the temper and character of the people,
though not in the law and constitution; as well as the most habitual, radical love of it, of any of them, as well as the most correct,
genteel, and artful pen. He is a man of refined policy, steadfast integrity, exquisite humanity, genteel erudition, obliging, engaging
manners, real as well as professed piety, and a universal good
character, unless it should be admitted that he is too attentive to
the public, and not enough so to himself and his family.

(WJA II 163–64)

(21 August 1811)

The talents and virtues of that great man were of the most exalted, though not of the most showy kind. His love of his country,

his exertions in her service through a long course of years, through the administrations of the Governors Shirley, Pownall, Bernard, Hutchinson, and Gage, under the royal government, and through the whole of the subsequent Revolution, and always in support of the same principles, his inflexible integrity, his disinterestedness, his invariable resolution, his sagacity, his patience, perseverance, and pure public virtue were never exceeded by any man in America.

(WJA I 673)

(15 April 1817)

In his common appearance he was a plain, simple, decent citizen, of middling stature, dress, and manners. He had an exquisite ear for music, and a charming voice, when he pleased to exert it. Yet his ordinary speeches in town meetings, in the House of Representatives, and in Congress exhibited nothing extraordinary; but, upon great occasions, when his deeper feelings were excited, he erected himself, or rather nature seemed to erect him, without the smallest symptom of affectation, into an upright dignity of figure and gesture, and gave a harmony to his voice which made a strong impression of spectators and auditors,—the more lasting for the purity, correctness, and nervous elegance of his style.

(WJA X 251)

(5 June 1817)

A man in his situation and circumstances must possess a large fund of sternness of stuff, or he will soon be annihilated. His piety ought not to be objected to him, or any other man. His bigotry, if he had any, was a fault; but he certainly had not more than Governor Hutchinson and Secretary Oliver, who, I know from personal conversation, were as staunch Trinitarians and Arminians with more contempt and scorn than he ever did. Mr. Adams lived and conversed freely with all sectarians, in philosophy and divinity. He never imposed his creed on anyone, or endeavored to make proselytes to his religious opinions. . . . Mr. Adams was an original—*sui generis, sui juris* [unique and independent].

(WJA X 262–63)

Marie Antoinette (1755–93)

Queen of France through her marriage to Louis XVI, she was beheaded during the French Revolution.

(7 June 1778)

She was an object too sublime and beautiful for my dull pen to describe. . . . Her dress was everything that art and wealth could make it. One of the maids of honor told me she had diamonds upon her person to the value of eighteen millions of livres; and I always thought her majesty much beholden to her dress. . . . She had a nice complexion, indicating perfect health, and was a handsome woman in her face and figure. But I have seen beauties much superior, both in countenance and form, in France, England, and America.

(WJA III 172–73)

Robert Auchmuty (d. 1788)

Loyalist and Judge of the Vice-Admiralty in Massachusetts and New Hampshire. He was cocounsel with John Adams during his defense of the British soldiers charged in the Boston Massacre. Auchmuty was forced to leave Boston in 1776 and settled in London.

(29 July 1766)

Auchmuty is employed in Sessions and everywhere; the same heavy, dull, insipid way of arguing everywhere; as many repetitions as a Presbyterian parson in his prayer. Volubility, voluble repetition and repeated volubility; fluent reiterations and reiterating fluency. Such nauseous eloquence always puts my patience to the torture. In what is this man conspicuous? In reasoning, in imagination, in painting, in the pathetic, or what? In confidence, in dogmatism, etc. His wit is flat, his humor is affected and dull. To have this man represented as the first at the bar, is a libel upon it, a reproach and disgrace to it.

(WJA II 198)

Edward Bancroft (1744–1821)

Writer and inventor who served as a minister to France with John Adams. Unbeknownst to the American negotiators, Bancroft was a spy for the British government.

(21 April 1778)

Bancroft was a meddler in the stocks as well as reviews, and frequently went into the alley, and into the deepest and darkest retirements and recesses of the brokers and jobbers, Jews as well as Christians, and found amusement as well, perhaps, as profit, by listening to all the news and anecdotes, true or false, that were there whispered or more boldly pronounced. This information I had from his own mouth. When Mr. Deane arrived in France, whether he wrote to Bancroft, or Bancroft to him, I know not, but they somehow or other sympathized with each other so well, that Bancroft went over to Paris, and became a confidential associate with his old friends, Franklin and Deane. Bancroft had a clear head and a good pen.

(WJA III 141–42)

Aaron Burr (1756–1836)

Revolutionary War colonel and vice president under Thomas Jefferson. In 1804, he challenged Alexander Hamilton and killed him in a duel, thereby destroying his own political career. He was later charged with treason for plotting to conquer part of Mexico for himself, but was acquitted.

(17 February 1815)

I have never known, in any country, the prejudice in favor of birth, parentage, and descent more conspicuous than in the instance of Colonel Burr. That gentleman was connected by blood with many respectable families in New England. He was the son of one president and the grandson of another president of Nassau Hall, or Princeton University; the idol of all the Presbyterians in New York, New England, New Jersey, Pennsylvania, Maryland, Virginia, and elsewhere. He had served in the army, and came out of it with the character of a knight without fear and an able officer. He had afterwards studied and practiced law with application and success. . . . I proposed to General Washington, in a conference between him and me . . . to nominate him for a brigadier general. Washington's answer to me was, "By all that I have known and heard, Colonel Burr is a brave and able officer; but the question is, whether he has not equal talents at intrigue". . . . I was not permitted to nominate Burr. If I had been, what would have been the consequence? Shall I say, that Hamilton would have been now alive, and Hamilton and Burr now at the head of our affairs? What then?

(WJA X 123)

John Dickinson (1732–1808)

Revolutionary publicist who gained widespread fame for his Letters from a Farmer, *which denounced British policies toward the American colonies.*

(31 August 1774)

He is a shadow; tall, but slender as a reed; pale as ashes; one would think at first sight that he could not live a month; yet, upon a more attentive inspection, he looks as if the springs of life were strong enough to last many years.

(WJA II 360)

(20 June 1779)
In conversation with Chevalier de la Luzerne, the French foreign minister.

He inquired after Mr. Dickinson, and the reason why he disappeared. I explained, as well as I could in French, the inconsistency of the Farmer's Letters, and his perseverance in that inconsistency in Congress, Mr. Dickinson's opposition to the Declaration of Independency. I ventured, as modestly as I could, to let him know that I had the honor to be the principal disputant in Congress against Mr. Dickinson upon that great question; that Mr. Dickinson had the eloquence, the learning, and the ingenuity, on his side of the question; but that I had the hearts of the Americans on mine; and, therefore, my side of the question prevailed. That Mr. Dickinson had a good heart, and an amiable character; but that his opposition to independency had lost him the confidence of the people, who suspected him of timidity and avarice, and that his opposition sprung from those passions; but that he had since turned out with the militia against the British troops, and, I doubted not, might in time regain the confidence of the people.

(WJA III 214–15)

Benjamin Franklin (1706–90)

American publisher, philosopher, diplomat, scientist, and inventor. Though Adams initially viewed Franklin in a favorable light, he later chafed at the heroic reputation Franklin achieved at home and abroad. Their relationship strained to the breaking point while they served as joint commissioners in Paris. Franklin was, in his opinion, too close to the French court, a pawn of the French foreign minister de Vergennes, and did not have an adequate grasp of American policy.

(23 July 1775)
During the Second Continental Congress in Philadelphia.

His conduct has been composed and grave, and, in the opinion of many gentlemen, very reserved. He has not assumed anything, nor affected to take the lead; but has seemed to choose that the Congress should pursue their own principles and sentiments, and adopt their own plans. Yet he has not been backward; has been very useful on many occasions, and discovered a disposition entirely American. He does not hesitate at our boldest measures, but rather seems to think us too irresolute and backward. He thinks us at present in an odd state, neither in peace nor war, neither dependent nor independent; but he thinks that we shall soon assume a character more decisive. He thinks that we have the power of preserving ourselves; and that even if we should be driven to the disagreeable necessity of assuming a total independency, and set up a separate state, we can maintain it. The people of England have thought that the opposition in America was wholly owing to Dr. Franklin; and I suppose their scribblers will attribute the temper and proceedings of Congress to him; but there cannot be a greater mistake. He has had but little share, further than to cooperate and to assist. He is, however, a great and good man.

(FL 83–84)

(16 April 1778)
While Adams and Franklin were serving as joint commissioners to the French court.

Doctor Franklin is reported to speak French very well, but I find, upon attending to him, that he does not speak it grammatically, and, indeed, upon inquiring, he confesses that he is wholly inattentive to the grammar. His pronunciation, too, upon which the French gentlemen and ladies compliment him, and which he seems to think is pretty well, I am sure is very far from being exact.

(WJA III 132)

(25 April 1778)
While living with Franklin at Passy, near Paris.

My venerable colleague enjoys a privilege here that is much to be envied. Being seventy years of age, the ladies not only allow him to embrace them as often as he pleases, but they are perpetually embracing him. I told him yesterday I would write this to America.

(FL 330)

(20 September 1779)
In early 1779, Adams learned that Congress had made Franklin the sole diplomatic representative to the French court. This was the result of a concerted effort by Franklin and Vergennes to have Adams removed.

Franklin is a wit and a humorist, I know. He may be a philosopher, for what I know. But he is not a sufficient statesman for all the business he is in. He knows too little of American affairs, of the politics of Europe, and takes too little pains to inform himself of either, to be sufficient for all these things, to be ambassador, secretary, admiral, consular agent, etc. Yet such is his name, on both sides the water, that it is best, perhaps, that he should be left there; but a secretary and consuls should be appointed to do the business, or it will not be done; or, if done, it will be by people who insinuate themselves into his confidence, without either such heads or hearts as Congress should trust. He is too old, too infirm, too indolent and dissipated, to be sufficient for the discharge of all the important duties of ambassador, board of war, board of treasury, commissary of prisoners, etc., etc., etc., as he is at present, in that department, besides an immense correspondence and acquaintance, each of which would be enough for the whole time of the most active man in the vigor of youth.

(WJA IX 485–86)

(17 November 1782)
In November, Adams returned to Paris from the Netherlands to assist with peace negotiations between the United States and Great Britain.

I must go further, and say that the least appearance of an independent spirit in any American minister has been uniformly cause enough to have his character attacked. Luckily, Mr. Deane out of the question, every American minister in Europe, except Dr. Franklin, has discovered a judgment, a conscience, and a resolution of his own, and, of consequence, every minister that has ever come, has been frowned upon. On the contrary, Dr. Franklin, who has been pliant and submissive in everything, has been constantly cried up to the stars, without doing anything to deserve it.

(WJA IX 516)

(15 May 1811)
Relating an infamous description of Adams that Franklin wrote to Robert Livingston in 1783.

One other letter I know he wrote, for I have seen it, more severe than this; and I regret that I have not a copy of it to send you. One sentence only I remember, and that may serve to designate it. . . . The sentence I mean is this: "Mr. Adams is always an honest man, and often a wise one, but he is sometimes completely out of his senses."

(WJA I 649)

(15 May 1811)

I must acknowledge, after all, that nothing in life has mortified or grieved me more than the necessity which compelled me to oppose him so often as I have. He was a man with whom I always wished to live in friendship, and for that purpose omitted no demonstration of respect, esteem, and veneration in my power, until I had unequivocal proofs of his hatred, for no other reason under the sun, but because I gave my judgment in opposition to his, in many points which materially affected the interests of our country, and in many more which essentially concerned our happiness, safety, and well-being.

(WJA I 664)

George III (1738–1820)

King of Great Britain during the American Revolution. See the account of their first meeting in the Appendix.

(3 December 1785)

The King, I really think, is the most accomplished courtier in his dominions. With all the affability of Charles II, he has all the domestic virtues and regularity of conduct of Charles I. He is the greatest talker in the world, and has a tenacious memory, stored with resources of small talk concerning all the little things of life, which are inexhaustible. But so much of his time is, and has been consumed in this, that he is, in all the great affairs of society and government, as weak, as far as I can judge, as we ever understood him to be in America. He is also as obstinate. The unbounded popularity, acquired by his temperance and facetiousness, added to the splendor of his dignity, gives him such a continual feast of flattery, that he thinks all he does is right; and he pursues his own ideas with a firmness which would become the best system of action. He has a pleasure in his own will and way, without which he would be miserable, which seems to be the true principle upon which he has always chosen and rejected ministers. He has a habitual contempt of patriots and patriotism, at least for what are called in this country by those names, and takes a delight in mortifying all who have any reputation for such qualities, and in supporting those who have a contrary character.

(WJA VIII 350–51)

Alexander Hamilton (1755–1804)

Member of the Continental Congress, captain in the American Revolution, secretary of the treasury under Washington, and one of the authors of The Federalist. *Though they were both Federalists, Hamilton did not agree with President Adams's policies, and schemed with members of Adams's cabinet to undermine his authority. In October 1800, Hamilton published "A Letter from Alexander Hamilton, Concerning the Public Conduct and Character of John Adams, Esq., President of the United States," a highly personal attack that contributed to Adams's defeat for a second term. Hamilton was killed in a duel with Aaron Burr.*

(3 December 1800)

I am not his enemy, and never was. I have not adored him, like his idolaters, and have had great cause to disapprove of some of his politics. He has talents, if he would correct himself, which might be useful. There is more burnish, however, on the outside, than sterling silver in the substance. He threatened his master, Washington, sometimes with pamphlets upon his character and conduct, and Washington, who had more regard to his reputation than I have, I say it with humility and mortification, might be restrained by his threats, but I dread neither his menaces of pamphlets nor the execution of them.

(WJA IX 576)

(1801)

Mr. Hamilton's erroneous conceptions of the public opinion may be excused by the considerations that he was not a native of the United States; that he was born and bred in the West Indies till he went to Scotland for education, where he spent his time in a seminary of learning till seventeen years of age, after which no man ever perfectly acquired a national character; then entered a college at New York, from whence he issued into the army as an aide-de-camp. In these situations he could scarcely acquire the opinions, feelings, or principles of the American people. His error may be excused by the further consideration, that his time was chiefly spent in his pleasures, in his electioneering visits, conferences, and correspondences, in propagating prejudices against every man whom he thought his superior in the public estimation, and in composing ambitious reports upon finance, while the real business of the treasury was done by Duer, by Wolcott, and even, for some time and in part, by Tench Coxe.

(WJA IX 277)

(11 February 1815)

One thing I know, that Cicero was not sacrificed to the vengeance of Antony by the unfeeling selfishness of the latter triumvirate more egregiously than John Adams was to the unbridled and unbounded ambition of Alexander Hamilton in the American triumvirate.

(WJA X 119)

John Hancock (1737–93)

Massachusetts statesman, signer of the Declaration of Independence, and governor of Massachusetts from 1787 to 1793. In one of the seminal events that led to the American Revolution, one of Hancock's merchant ships, Liberty, was seized by Boston customs officials in 1768. A large naval force and two regiments of troops were sent to Boston to suppress rioting, setting into motion the chain of events that culminated in the Boston Massacre.

(1 June 1817)

I can say, with truth, that I profoundly admired him, and more profoundly loved him. If he had vanity and caprice, so had I. And if his vanity and caprice made me sometimes sputter, as you know they often did, mine, I well know, had often a similar effect upon him. But these little flickerings of little passions determine nothing concerning essential characters. I knew Mr. Hancock from his cradle to his grave. He was radically generous and benevolent. . . . Mr. Hancock had a delicate constitution. He was very infirm; a great part of his life was passed in acute pain. He inherited from his father, though one of the most amiable and beloved of men, a certain sensibility, a keenness of feeling, or, in more familiar language, a peevishness of temper, that sometimes disgusted and afflicted his friends. Yet it was astonishing with what patience, perseverance, and punctuality he attended to business to the last. Nor were his talents or attainments inconsiderable. They were far more superior to many who have been much more celebrated. He had a great deal of political sagacity and penetration into men. He was by no means a contemptible scholar or orator. Compared with Washington, Lincoln, or Knox, he was learned.

(WJA X 259–61)

Stephen Hopkins (1707–85)

Rhode Island statesman, member of the Continental Congress, and signer of the Declaration of Independence.

(8 March 1805)

Mr. Lee, Mr. Gadsden, were sensible men, and very cheerful, but Governor Hopkins of Rhode Island, above seventy years of age, kept us all alive. Upon business, his experience and judgment were very useful. But when the business of the evening was over, he kept us in conversation till eleven, and sometimes twelve o'clock. His custom was to drink nothing all day, nor till eight o'clock in the evening, and then his beverage was Jamaica spirit and water. It gave him wit, humor, anecdotes, science, and learning. He had read Greek, Roman, and British history, and was familiar with English poetry, particularly Pope, Thomson, and Milton, and the flow of his soul made all his reading our own, and seemed to bring to recollection in all of us, all we had ever read. I could neither eat nor drink in these days. The other gentlemen were very temperate. Hopkins never drank to excess, but all he drank was immediately not only converted into wit, sense, knowledge, and good humor, but inspired us with similar qualities.

(WJA III 12)

Ralph Izard (1742–1804)

South Carolina delegate to the Continental Congress and U.S. senator from 1789 to 1795.

(21 April 1778)

Mr. Ralph Izard was a native of South Carolina. . . . When he came to the possession of his fortune, he married Miss De Lancey, a daughter of Chief Justice De Lancey, who was so long at the head of the party in New York, in opposition to the Livingstons, a lady of great beauty and fine accomplishments, as well as perfect purity of conduct and character through life. This accomplished pair had a curiosity to travel. They went to Europe, and passed through Italy, Germany, Holland, and I know not how many other countries. When the American war commenced, they were in England, and Mr. Izard, embracing the cause of his country with all the warmth of his character, passed with his family over to France, on his way to America. . . . Mr. Izard was nominated by Mr. Arthur Middleton, in the name of South Carolina, and highly recommended for his integrity, good sense, and information. . . . With a high sense of honor and great benevolence of heart as well as integrity of principle, Mr. Izard had a warmth of temper and sometimes a violence of passions, that were very inconvenient to him and his friends, and not a little dangerous to his enemies.

(WJA III 141)

Thomas Jefferson (1743–1826)

Virginia statesman, member of the Continental Congress, author of the Virginia Resolves and the Declaration of Independence, and founder of the University of Virginia. Jefferson became the third president of the United States by narrowly defeating John Adams in the election of 1800. Adams and his wife, Abigail, formed a very close friendship with Jefferson during the Second Continental Congress, but Jefferson's positive opinions of the French Revolution and his underhanded attempts to discredit Adams's reputation strained their relationship to the breaking point. During the time that Jefferson served as vice president, Adams rarely consulted with him. After Jefferson's presidential inauguration, the two men did not communi-

cate with each other for over eleven years. They resumed their relationship in 1812, exchanging a body of correspondence that is unmatched in American letters. Adams and Jefferson died within hours of each other, on July 4, 1826, the fiftieth anniversary of the signing of the Declaration of Independence.

(13 April 1785)
During the time that they were in France to make treaties, the slow pace of progress was not to Adams's liking.

I am very happy in my friend Mr. Jefferson, and have nothing but my inutility to disgust me with a residence here.

(WJA VIII 236)

(29 July 1791)
In 1791, Jefferson wrote negative remarks about Adams that appeared in the introduction to a new work by Thomas Paine.

The friendship that has subsisted for fifteen years without the smallest interruption, and, until this occasion without the slightest suspicion, ever has been and still is very dear to my heart.

(WJA VIII 508–9)

(1801)

With this gentleman I had lived on terms of intimate friendship for five-and-twenty years, had acted with him in dangerous times and arduous conflicts, and always found him assiduous, laborious, and as far as I could judge, upright and faithful. Though by this time I differed from him in opinion by the whole horizon concerning the practicability and success of the French revolution, and some other points, I had no reason to think that he differed materially from me with regard to our national Constitution. . . . I will not take leave of Mr. Jefferson in this place, without declaring my opinion that the accusations against him of blind devotion to France, of hostility to England, of hatred to commerce, of partiality and duplicity in his late negotiations with the belligerent powers, are without foundation.

(WJA IX 284–5)

(25 December, 1811)
To Benjamin Rush, who was trying to reconcile Adams and Jefferson after a ten-year silence.

You gravely advise me "to receive the olive branch," as if there had been war; but there has never been any hostility on my part, nor that I know, on his. When there has been no war, there can be no room for negotiations of peace.

(WJA X 10)

(25 December 1811)
Adams's analysis of the difference between his and Jefferson's presidential styles.

In point of republicanism, all the difference I ever knew or could discover between . . . Jefferson and me, consisted,

1. In the difference between speeches and messages. I was a monarchist because I thought a speech more manly, more respectful to Congress and the nation. Jefferson and Rush preferred messages.
2. I held levees once a week, that all my time might not be wasted by idle visits. Jefferson's whole eight years was a levee.
3. I dined a large company once or twice a week. Jefferson dined a dozen every day.
4. Jefferson and Rush were for liberty and straight hair. I thought curled hair was as republican as straight.

In these, and a few other points of equal importance, all miserable frivolities, that Jefferson and Rush ought to blush that they ever laid any stress upon them, I might differ; but I never knew any points of more consequence, on which there was any variation between us.

(WJA X 11)

(6 August 1822)
Adams's explanation of why Jefferson was picked to write the draft of the Declaration of Independence.

Mr. Jefferson came into Congress, in June, 1775, and brought with him a reputation for literature, science, and a happy talent of composition. Writings of his were handed about, remarkable for the peculiar felicity of expression. Though a silent member in Congress, he was so prompt, frank, explicit, and decisive upon committees and in conversation, not even Samuel Adams was more so, that he soon seized upon my heart; and upon this occasion I gave him my vote, and did all in my power to procure the votes of others. I think he had one more vote than any other, and that placed him at the head of the committee. I had the next highest number, and that placed me the second. The committee met, discussed the subject, and then appointed Mr. Jefferson and me to make the draught, I suppose because we were the two first on the list.

(WJA II 513–14)

John Paul Jones (1747–92)

Naval hero of the American Revolution.

(3 May 1779)

This is the most ambitious and intriguing officer in the American navy. Jones has art and secrecy, and aspires very high. You see the character of the man in his uniform, and that of his officers and marines, variant from the uniforms established by Congress,— golden button-holes for himself, two epaulettes,—marines in red and white, instead of green. Eccentricities and irregularities are to be expected from him. They are in his character, they are visible in his eyes. His voice is soft and still and small; his eye has keenness and wildness and softness in it.

(WJA III 202)

Arthur Lee (1740–92)

Member of the Virginia State legislature and delegate to the Continental Congress. He was the brother of Richard Henry Lee and Francis Lightfoot Lee. Lee served with John Adams as a minister to the French court.

(21 April 1778)

Animated with great zeal in the cause of his native country, he took a decided part in her favor, and became a writer of some celebrity by his Junius Americanus and other publications. Becoming known in America as a zealous advocate of our cause, the two Houses of the Legislature of Massachusetts Bay appointed him provisionally their agent to the court of Great Britain, in case of the death, absence, or disability of Dr. Franklin, in which capacity he corresponded with some of the members of that assembly, particularly with Mr. Samuel Adams, and with the assembly itself, transmitting from time to time information of utility and importance. After a Congress was called in 1774–5 and 6, he continued to transmit to us some of the best and most authentic intelligence which we received from England. In 1776, when the election of ministers to the court of France was brought forward, and after I had declined the nomination, and Mr. Jefferson had refused the election and appointment sent him by Congress, Mr. Arthur Lee was elected in his place. He came immediately over to Paris, and joined his colleagues in commission. His manners were polite, his reading extensive, his attention to business was punctual, and his integrity without reproach.

(WJA III 140)

Richard Henry Lee (1732–94)

Virginia delegate to the Second Continental Congress, signer of the Declaration of Independence, and U.S. senator from Virginia from 1789 to 1792.

(24 February 1821)

He was a gentleman of fine talents, of amiable manners, and great worth. As a public speaker, he had a fluency as easy and graceful as it was melodious, which his classical education enabled him to decorate with frequent allusion to some of the finest passages of antiquity. With all his brothers he was always devoted to the cause of his country.

(WJA X 395–96)

Louis XVI (1754–93)

King of France, guillotined during the French Revolution.

(8 May 1778)

This monarch is in the twenty-fourth year of his age, having been born the 23d day of August, 1754. He has the appearances of a strong constitution, capable of enduring to a great age. His reign has already been distinguished by an event that will reflect a glory upon it in future ages, I mean the treaty with America. . . . The King and Queen must speak to everybody. This has made him the greatest talker in Christendom; but it is a slavery to which no human being should be subjected. It is but justice to say, that it was agreeable and instructive to hear him; for . . . his Majesty said as many things which deserved to be remembered, as any sage I ever heard.

(WJA III 155–56)

(2 June 1778)

This very monarch had in him the milk of human kindness, and, with all his open, undisguised vices, was very superstitious. Whenever he met the host, he would descend from his coach, and down upon his knees in the dust, or even in the mud, and compel all his courtiers to follow his example. Such are the inconsistencies in the human character!

(WJA III 171)

John Milton (1608–74)

English poet and author of Paradise Lost.

(30 April 1756)

That man's soul, it seems to me, was distended as wide as creation. His power over the human mind was absolute and unlimited. His genius was great beyond conception, and his learning without bounds. I can only gaze at him with astonishment, without comprehending the vast compass of his capacity.

(WJA II 14)

John Montague (1719–95)

Vice admiral in the British Royal Navy and commander-in-chief of the North America station from 1771 to 1774.

(29 December 1772)

A coachman, a jack-tar before the mast, would be ashamed, nay, a porter, a shoeblack, or chimney sweeper, would be ashamed of the coarse, low, vulgar dialect of this sea officer, though a rear admiral of the blue, and though a second son of a genteel if not a noble family in England. An American freeholder, living in a log house twenty feet square without a chimney in it, is a well-bred man, a polite accomplished person, a fine gentleman, in comparison of this beast of prey. This is not the language of prejudice, for I have none against him, but of truth. His brutal, hoggish manners are a disgrace to the royal navy and to the King's service.

(WJA II 306)

Montesquieu (1689–1775)

French political philosopher and writer whose theories contributed to the Constitution of the United States.

(22 April 1817)

I am not an implicit believer in the inspiration or infallibility of Montesquieu. On the contrary, it must be acknowledged, that some of these philosophers have detected many errors in his writings. But all their heads consolidated into one mighty head, would not equal the depth of his genius, or the extent of his views. Voltaire, alone, excels or equals him.

(WJA X 257)

Robert Morris (1734–1806)

Pennsylvania delegate to the Continental Congress, signer of the Declaration of Independence, and financier of the American Revolution.

(16 February 1809)

Robert Morris . . . was a frank, generous, and manly mortal. He rose from nothing but a naked boy, by his industry, ingenuity, and fidelity, to great business and credit as a merchant. At the beginning of our revolution, his commerce was stagnated, and as he had over-traded, he was much embarrassed. He took advantage of the times, united with the Whigs, came into Congress, and united his credit, supported by my loans in Holland, and resources of the United States. By this means he supported his credit for many years; but at last grew extravagant, as all conquerors and extraordinary characters do, and died as he had lived, as I believe, all his days, worth very little solid capital.

(WJA IX 609)

James Otis (1725–83)

Member of the Stamp Act Congress, leader of the Massachusetts committee of correspondence, and publicist. Adams believed that a speech by Otis against illegal ship searches by British officials in 1761 was one of the most influential causes of the American Revolution, and he always mentioned Otis as a central figure in the struggle for independence. In 1769, Otis began displaying symptoms of mental illness that eventually prevented him from participating in politics.

(1768)

Otis is fiery and feverous; his imagination flames, his passions blaze; he is liable to great inequalities of temper; sometimes in despondency, sometimes in a rage. The rashnesses and imprudencies into which his excess of zeal have formerly transported him, have made him enemies, whose malicious watch over him occasion more caution, and more cunning, and more inexplicable passages in his conduct than formerly; and, perhaps, views at the

chair or the board, or possibly more expanded views beyond the
Atlantic, may mingle now with his patriotism.

(WJA II 163)

(1770)
*After receiving a serious head injury during a fight with a customs official,
Otis started to display symptoms of mental illness.*

In one word, Otis will spoil the club. He talks so much, and takes
up so much of our time, and fills it with trash, obsceneness, profaneness, nonsense, and distraction, that we have none left for rational amusements or inquiries. . . . In short, I never saw such an
object of admiration, reverence, contempt, and compassion, all at
once, as this. I fear, I tremble, I mourn, for the man and for his
country; many others mourn over him, with tears in their eyes.

(WJA II 227)

(29 March 1817)

Mr. Otis's popularity was without bounds. In May, 1761, he was
elected into the House of Representatives by an almost unanimous vote. On the week of his election, I happened to be in
Worcester, attending the Court of Common Pleas, of which
Brigadier Ruggles was Chief Justice. . . . That election has shaken
two continents, and will shake all four. For ten years Mr. Otis, at
the head of his country's cause, conducted the town of Boston,
and the people of the province, with a prudence and fortitude, at
every sacrifice of personal interest, and amidst unceasing persecution, which would have done honor to the most virtuous patriot or martyr of antiquity.

(WJA X 248)

(25 February 1818)

I have been young, and now am old, and I solemnly say, I have
never known a man whose love of his country was more ardent or
sincere; never one, who suffered so much; never one, whose services for any ten years of his life were so important and essential
to the cause of his country, as those of Mr. Otis from 1760 to 1770.

(WJA X 291)

Thomas Paine (1737–1809)

Political and religious theorist and publicist. Paine wrote Common Sense, *which was the first widely publicized call for independence in America. Adams saw Paine's political theories as naïve, and grew to detest Paine after he published works that were considered atheistic and favorable to the French Revolution.*

(28 April 1776)

The writer of "Common Sense" and "The Forester" is the same person. His name is Paine, a gentleman about two years ago from England, a man who, General Lee says, has genius in his eyes.

(FL 167)

(21 January 1810)

His political writings, I am singular enough to believe, have done more harm than his irreligious ones. He understood neither government nor religion. From a malignant heart he wrote virulent declamations, which the enthusiastic fury of the times intimidated all men, even Mr. Burke, from answering as he ought. His deism, as it appears to me, has promoted rather than retarded the cause of revolution in America, and indeed in Europe. His billingsgate, stolen from Blount's Oracles of Reason, from Bolingbroke, Voltaire, Bérenger, etc., will never discredit Christianity, which will hold its ground in some degree as long as human nature shall have anything moral or intellectual left in it.

(WJA IX 627)

(11 August 1800)

The German letter proposing to introduce into this country a company of schoolmasters, painters, poets, etc., all of them disciples of Mr. Thomas Paine, will require no answer. I had rather countenance the introduction of Ariel and Caliban, with a troop of spirits the most mischievous from fairy land.

(WJA IX 73)

Charles Willson Peale (1741–1827)

American portrait painter and naturalist. Peale made a portrait of then Vice President John Adams in 1791.

(21 August 1776)

Yesterday morning I took a walk into Arch Street to see Mr. Peale's painter's room. Peale is from Maryland, a tender, soft, affectionate figure. . . . He showed me one moving picture. His wife, all bathed in tears, with a child about six months old laid out upon her lap. This picture struck me prodigiously. He has a variety of portraits, very well done, but not so well done as Copley's portraits. . . . He is ingenious. He has vanity, loves finery, wears a sword, gold lace, speaks French, is capable of friendship, and strong family attachments and natural affections.

(FL 215–16)

William Pitt (1759–1806)

Prime minister of Great Britain from 1783 to 1801.

(3 December 1785)
In 1785, Adams was named as the first United States ambassador to Great Britain.

Mr. Pitt is very young. He has discovered abilities and firmness upon some occasions; but I have never seen in him any evidence of greater talents than I have seen in members of Congress, and in other scenes of life in America, at his age. I have not yet seen any decided proofs of principle, or patriotism, or virtue; on the contrary, there are many symptoms of the want of these qualities, without which, no statesman ever yet appeared uniformly great, or wrought out any memorable salvation for any country. In American affairs he has oscillated like a pendulum, and no one can yet guess when he will be fixed.

(WJA VIII 351)

Plato (428?–348? B.C.)

Greek philosopher.

(16 July 1814)

Some thirty years ago, I took upon me the severe task of going through all his works. With the help of two Latin translations and one English and one French translation, and comparing some of the most remarkable passages with the Greek, I labored through the tedious toil. My disappointment was very shocking. Two things only did I learn from him. First, that Franklin's ideas of exempting husbandmen and mariners, etc., from the depredations of war, were borrowed from him; and second, that sneezing is a cure for the hiccough. Accordingly, I have cured myself and all of my friends of that provoking disorder, for thirty years, with a pinch of snuff.

(WJA X 102–3)

David Rittenhouse (1732–96)

Philadelphia surveyor, astronomer, and clock maker.

(14 March 1814)

Rittenhouse was a virtuous and amiable man; an exquisite mechanician, a master of the astronomy known in his time, an expert mathematician, a patient calculator of numbers. . . . In politics, Rittenhouse was good, simple, ignorant, well-meaning, Franklinian, democrat, totally ignorant of the world, as an anchorite, an honest dupe of the French revolution, a mere instrument of Jonathan Sargeant, Dr. Hutchinson, Genet, and Mifflin. I give him all the credit of his planetarium. The improvement of the orrery to the planetarium was an easy, natural thought, and nothing was wanting but calculations of orbits, distances, and periods of revolutions, all of which were made to his hands long before he existed. Patience, perseverance, and sleight of hand, is his undoubted merit and praise.

(WJA X 90)

Caesar Rodney (1728–84)

Member of the Delaware legislature, delegate to the Stamp Act Congress and the Continental Congress, signer of the Declaration of Independence, and a major general during the American Revolution.

(3 September 1774)

Caesar Rodney is the oddest looking man in the world; he is tall, thin and slender as a reed, pale; his face is not bigger than a large apple, yet there is sense and fire, spirit, wit, and humor in his countenance.

(WJA II 364)

Edward Rutledge (1749–1800)

South Carolina statesman and signer of the Declaration of Independence.

(15 September 1775)

Rutledge is a very uncouth and ungraceful speaker; he shrugs his shoulders, distorts his body, nods and wriggles with his head, and looks about with his eyes from side to side, and speaks through his nose, as the Yankees sing.

(WJA II 422)

William Shakespeare (1564–1616)

British playwright and poet.

(30 March 1786)
In April, John Adams and Thomas Jefferson took a break from treaty negotiations to travel through the English countryside.

Stratford upon Avon is interesting, as it is the scene of the birth, death, and sepulcher of Shakespeare. Three doors from the inn is the house where he was born, as small and mean as you can conceive. They showed us an old wooden chair in the chimney corner where he sat. We cut off a chip according to custom. A mulberry tree that he planted has been cut down, and is carefully preserved for sale. The house where he died has been taken down, and the spot is now only yard or garden. The curse upon him who should remove his bones, which is written on his gravestone, alludes to a pile of some thousands of human bones which lie exposed in that church. There is nothing preserved of this great genius which is worth knowing; nothing which might inform us what education, what company, what accident, turned his mind to letters and the drama. His name is not even on his gravestone. An ill-sculptured head is set up by his wife, by the side of his grave in the church. But paintings and sculpture would be thrown away upon his fame. His wit, fancy, his taste and judgment, his knowledge of nature, of life and character, are immortal.

(WJA III 394)

Roger Sherman (1721–93)

Connecticut delegate to the Continental Congress and signer of the Declaration of Independence. Sherman served on the committee to draft the Declaration of Independence with Adams and Jefferson.

(15 September 1775)

Sherman's air is the reverse of grace; there cannot be a more striking contrast to beautiful action, than the motions of his hands; generally he stands upright, with his hands before him, the fingers of his left hand clenched into a fist, and the wrist of it grasped with his right. But he has a clear head and sound judgment; but when he moves a hand in any thing like an action, Hogarth's genius could not have invented a motion more opposite to grace; it is stiffness and awkwardness itself, rigid as starched linen or buckram; awkward as a junior bachelor or a sophomore.

(WJA II 423)

Oxenbridge Thatcher (1681–1765)

Prominent Boston lawyer and member of the Massachusetts House of Representatives.

(13 February 1818)

There was not a citizen of that town more universally beloved for his learning, ingenuity, every domestic and social virtue, and conscientious conduct in every relation of life. His patriotism was as ardent as his progenitors had been ancient and illustrious in this country. . . . From 1758 to 1765, I attended every superior and inferior court in Boston, and recollect not one, in which he did not invite me home to spend evenings with him, when he made me converse with him as well as I could, on all subjects of religion, morals, law, politics, history, philosophy, belles letters, theology, mythology, cosmogony, metaphysics,—Locke, Clark, Leibnitz, Bolingbroke, Berkeley,—the preestablished harmony of the universe, the nature of matter and of spirit, and the eternal establishment of coincidences between their operations; fate, foreknowledge absolute; and we reasoned on such unfathomable subjects as high as Milton's gentry in pandemonium; and we understood them as well as they did, and no better. To such mighty mysteries he added the news of the day, and the tittle-tattle of the town. But his favorite subject was politics, and the impending, threatening, system of parliamentary taxation and universal government over the colonies. On this subject he was so anxious and agitated that I have no doubt it occasioned his premature death.

(WJA X 286)

Voltaire (1694–1778)

French author and philosopher of the Enlightenment.

(3 May 1816)
Fiercely critical of the church during his lifetime, Voltaire was rumored to have recanted and signed a confession of faith while on his deathbed.

Voltaire, the greatest genius of them all, behaved like the greatest coward of them all, at his death, as he had like the wisest fool of them all in his lifetime.

(WJA X 214)

George Washington (1732–99)

Commander-in-chief of the Continental Army during the American Revolution and first president of the United States. In June 1775, Adams recommended Washington to lead the fledgling Continental Army. As the man with the second-highest number of votes during the first presidential election, Adams became vice president and held the position through Washington's second term.

(21 April 1789)
From a speech while Adams was vice president.

Were I blessed with powers to do justice to his character, it would be impossible to increase the confidence or affection of his country, or make the smallest addition to his glory. This can only be affected by a discharge of the present exalted trust, on the same principles, with the same abilities and virtues, which have uniformly appeared in all his former conduct, public or private. May I, nevertheless, be indulged to inquire, if we look over the catalog of the first magistrates of nations, whether they have been denominated presidents or consuls, kings or princes, where shall we find one, whose commanding talents and virtues, whose overruling good fortune, have so completely united all hearts and voices in his favor, who enjoyed the esteem and admiration of foreign nations and fellow citizens with equal unanimity? Qualities, so uncommon, are no common blessings to the country that possesses them. By those great qualities, and their benign effects, has Providence marked out the head of this nation with a hand, so distinctly visible, as to have been seen by all men, and mistaken by none.

(WJA VIII 486–87)

(8 March 1797)
Adams's first Inaugural Speech.

In that retirement which is his voluntary choice, may he long live to enjoy the delicious recollection of his services, the gratitude of mankind, the happy fruits of them to himself and the world, which are daily increasing, and that splendid prospect of the future fortunes of his country, which is opening from year to year! His name may be still a rampart, and the knowledge that he lives, a bulwark against all open or secret enemies of his country's peace.

(WJA IX 108)

(23 December 1799)
Reply to Congress after Washington's death.

The attributes and decorations of royalty could have only served to eclipse the majesty of those virtues which made him, from being a modest citizen, a more resplendent luminary. Misfortune, had he lived, could hereafter have sullied his glory only with those superficial minds, who, believing that characters and actions are marked by success alone, rarely deserve to enjoy it. Malice could never blast his honor, and envy made him a singular exception to her universal rule. For himself he had lived long enough to life and to glory. For his fellow-citizens, if their prayers could have been answered, he would have been immortal. For me, his departure is at a most unfortunate moment. Trusting, however, in the wise and righteous dominion of Providence over the passions of men and the results of their counsels and actions, as well as over their lives, nothing remains for me but humble resignation.

(WJA I 564)

School Children

(15 March 1756)
Upon graduating from Harvard, Adams taught grammar school in Worcester, Massachusetts.

I sometimes in my sprightly moments consider myself, in my great chair at school, as some dictator at the head of a commonwealth. In this little state I can discover all the great geniuses, all the surprising actions and revolutions of the great world, in miniature. I have several renowned generals but three feet high, and several deep projecting politicians in petticoats. I have others catching and dissecting flies, accumulating remarkable pebbles, cockle shells, etc., with as ardent curiosity as any virtuoso in the Royal Society. Some rattle and thunder out A, B, C, with as much fire and impetuosity as Alexander fought, and very often sit down and cry as heartily upon being outspelt, as Caesar did, when at Alexander's sepulcher he recollected that the Macedonian hero had conquered the world before his age. At one table sits Mr. Insipid, foppling and fluttering, spinning his whirligig, or playing with his fingers, as gaily and wittily as any Frenchified coxcomb brandishes his cane or rattles his snuff-box. At another, sits the polemical divine, plodding and wrangling in his mind about "Adam's fall, in which we sinned all," as his Primer has it. In short, my little school, like the great world, is made up of kings, politicians, divines, L. D.'s, fops, buffoons, fiddlers, sycophants, fools, coxcombs, chimney sweepers, and every other character drawn in history, or seen in the world.

(WJA II 9)

15

Places

France

(11 April 1778)

The Palace of Versailles was then shown to me, and I happened to be present when the king passed through, to council. His Majesty, seeing my colleagues, graciously smiled and passed on. The galleries and royal apartments, and the king's bedchamber were shown to me. The magnificence of these scenes is immense; the statues, the paintings, the everything, is sublime.

(WJA III 125)

(12 April 1778)

The delights of France are innumerable. The politeness, the elegance, the softness, the delicacy, are extreme. In short, stern and haughty republican as I am, I cannot help loving these people for their earnest desire and assiduity to please.

(FL 329)

(20 May 1778)

The French opera is an entertainment which is very pleasing for a few times. There is everything which can please the eye or the ear. But the words are unintelligible, and, if they were not, they are said to be very insignificant. I always wish, in such an amusement, to learn something. The imagination, the passions, and the understanding, have too little employment in the opera.

(WJA III 158)

(20 May 1778)

I am wearied to death with gazing, wherever I go, at a profusion of unmeaning wealth and magnificence. . . . Gold, marble, silk, velvet, silver, ivory, and alabaster, make up the show everywhere.

(WJA III 158)

(2 June 1778)

Instead of wondering that the licentiousness of women was so common and so public in France, I was astonished that there should be any modesty or purity remaining in the kingdom, as there certainly was, though it was rare. Could there be any morality left among such a people, where such examples were set up to the view of the whole nation? Yes. There was a sort of morality. There was a great deal of humanity, and what appeared to me real benevolence. There was a great deal of charity and tenderness for the poor.

(WJA III 170–71)

Holland

(15 September 1780)

The country where I am is the greatest curiosity in the world. . . . Their industry and economy ought to be examples to the world. They have less ambition, I mean that of conquest and military glory, than their neighbors, but I don't perceive that they have more avarice. And they carry learning and arts, I think, to greater extent. The collections of curiosities, public and private, are innumerable.

(FL 386)

(18 December 1780)

The Dutch say that without the habit of thinking of every [cent] before you spend it, no man can be a good merchant, or conduct trade with success. This I believe is a just maxim in general, but I would never with a son of mine govern himself by it. It is the sure and certain way for an industrious man to be rich. It is the only possible way for a merchant to become the first merchant or the richest man in the place. But this is an object that I hope none of my children will ever aim at.

(FL 389)

Maryland

(14 June 1776)

I have never had the honor of knowing many people from Maryland, but by what I have learned of them and seen of their delegates, they are an open, sincere, and united people. A little obstinate, to be sure, but that is very pardonable, when accompanied with frankness.

(WJA IX 397)

(2 February 1777)

I think I have never been better pleased with any of our American States than with Maryland. We saw the most excellent farms all along the road, and what was more striking to me, I saw more sheep and flax in Maryland than I ever saw riding a like distance in any other State.

(FL 238)

(2 February 1777)

Baltimore is a very pretty town, situated on Patapsco River, which empties into the great bay of Chesapeake. . . . The streets are very dirty and miry, but everything else is agreeable, except the monstrous prices of things.

(FL 237)

(23 February 1777)

The manners of Maryland are somewhat peculiar. They have but few merchants. They are chiefly planters and farmers; the planters are those who raise tobacco, and the farmers such as raise wheat, etc. The lands are cultivated, and all sorts of trades are exercised by Negroes, or by transported convicts, which has occasioned the planters and farmers to assume the title of gentlemen; and they hold their negroes and convicts, that is, all laboring people and tradesmen, in such contempt, that they think themselves a distinct order of beings. Hence they never will suffer their sons to labor or learn any trade but they bring them up in idleness, or, what is worse, in horse-racing, cock-fighting, and card-playing.

(WJA II 436)

(28 February 1777)

The object of the men of property here, the planters, etc., is universally wealth. Every way in the world is sought to get and save money. Landjobbers, speculators in land; little generosity to the public, little public spirit.

(WJA II 436)

New York City

(23 August 1774)

With all the opulence and splendor of this city, there is very little good breeding to be found. We have been treated with an assiduous respect; but I have not seen one real gentleman, one well-bred man, since I came to town. At their entertainments, there is no conversation that is agreeable; there is no modesty, no attention to one another. They talk very loud, very fast, and altogether. If they ask you a question, before you can utter three words of your answer, they will break out upon you again, and talk away.

(WJA II 353)

New England

(29 October 1775)

New England has, in many respects, the advantage of every other colony in America, and, indeed, of every other part of the world that I know anything of.

(FL 120)

(25 November 1775)

The characters of gentlemen in the four New England colonies, differ as much from those in the others, as that of the common people differs; that is, as much as several distinct nations almost. Gentlemen, men of sense or any kind of education, in the other colonies, are much fewer in proportion than in New England.

(WJA IX 1775)

Philadelphia

(9 October 1774)

Philadelphia, with all its trade and wealth and regularity, is not Boston. The morals of our people are much better; their manners are more polite and agreeable; they are purer English; our language is better, our taste is better, our persons are handsomer; our spirit is greater, our laws are wiser, our religion is superior, our education is better. We exceed them in every thing but in a market, and in charitable, public foundations.

(WJA II 395)

South America

(30 March 1815)

What would I think of revolutions and constitutions in South America? A people more ignorant, more bigoted, more superstitious, more implicitly credulous in the sanctity of royalty, more blindly devoted to their priests, in more awful terror of the Inquisition, than any people in Europe, even in Spain, Portugal, or the Austrian Netherlands, and infinitely more than in Rome itself, the immediate residence of the head of the holy church.

(WJA X 150)

Washington, D.C.

(22 November 1800)

Immediately after the adjournment of Congress at their last session in Philadelphia I gave directions, in compliance with the laws, for removal of the public offices, records, and property [to the new seat of government in Washington].

May this territory be the residence of virtue and happiness! In this city may that piety and virtue, that wisdom and magnanimity, that constancy and self-government, which adorned the great character whose name it bears, be forever held in veneration! Here, and throughout our country, may simple manners, pure morals, and true religion flourish forever!

(WJA I 592)

APPENDIX

Letter to Abigail Adams.

Philadelphia, 3 July, 1776

Your favor of 17 June, dated at Plymouth, was handed me by yesterday's post. I was much pleased to find that you had taken a journey to Plymouth, to see your friends, in the long absence of one whom you may wish to see. The excursion will be an amusement, and will serve your health. How happy would it have made me to have taken this journey with you!

I was informed, a day or two before the receipt of your letter, that you was gone to Plymouth, by Mrs. Polly Palmer, who was obliging enough, in your absence, to send me the particulars of the expedition to the lower harbor against the men-of-war. Her narration is executed with a precision and perspicuity, which would have become the pen of an accomplished historian.

I am very glad you had so good an opportunity of seeing one of our little American men-of-war. Many ideas new to you must have presented themselves in such a scene; and you will, in future, better understand the relationship of sea engagements.

I rejoice extremely at Dr. Bulfinch's petition to open a hospital. But I hope the business will be done upon a larger scale. I hope that one hospital will be licensed in every county, if not in every town. I am happy to find you resolved to be with the children in the first class. Mr. Whitney and Mrs. Katy Quincy are cleverly through inoculation in this city.

The information you give me of our friend's refusing his appointment has given me much pain, grief, and anxiety. I believe I shall be obliged to follow his example. I have not fortune enough to support my family and, what is of more importance, to support the dignity of that exalted station. It is too high a lifted up for me who delight in nothing so much as retreat, solitude, silence, and obscurity. In private life, no one has a right to censure me for following my own inclinations in retirement, simplicity, and frugality. In public life, every man has a right to remark as he pleases. At least he thinks so.

Yesterday, the greatest question was decided which ever was debated in America, and a greater, perhaps, never was nor will be decided among men. A Resolution was passed without one dissenting colony "that these United Colonies are, and of right ought to be, free and independent States, and as such they have, and of right ought to have, full power to make war, conclude peace, establish commerce, and to do all other acts and things which other States may rightfully do." You will see, in a few days, a Declaration setting forth the causes which have impelled us to this mighty revolution, and the reasons which will justify it in the sight of God and man. A plan of confederation will be taken up in a few days.

When I look back to the year 1761, and recollect the argument concerning writs of assistance in the superior court, which I have hitherto considered as the commencement of this controversy between Great Britain and America, and run through the whole period from that time to this, and recollect the series of political events, the chain of causes and effects, I am surprised at the suddenness as well as greatness of this revolution. Britain has been filled with folly, and America with wisdom; at least, this is my judgment. Time must determine. It is the will of Heaven that the two countries should be sundered forever. It may be the will of Heaven that America shall suffer calamities still more wasting, and distresses yet more dreadful. If this is to be the case, it will have this good effect at least. It will inspire us with many virtues which we have not, and correct many errors, follies, and vices which threaten to disturb, dishonor, and destroy us. The furnace of affliction produces refinement in states as well as individuals. And the new Governments we are assuming in every part will require a purification from our vices, and an augmentation of our virtues, or they will be no blessings. The people will have unbounded power, and the people are extremely addicted to corruption and venality, as well as the great. But I must submit all my hopes and fears to an overruling Providence, in which, unfashionable as the faith may be, I firmly believe.

With great respect, etc.

John Adams

Account of John Adams's meeting with King George III, during his time as the first U.S. ambassador to Great Britain.

To Secretary John Jay   Westminster, 2 June, 1785

Dear Sir,—During my interview with the Marquis of Carmarthen, he told me that it was customary for every foreign minister, at his first presentation to the King, to make his Majesty some compliments conformable to the spirit of his letter of credence; and when Sir Clement Cottrell Dormer, the master of ceremonies, came to inform me that he should accompany me to the secretary of state and to Court, he said that every foreign minister whom he had attended to the Queen had always made a harangue to her Majesty, and he understood, though he had not been present, that they always harangued the King.

On Tuesday evening, the Baron de Lynden called upon me, and said he came from the Baron de Nolken, and they had been conversing upon the singular situation I was in, and they agreed in opinion that it was indispensable that I should make a speech, and that that speech should be as complimentary as possible. All this was conformable to the advice lately given by the Count de Vergennes to Mr. Jefferson; so that, finding it was a custom established at both these great Courts, and that this Court and the foreign ministers expected it, I thought I could not avoid it, although my first thought and inclination had been to deliver my credentials silently and retire.

At one, on Wednesday, the master of ceremonies called at my house, and went with me to the secretary of state's office, in Cleveland Row, where the Marquis of Carmarthen received me, and introduced me to his under secretary, Mr. Fraser, who has been, as his Lordship told me, uninterruptedly in that office, through all the changes in administration for thirty years, having first been appointed by the Earl of Holderness. After a short conversation upon the subject of importing my effects from Holland

and France free of duty, which Mr. Fraser himself introduced, Lord Carmarthen invited me to go with him to his coach to Court. When we arrived in the antechamber, the *oeil de boeuf* of St. James's, the master of ceremonies met me and attended me, while the secretary of state went to take the commands of the King. While I stood in this place, where it seems all ministers stand upon such occasions, always attended by the master of ceremonies, the room very full of ministers of state, lords, and bishops, and all sorts of courtiers, as well as the next room, which is the King's bedchamber, you may well suppose I was the focus of all eyes. I was relieved, however, from the embarrassment of it by the Swedish and Dutch ministers, who came to me, and entertained me in a very agreeable conversation during the whole time. Some other gentlemen, whom I had seen before, came to make their compliments too, until the Marquis of Carmarthen returned and desired me to go with him to his Majesty. I went with his Lordship through the levee room into the King's closet. The door was shut, and I was left with his Majesty and the secretary of state alone. I made three reverences,—one at the door, another about half way, and a third before the presence,—according to the usage established at this and all the northern Courts of Europe, and then addressed myself to his Majesty in the following words:—

"Sir,—The United States of America have appointed me their minister plenipotentiary to your Majesty, and have directed me to deliver to your Majesty this letter which contains the evidence of it. It is in obedience to their express commands, that I have the honor to assure your Majesty of their unanimous disposition and desire to cultivate the most friendly and liberal intercourse between your Majesty's subjects and their citizens, and of their best wishes for your Majesty's health and happiness, and for that of your royal family. The appointment of a minister from the United States to your Majesty's Court will form an epoch in the history of England and of America. I think myself more fortunate than all my fellow citizens, in having the distinguished honor to be the first to stand in your Majesty's royal presence in a diplomatic character; and I shall esteem myself the happiest of men, if I can be instrumental in recommending my country more and more to your Majesty's royal benevolence, and of restoring an entire esteem, confidence, and affection, or, in better words, the old good nature and the old good humor between people, who, though separated by an ocean, and under different governments, have the same language, a similar religion, and kindred blood.

I beg your Majesty's permission to add, that, although I have some time before been entrusted by my country, it was never in my whole life in a manner so agreeable to myself."

The King listened to every word I said, with dignity, but with an apparent emotion. Whether it was the nature of the interview, or whether it was my visible agitation, for I felt more than I did or could express, that touched him, I cannot say. But he was much affected, and answered me with more tremor than I had spoken with, and said:—

"Sir:—The circumstances of this audience are so extraordinary, the language you have now held is so extremely proper, and the feelings you have discovered so justly adapted to the occasion, that I must say that I not only receive with pleasure the assurance of the friendly dispositions of the United States, but that I am very glad the choice has fallen upon you to be their minister. I wish you, sir, to believe, and that it may be understood in America, that I have done nothing in the late contest but what I thought myself indispensably bound to do, by the duty which I owed to my people. I will be very frank with you. I was the last to consent to the separation; but the separation having been made, and having become inevitable, I have always said, as I say now, that I would be the first to meet the friendship of the United States as an independent power. The moment I see such sentiments and language as yours prevail, and a disposition to give to this country the preference, that moment I shall say, let the circumstances of language, religion, and blood have their natural and full effect."

I dare not say that these were the King's precise words, and, it is even possible, that I may have in some particular mistaken his meaning; for, although his pronunciation is as distinct as I ever heard, he hesitated some time between his periods, and between the members of the same period. He was indeed much affected, and I confess I was not less so, and, therefore I cannot be certain that I was so cool and attentive, heard so clearly, and understood so perfectly, as to be confident of all his words or sense; and, I think, that all which he said to me should at present be kept secret in America, unless his Majesty or his secretary of state, who alone was present, should judge proper to report it. This I do say, that the foregoing is his Majesty's meaning as I then understood it, and his own words as nearly as I can recollect them.

The King then asked me whether I came last from France, and upon my answering in the affirmative, he put on an air of familiarity, and, smiling, or rather laughing, said, "there is an opinion among some people that you are not the most attached of all your countrymen to the manners of France." I was surprised at this, because I thought it an indiscretion and a departure from the dignity. I was a little embarrassed, but determined not to deny the truth on one hand, nor leave him to infer from it any attachment to England on the other. I threw off as much gravity as I could, and assumed an air of gayety and a tone of decision as far as was decent, and said, "that opinion, sir, is not mistaken; I must avow to your Majesty, I have no attachment but to my own country." The King replied, as quick as lightning, "an honest man will never have any other."

The King then said a word or two to the secretary of state, which, being between them, I did not hear, and then turned round and bowed to me, as is customary with all kings and princes when they give the signal to retire. I retreated, stepping backward, as is the etiquette, and, making my last reverence at the door of the chamber, I went my way. The master of ceremonies joined me the moment of my coming out of the King's closet, and accompanied me through the apartments down to my carriage, several stages of servants, gentlemen porters and under porters, roaring out like thunder, as I went along, "Mr. Adams's servants, Mr. Adams's carriage, etc." I have been thus minute, as it may be useful to others hereafter to know.

The conversation with the King Congress will form their own judgment of. I may expect from it a residence less painful than I once expected, as so marked an attention from the King will silence many grumblers; but we can infer nothing from all this concerning the success of my mission.

There are a train of other ceremonies yet to go through, in presentations to the Queen, and visits to and from ministers and ambassadors, which will take up much time, and interrupt me in my endeavors to obtain all that I have at heart,—the objects of my instructions. It is thus the essence of things is lost in ceremony in every country of Europe. We must submit to what we cannot alter. Patience is the only remedy.

With great respect, etc.

John Adams

(WJA VIII 255–59)

John Adams's first Inaugural Speech, March 4, 1797.

When it was first perceived, in early times, that no middle course for America remained between unlimited submission to a foreign legislature and a total independence of its claims, men of reflection were less apprehensive of danger from the formidable power of fleets and armies they must determine to resist than from those contests and dissensions which would certainly arise concerning the forms of government to be instituted over the whole and over the parts of this extensive country. Relying, however, on the purity of their intentions, the justice of their cause, and the integrity and intelligence of the people, under an overruling Providence which had so signally protected this country from the first, the representatives of this nation, then consisting of little more than half its present number, not only broke to pieces the chains which were forging and the rod of iron that was lifted up, but frankly cut asunder the ties which had bound them, and launched into an ocean of uncertainty.

The zeal and ardor of the people during the revolutionary war, supplying the place of government, commanded a degree of order sufficient at least for the temporary preservation of society. The Confederation which was early felt to be necessary was prepared from the models of the Batavian and Helvetic confederacies, the only examples which remain with any detail and precision in history, and certainly the only ones which the people at large had ever considered. But reflecting on the striking difference in so many particulars between this country and those where a courier may go from the seat of government to the frontier in a single day, it was then certainly foreseen by some, who assisted in Congress at the formation of it, that it could not be durable.

Negligence of its regulations, inattention to its recommendations, if not disobedience to its authority, not only in individuals but in States, soon appeared with their melancholy consequences; universal languor, jealousies and rivalries of States, decline of navigation and commerce; discouragement of necessary manufactures; universal fall in the value of lands and their produce; contempt of public and private faith; loss of consideration and credit with foreign nations; and at length in discontents, animosities, combinations, partial conventions, and insurrection, threatening some great national calamity.

In this dangerous crisis the people of America were not abandoned by their usual good sense, presence of mind, resolution, or integrity. Measures were pursued to concert a plan to form a more perfect union, establish justice, insure domestic tranquility, provide for the common defense, promote the general welfare, and secure the blessings of liberty. The public disquisitions, discussions, and deliberations issued in the present happy Constitution of government.

Employed in the service of my country abroad during the whole course of these transactions, I first saw the Constitution of the United States in a foreign country. Irritated by no literary altercation, animated by no public debate, heated by no party animosity, I read it with great satisfaction, as the result of good heads prompted by good hearts, as an experiment better adapted to the genius, character, situation, and relations of this nation and country than any which had ever been proposed or suggested. In its general principles and great outlines it was conformable to such a system of government as I had ever most esteemed, and in some States, my own native State in particular, had contributed to establish. Claiming a right of suffrage, in common with my fellow-citizens, in the adoption or rejection of a constitution which was to rule me and my posterity, as well as them and theirs, I did not hesitate to express my approbation of it on all occasions, in public and in private. It was not then, nor has been since, any objection to it in my mind that the Executive and Senate were not more permanent. Nor have I ever entertained a thought of promoting any alteration in it but such as the people themselves, in the course of their experience, should see and feel to be necessary or expedient, and by their representatives in Congress and the State legislatures, according to the Constitution itself, adopt and ordain.

Returning to the bosom of my country after a painful separation from it for ten years, I had the honor to be elected to a station under the new order of things, and I have repeatedly laid myself under the most serious obligations to support the Constitution. The operation of it has equaled the most sanguine expectations of its friends, and from an habitual attention to it, satisfaction in its administration, and delight in its effects upon the peace, order, prosperity, and happiness of the nation I have acquired an habitual attachment to it, and veneration for it.

What other form of government, indeed, can so well deserve our esteem and love?

There may be little solidity in an ancient idea, that congregations of men into cities and nations are the most pleasing objects in the sight of superior intelligences; but this is very certain, that, to a benevolent human mind, there can be no spectacle presented by any nation, more pleasing, more noble, majestic, or august, than an assembly like that which has so often been seen in this and the other Chamber of Congress; of a government, in which the executive authority, as well as that of all the branches of the legislature, are exercised by citizens selected at regular periods by their neighbors, to make and execute laws for the general good. Can anything essential, anything more than mere ornament and decoration, be added to this by robes and diamonds? Can authority be more amiable and respectable, when it descends from accidents or institutions established in remote antiquity than when it springs fresh from the hearts and judgments of an honest and enlightened people? For it is the people only that are represented; it is their power and majesty that is reflected, and only for their good, in every legitimate government, under whatever form it may appear. The existence of such a government as ours, for any length of time, is a full proof of a general dissemination of knowledge and virtue throughout the whole body of the people. And what object or consideration, more pleasing than this, can be presented to the human mind? If national pride is ever justifiable or excusable, it is when it springs, not from power or riches, grandeur or glory, but from conviction of national innocence, information, and benevolence.

In the midst of these pleasing ideas, we should be unfaithful to ourselves, if we should ever lose sight of the danger to our liberties, if anything partial or extraneous should infect the purity of our free, fair, virtuous, and independent elections. If an election is to be determined by a majority of a single vote, and that can be procured by a party through artifice or corruption, the government may be the choice of a party, for its own ends, not of the nation, for the national good. If that solitary suffrage can be obtained by foreign nations, by flattery or menaces; by fraud or violence; by terror, intrigue, or venality; the government may not be the choice of the American people, but of foreign nations. It may be foreign nations who govern us, and not we, the people, who govern ourselves; and candid men will acknowledge, that, in such cases, choice would have little advantage to boast of over lot or chance.

Such is the amiable and interesting system of government (and such are some of the abuses to which it may be exposed) which the people of America have exhibited, to the admiration and anxiety of the wise and virtuous of all nations, for eight years; under the administration of a citizen, who, by a long course of great actions, regulated by prudence, justice, temperance, and fortitude, conducting a people, inspired with the same virtues, and animated with the same ardent patriotism and love of liberty, to independence and peace, to increasing wealth and unexampled prosperity, has merited the gratitude of his fellow-citizens, commanded the highest praises of foreign nations, and secured immortal glory with posterity.

In that retirement which is his voluntary choice, may he long live to enjoy the delicious recollection of his services, the gratitude of mankind, the happy fruits of them to himself and the world, which are daily increasing, and that splendid prospect of the future fortunes of this country which is opening from year to year! His name may be still a rampart, and the knowledge that he lives, a bulwark against all open or secret enemies of his country's peace.

This example has been recommended to the imitation of his successors by both Houses of Congress, and by the voice of the legislatures and the people throughout the nation.

On this subject it might become me better to be silent or to speak with diffidence; but, as something may be expected, the occasion, I hope, will be admitted as an apology, if I venture to say, that, if a preference, upon principle, of a free republican government, formed upon long and serious reflection, after a diligent and impartial inquiry after truth; if an attachment to the Constitution of the United States, and a conscientious determination to support it, until it shall be altered by the judgments and wishes of the people, expressed in the mode prescribed in it; if a respectful attention to the constitutions of the individual States and a constant caution and delicacy toward the State governments; if an equal and impartial regard to the rights, interest, honor, and happiness of all the States in the Union, without preference or regard to a northern or southern, an eastern or western position, their various political opinions on essential points or their personal attachments; if a love of virtuous men of all parties and denominations; if a love of science and letters, and a wish to patronize every rational effort to encourage schools, colleges, universities, academies, and every institution for propagating knowledge, virtue, and religion among all classes of the people, not only for their benign influence on the happiness of life in all its stages and classes and of society in all its forms, but as the only means of preserving our Constitution from its natural enemies, the spirit of sophistry, the spirit of party, the spirit of intrigue, profligacy, and corruption, and the pestilence of foreign influence, which is the angel of destruction to elective governments; if a love of equal laws, of justice, and humanity in the interior administration; if an inclination to improve agriculture, commerce, and manufacturers for necessity, convenience, and defense; if a spirit of equity and humanity toward the aboriginal nations of America, and a disposition to meliorate their condition by inclining them to be more friendly to us, and our citizens to be more friendly to them; if an inflexible determination to maintain peace and inviolable faith with all nations, and that system of neutrality and impartiality among the belligerent powers of Europe, which has been adopted by the government, and so solemnly sanctioned by both Houses of Congress, and applauded by the legislatures of the States and the public opinion, until it shall be otherwise ordained by Congress; if a personal esteem for the French nation, formed in a residence of seven years chiefly among them, and a sincere desire to preserve the friendship which has been so much for the honor and interest of both nations; if, while the conscious honor and integrity of the people of America, and the internal sentiment of their own power and energies must be preserved, an earnest endeavor to investigate every just cause and remove every colorable pretense of complaint; if an intention to pursue by amicable negotiation, a reparation for the injuries that have been committed on the commerce of our fellow-citizens by whatever nation, and (if success cannot be obtained), to lay the facts before the legislature, that they may consider what further measures the honor and interest of the government and its constituents demand; if a resolution to do justice, as far as may depend upon me, at all times, and to all nations, and maintain peace, friendship, and benevolence with all the world; if an unshaken confidence in the honor, spirit, and resources of the American people, on which I have so often hazarded my all, and never been deceived; if elevated ideas of the high destinies of this country, and of my own duties toward it, founded on a knowledge of the moral principles and intellectual improvements of the people, deeply engraved on my mind in early life, and not obscured, but exalted by experience and age; and with humble reverence I feel it to be my duty to add, if a veneration for the religion of a people, who profess and call themselves Christians, and a fixed resolution to consider a decent respect for Christianity among the best recommendations for the public service;—can enable me in any degree to comply with your wishes, it shall be my strenuous endeavor that this sagacious injunction of the two Houses shall not be without effect.

With this great example before me, with the sense and spirit, the faith and honor, the duty and interest of the same American people, pledged to support the Constitution of the United States, I entertain no doubt of its continuance in all its energy; and my mind is prepared without hesitation, to lay myself under the most solemn obligations to support it to the utmost of my power.

And may that Being, who is supreme over all, the Patron of Order, the Fountain of Justice, and the Protector, in all ages of the world, of virtuous liberty, continue His blessing upon this nation and its government and give it all possible success and duration, consistent with the ends of His providence.

(WJA IX 105–11)

Selected Bibliography

Key to Sources

DC: *The Diplomatic Correspondence of the American Revolution.* Vols. IV, V.

FL: *Familiar Letters of John Adams and His Wife Abigail Adams, During the Revolution.*

WJA: *The Works of John Adams, Second President of the United States: With a Life of the Author, Notes and Illustrations.* 10 Vols.

Adams, Charles Francis, ed. *Familiar Letters of John Adams and His Wife Abigail Adams, During the Revolution.* Boston: Houghton, Mifflin and Co., 1875.

Adams, Charles Francis, ed. *The Works of John Adams, Second President of the United States: With a Life of the Author, Notes and Illustrations.* 10 Vols. Boston: Charles C. Little and James Brown, 1850.

Brown, Ralph Adams. *The Presidency of John Adams.* Lawrence: University Press of Kansas, 1975.

Dictionary of American Biography. New York: Scribner's, 1964.

Ellis, Joseph. *Passionate Sage: The Character and Legacy of John Adams.* New York: Norton, 1993.

Journals of the Continental Congress, 1774–1789, ed. Worthington C. Ford et al. (Washington, D.C., 1904–37).

McCullough, David. *John Adams.* Boston: Simon and Schuster, 2001.

Sparks, Jared. *The Diplomatic Correspondence of the American Revo-*

lution. Vols. IV, V. Boston: Nathan Hale and Gray & Bowen, 1829.

Thompson, C. Bradley. *John Adams and the Spirit of Liberty*. Lawrence: University Press of Kansas, 1998.

Online Resources

John Adams, C-SPAN.
americanpresidents.org/presidents/president.asp?President Number=2

John Adams, The White House.
www.whitehouse.gov/history/presidents/ja2.html

The Adams Papers, Massachusetts Historical Society.
www.masshist.org/adams.html

The Papers of John Adams, Yale Law School.
www.yale.edu/lawweb/avalon/president/adamspap.htm

Index